AF615821

MY THIRTY-THREE YEARS' DREAM

PRINCETON LIBRARY OF ASIAN TRANSLATIONS

ADVISORY COMMITTEE (Japan): Marius Jansen, Earl Miner, James Morley, J. Thomas Rimer

TITLES PUBLISHED

Ōkagami (The Great Mirror), TRANSLATED BY Helen McCullough.

Told Round a Brushwood Fire (The Autobiography of Arai Hakuseki), TRANSLATED BY Joyce Ackroyd.

The Ten Thousand Leaves: A translation of the Man'yōshū, Japan's Premier Anthology of Classical Poetry, Volume One, TRANSLATED BY Ian Hideo Levy

The Zen Poems of Ryōkan, SELECTED AND TRANSLATED BY Nobuyuki Yuasa

MY THIRTY-THREE YEARS' DREAM

The Autobiography of Miyazaki Tōten

Translated, with an introduction, by

ETŌ SHINKICHI
AND
MARIUS B. JANSEN

PRINCETON UNIVERSITY PRESS

Copyright © 1982 by Princeton University Press
Published by Princeton University Press, 41 William Street,
Princeton, New Jersey
In the United Kingdom: Princeton University Press, Guildford, Surrey

ALL RIGHTS RESERVED
Library of Congress Cataloging in Publication Data will be
found on the last printed page of this book

This book has been composed in Linotron Bembo
Designed by Barbara Werden

Clothbound editions of Princeton University Press books
are printed on acid-free paper, and binding materials are
chosen for strength and durability

Printed in the United States of America by
Princeton University Press, Princeton, New Jersey

FOR KAZUKO AND JEAN

[Translators' Foreword]

When we first met in 1951, Miyazaki Tōten's *Thirty-Three Years' Dream* provided the first item in the discovery of common interests. In our numerous encounters and discussions during the almost thirty-three years since then, a host of other topics relating to Sino-Japanese relations have come up, but none more engaging than the autobiography of this Japanese China enthusiast with its insights into the thought world of young men in Meiji Japan.

Some fifteen years ago we first began to discuss cooperating in an English edition and translation. We were not the first to discuss such cooperation; in postwar days Kuwabara Takeo and E. H. Norman talked about doing it too. Collaboration seemed to Kuwabara and Norman, and to us, the indicated path, for Tōten's Meiji Japanese is heavily tinted with the usages of his native Kumamoto, which is also, by good fortune, the ancestral Etō point of origin. In 1967 one of us had occasion to edit and annotate a new Japanese edition of the text for Heibonsha Publishers, and this provided new impetus for the project.

We began experimentally with the chapter on Sun Yatsen, and thereafter continued to work together whenever our travels and schedules, both filled with other commitments, permitted. Periods of work together were made possible by assistance from the Princeton University Council of the Humanities (1971), the Japan Foundation (1976), the Henry Luce Foundation's Fund for Asian Studies (1979), and the Guggenheim Foundation (1979). We have benefited also from the help of friends and colleagues who provided counsel on points of chronology, geography, and identification; these include Ta-tuan Ch'en in Princeton, Mr. and Mrs. Miyazaki Tomoo in Tokyo, Nishino Junjirō in Tokyo, Prasert Chittiwatanapong in Bangkok, Sugii Mutsurō in Kyoto, Tamai Kensuke, then in Bangkok, and Wang Gung-wu in Canberra. We are particularly grateful for the close reading and helpful comments that Dr. Joshua Fogel of Columbia University and Professor Akira Iriye of the University of Chicago gave the manuscript. For the illustrations we are grateful to Professor Miyazaki Tomoo and Mrs. Miyazaki Fuki. The maps were drawn by Ms. Onoue Kei, Momota Kimiko, and Kondō Shōko. We are also happy to acknowledge the interest and encouragement of Miriam Brokaw and her associates at Princeton University Press, whose enthusiasm for its Asian Translation series made this the perfect home for the manuscript.

Throughout the translation and notes we have retained the East Asian sequence of surname before family name. Our notes refer to the author by his literary name (*gō*) of Tōten, but for the many individuals he refers to by secondary or assumed names we have retained real names to avoid unnecessary confusion and facilitate reference. We have used Mandarin Chinese readings, in Wade-Giles romanization, for all personal and place names, though in the case of South China locations Cantonese readings have been added in parentheses after the first mention.

After so extended a collaboration we do not see Tōten leave our desks without some sense of regret, but we are confident that he will return to claim our attention in the enthusiasm of colleagues and students who can now encounter him on his own terms for the first time.

Etō Shinkichi
The University of Tokyo

Marius B. Jansen
Princeton University

[Contents]

[List of Illustrations]

Figures

Maps

1. Tōten at the time of the Revolution of 1911.

[Introduction]

Miyazaki Tōten: The Dream and The Life

Miyazaki Torazō, better known as Tōten, the pen name he used during a career that revolved around Sun Yat-sen and the Chinese revolution, published his *Thirty-Three Years' Dream* to explain the failure of efforts to mount a revolution in south China in 1900. Then and later he was the most important of a small group of Japanese enthusiasts who devoted their lives to helping their Chinese friends overthrow the Manchu dynasty. Tōten saw that overthrow as an essential first step in a world-wide crusade for freedom and justice in which his role was that of a chivalrous Lafayette to Sun Yat-sen's Washington. A decade later, after the Chinese revolution had succeeded, only to be betrayed by Yüan Shih-k'ai, he indignantly rejected overtures of reward from Yüan as inappropriate to the purity of his motives. The account translated here was published in 1902, however, at a time when success still seemed distant, and as a result the autobiography gives a romantic and often melancholy account of the fate of pure motives in the impure world of Japan at the end of the nineteenth century.

Tōten's autobiography stands quite alone among others of its time. Almost without exception, the subjects of Meiji biography and autobiography are presented as exemplars of devotion and duty. Their tales are those of success, and they or their biographers stress the qualities that made for such success. As they remember it, country and emperor dominated their waking thoughts. Patriotism, diligence, filiality, and loyalty are the stuff of which the establishment was built. Tōten, however, considered himself a failure when he wrote his book; as he looked back on a series of forlorn hopes and attempts three decades of effort seemed wasted. He devoted a rueful backward glance to the high aspirations of his youth only to contrast them with the meager achievements of his maturity, and concluded his story with his decision to give up his dreams and take up a new career as an entertainer. His opening imagery of fallen blossoms symbolized his failures and foreshadowed his efforts to sing of them in ballads of despair. Without a story of success to chronicle, Tōten needed no catalogue of virtues as explanation. Instead he was relentlessly honest in his self-examination and pitiless in his skepticism. Weakness, dalliance, and self-indulgence occupy page after page; "sex and *sake*," he confesses at one point "were my consolation." There is no mention of emperor, and little of country. His concern, we learn, was with all mankind, and especially with Asia and the "yellow races." His is, above all, a story of crusade for China and for Asia: one that seemed to be ending in failure when he wrote it, but one that was changing to triumph by the time he died in 1922.

Tōten's is a romance of idealism and optimism, beautifully told and full of humanity and humor. In addition to all this, his story provides invaluable insights into at least three aspects of modern East Asian history: the psychological, social, and intellectual turbulence of Japan in the 1880's, the late nineteenth-century Japanese perception of world affairs, and the coming of the Chinese revolution.

Early Meiji Japan and the "New Generation"

Kenneth Pyle's discussion of the "new generation" of early Meiji Japan[1] focused attention on the generation of young Japanese who grew to manhood at a time when the established verities of Confucian and feudal custom were under attack from the Western world. One of Pyle's examples was Tōten's early teacher, the Kumamoto educator, journalist, and critic, Tokutomi Iichirō (1863-1957). The experience Tōten describes advances and sharpens the argument and

[1] Kenneth B. Pyle, *The New Generation in Meiji Japan: Problems of Cultural Identity, 1885-1895* (Stanford University Press, 1969).

provides an important view of the times. The ebb and flow of stimuli from the West in the disarray of "traditional" influence and inspiration contain few examples better suited to illustrate the volatility and intensity of that generation during its formative years.

Tōten was born in 1870 in the province of Higo, the Tokugawa domain of Kumamoto. Kumamoto was poorly represented in the dramatic events that brought about the Meiji Restoration of 1868, and its feudal leaders tried to make up for this by establishing a Western-style military school to which they brought as teacher an American Civil War artillery officer, L. L. Janes, in 1871. Janes proved to be a fervent Christian as well as soldier, and his first students, who included Tōten's teacher Tokutomi, provided the members of the "Kumamoto Band" who vowed to win their countrymen to Christ. Kozaki Hiromichi, Tōten's future counselor in the new faith, was also one of their number. In addition Kumamoto produced, in the "Divine Wind Party," an equally fervent reactionary movement that rebelled against such currents of change in a spectacular but unsuccessful rebellion in 1876. Tōten's account tells us of finding survivors of this group, their samurai topknots still in place, as his teachers in primary school.

Comparable patterns of total acceptance and extreme rejection of the new Western influence characterized the response of Tōten and many of his generation to the new influences with which their country was being inundated.

The family into which Tōten was born was of *gōshi* rank. These "rural samurai" lived in the countryside as opposed to the higher-ranking, full-time samurai who were assigned residences in the castle town and served the feudal administration as bureaucrats in Kumamoto or on rotation duty in the shogunal capital of Edo (modern Tokyo). *Gōshi* were thus second-class members of the ruling class, but they were frequently large landowners. The Miyazakis fitted this pattern with 48 *chō* (120 acres) of paddy and upland in their native village of Arao in addition to land producing 50 bales of tenant rice income in the neighboring village of Hirai. The family's land tax assessment under the system worked out in 1873 was 133 *yen*. Since the 1889 provisions for elections, which limited suffrage to taxpayers assessed to pay 15 *yen*, produced a national electorate of fewer than one half million voters, the Miyazakis were clearly members of a genuine rural elite. Unlike castle-town samurai, whose dependence on government-provided stipends (and, later, pensions and bonds) left them totally at the mercy of officials' decisions, rural leaders like the Miyazakis could look on aspirants to official employment with fastidious disdain and aspire to other goals.

Tōten was the youngest of eleven children. One brother, Hachirō, was killed in the Satsuma Rebellion of 1877; two older brothers and two sisters survived to maturity. The father, a self-styled expert in traditional martial arts, died in 1879. Tōten's childhood memories included his father's contempt for money and his fondness for drink. The father had adopted a son to carry on the family responsibilities so that his own children would be free to follow their inclinations after they had been educated, but that adoptive son had himself forsaken his newly incurred duties to participate, and die, in the violence that preceded the Meiji Restoration. Thus the family heritage was one of insouciance about material things, elite consciousness, and sacrifice in Restoration and early Meiji political struggles. Tōten's childhood influences included admonitions to be a hero like his brother, and his mother's injunctions to die like a hero and not in bed. Years later, when her sons avoided army duty after war broke out with China in 1894, the mother's blazing indignation would serve as reminder of her code of values.

Even landlord fortunes could ill survive such casual attention, however, and Tōten's youthful days were affected by shortage and poverty, though no doubt at a level well above the ordinary. His mother's sacrificial management of the property held things together during his schoolboy days, but in later days his own indifference to practical concerns was to place his wife and children at the mercy of pawnshop operators and vengeful bill-collectors.

From the first, practicality took second place to identification of a life-objective for Tōten. From elementary school on he seems to have been a rebel, unable or unwilling to accept the values of those around him and skeptical of their sincerity. Like his brothers, he began with distrust of and dislike for the new national government, whose ruling clique was drawn from the neighboring domains of Satsuma and Chōshū. For ambitious young men in the 1870's and 1880's values were political and hopes tended to be expressed in terms of service as an official—if not in the present government, then in its successor, which was expected to come out of the rather amorphous rhetoric of popular participation and "people's rights" that entered with Western political thought. Hachirō, Tōten's elder brother who fell with Saigō Takamori in 1877, had returned to Kumamoto from Tokyo to organize such sentiment, and had seen in the Satsuma Rebellion a way of moving a step closer to those goals by unhorsing the unpopular government. The Miyazaki brothers considered themselves adherents of this liberal tradition. Public schools populated by boys determined to become government officials thus served young Tōten poorly.

The far more liberal private academy established by Tokutomi to which Tōten next transferred, however, provided only temporary relief. Its atmosphere was temporarily exhilarating, but the kind of affirmation required in its public-speaking exercises drove young Miyazaki to avoid his turn, then to doubt the sincerity of his peers and his teachers, next to despair, and finally to flight. Once arrived in Tokyo, he languished, as he describes in striking pages, on the brink of total despair and self-rejection. He was saved from this abyss by a regeneration of conviction and rebirth as a Christian convert. The new faith, encountered in an accidental visit to a mission church, was nurtured through instruction at the hands of Kozaki Hiromichi of the "Kumamoto Band." Meanwhile, further schooling at what was to become Waseda and in several language schools culminating in the Nagasaki Cobleigh Academy produced the thought of traveling to Hawaii for education abroad.

Tōten's fervor as a Christian convert was total. He laid siege to and overcame his mother's defenses, and he also persuaded his brother Yazō to join him in the faith. When the depression years of the early 1880's made it necessary for the three brothers to return home for several years to conserve resources, Tōten was the leader in debate and the preacher in informal services he arranged for young people in the village. It was natural that such gatherings should be at the big Miyazaki family residence.

Yet Christianity did not long suffice to contain and channel Tōten's intensity. The Kumamoto depression years that had brought renewed association with his brothers found him turning to other concerns under their influence. Yazō, long a rather reluctant convert, undermined his brother's defenses with doubts about the Trinity; Tamizō, always a rationalist, argued that social problems should take precedence over otherwordly teachings. Tamizō's preoccupation with the inequalities of landholding grew naturally out of a setting in which tenants came in tears protesting their inability to pay their rent. He prevailed upon them to bear with things until the brothers' education, study, and reason had worked out a solution, something to which they, astonishingly enough, agreed. The solution Tamizō reached was provided by Henry George's single-tax proposal with the unearned increment reverting to society. Young Tōten—he was now in his early teens—gradually came to accept the priority of food over evangelizing, but he did so under the influence of his other brother, Yazō, who emphasized the importance of a solution that would embrace all Asia, and not just Japan alone.

What strikes the reader in these engrossing chapters is the immense vitality and terrible intensity with which these young people sought answers and accepted, then rejected, solutions. Young Tōten seems to have been unable to live with ambiguity. There was a directness and sincerity about him that required a total commitment and action on that commitment. Nothing less than total truth would do, and nothing less than an ultimate solution to the human predicament was worth his allegiance. For that program, once he found it, he was prepared to sacrifice all lesser goods of family, position, and ease.

The Mid-Meiji Perception of the World

The goal Tōten adopted for his life was nothing less than the revival of Asia. His brother Yazō had convinced him that Asia was being oppressed by the Western powers, of which Russia was only the most malevolent and the most visible aggressor. Asia's restoration to sovereignty and dignity depended upon the revival of China, its largest and most important state. That revival in turn was tied in with social reconstruction, for Tamizō's views of the evil of the system of landholding throughout the world made it possible to see reconstruction in China as essential to the solution of the problems of the poor of all the world. Heroism, compassion, universality, and self-sacrifice were all present in this dream, which drew upon each of the influences Tōten had known. He had not yet become one with "the Way," he wrote his wife in 1897, nor with truth; but he knew he had compassion. Theories might change, but one thing was indisputable: "Today millions of the poor throughout the world weep by the side of the road. That is completely clear. A compassionate hero who accepts a common fate with those millions and sets out to wage war on the injustice of false objectivity, does so not from falsehood, from error, or from duty, but because he cannot help himself, thanks to the sincerity that moves him to do the right."[2]

[2] Letter dated June 22, 1897, *Zenshū*, Vol. 5, pp. 348-50. This is also one of several excerpted and translated into Chinese and English by Chen Pengjen in *China Forum*, 6:1 (January 1979), as "Selected Letters of Miyazaki Torazō," pp. 293ff., and called to our attention by C. Martin Wilbur. The English translations are, however, quite unreliable.

Thus solutions to the social problem, the East Asian problem, and in fact the world problem, all lay in China. China's resurrection from weakness and humiliation, however, would require a political and social revolution to free it from the shackles of the Manchu dynasty. That revolution, in turn, depended upon the identification of a hero who could call the country back to health and strength. Yazō and Tōten thus set themselves the task of finding and helping such a hero. If none was to be found, Yazō said at one point, he would have to do it himself.

These goals were contemporary in their identification of the need for social reconstruction along lines of equality and revolution, and in their application of a Darwinian imagery of survival and struggle to the international environment. The brothers' idealistic view of their own compassionate and selfless role in the events to come was well within Meiji currents of romanticism and idealism. They were also contemporary in their acceptance and extension of the liberal movement's readiness to expand its analysis of Japan's problems to its neighbors. But they were also in touch with tradition. Tōten's childhood memories of injunctions to be a "hero" and a "general" were echoed in the quixotic role he envisaged for himself as midwife at the birth of the new China, and his constant invocation of "chivalry" and "chivalrous attitudes" drew on the samurai-Bushidō tradition of his own land as well as the knight-errant tradition and language of the great romantic novels of China. His conspirators' lair he dubbed the *ryōzanpaku*, a term used for the remote hideout of the heroes in the classic, *Water Margin* (or, as Pearl Buck preferred the title, *All Men Are Brothers*).

Japanese perceptions of the international environment in the 1880's and 1890's were commonly, and reasonably, akin to those that Miyazaki Yazō sketched out for his younger brother. The Western powers did seem a set of ravenous wolves whose strength grew as they fed on the riches and labor of the Asian lands they had subjected. The greater part of the Meiji governmental establishment, however, concluded that the only possible course for a modernizing Japan was to try to join the imperialist club and distance itself from Asia in policy and in Western imagination. War against China in 1894–95 brought control over Taiwan, a full share of imperialist privileges at the feast in Manchu China, and assurance that Korea would not be tied to the fortunes of the faltering regime in Peking. The twentieth century, which began with Japanese participation in suppression of the Boxer Rebellion, alliance with England, and victory over Tsarist Russia, seemed to most Japanese to confirm the correctness of that estimate.

For other Japanese, however, an affiliation with the West should never be more than tactical. Japan's mission was to be an Asian power, and its autonomy and strength, once established in Western eyes, should be devoted to working out a role of leadership in Asian change against the West. This kind of Asian consciousness could easily converge with Japanese nationalism to encourage expansion, and many "Asia firsters" who began with a position of anti-government liberalism ended by urging their government to take a firmer line on the nearby continent.

Tōten, however, did not. Although his career, like his interests, saw frequent overlap and occasional cooperation with advocates of national strength and national expansion, he remained independent and distrustful of them. He was won to the cause of Asia not by popular sentiment in the 1880's but rather by the arguments of his brother Yazō and, secondarily, by the eccentric counsel of an old European hobo named Isaac Abraham whom he met in Nagasaki. These individuals, and not press or political cries of alarm for the future of Japan in a divided world, swayed him. He saw himself, romantically as always, as a chivalrous hero working for the colored races of mankind, and not as the servant of his country nor his emperor. A temporary government assignment made it possible for him to find Sun Yat-sen in 1897, but it was the government that facilitated his needs, and not he that served the Meiji government.

The early stages of Tōten's Asian quest, without exception, ended in disaster. Yazō, a quiet bookish type, decided to go underground in the Chinese community in Japan to prepare himself for working for change in China. A letter to his mother before he broke off further contact with his family gives some sense of the romantic dedication and desperate determination of that effort. Yazō held out to her the challenge of serving as mother of the Gracchi, and then went on, ". . . this is the path of justice. The world situation is already urgent, and moreover we cannot do otherwise, for we believe that we are carrying out the will of the ruler of all the universe, which we dare not ignore, even if it costs our lives. . . . If our spirit is right, God will go with us, and God is lord of all things. . . ." Tōten himself invested what was left of his share of the family patrimony in a trip to China to learn Chinese, only to be cheated by old friends to whom he lent the money. He tried to work through Korea, only to lose his contact with the murder of the Korean reformer Kim Ok-kiun in 1894. A trip to Hakodate in the hope of finding a Chinese teacher failed because of the exodus of the Chinese community there during the Sino-Japanese War. Involvement in an immigration venture to Siam failed because of the collapse of the immigration company and very nearly cost him his life to cholera. And finally, and most tragically for Tōten, the death of his brother Yazō in Yokohama, where he was desperately trying to learn Chinese while pretending to be Chinese, brought him close to despair.

It was at this juncture that Tōten decided he would have to accept government money. In 1897 he wrote his wife of a visit to Yazō's tomb in Tokyo. He had poured out his heart in search of guidance without receiving any. "I realized then," he wrote, "that I could not achieve my great purpose as an individual"; accordingly he had "entered the gates of the powerful," and now mixed with politicians and talked "brazenly about politics and East Asian problems with them. I defer to their opinions and try to please them." He thought he must seem, in people's eyes, to have exchanged his ideals for the shallow rewards of power, flattery, and self-indulgence. "Alas," he granted; "I have become a geisha myself, and have had the baptism of vulgarity."[3] Yet a few months later these contacts and the financing they brought made it possible for Tōten to make the acquaintance of Sun Yat-sen. He had found his hero; his life was back on course.

Participation in the Chinese Revolution

Tōten became an actor in one of the great dramas of twentieth-century East Asian history through his participation in the cause of Sun Yat-sen. With one meeting, in which the discussion immediately turned to the revival of China and the salvation of Asia, he became Sun's disciple and confidant, certain that he had made the acquaintance of one of the great men of modern times.

The importance of this event for Chinese history was very great. Japanese support was an important part of Sun Yat-sen's ability to remain active and visible after the failure of his abortive rising in Canton in 1895. Tōten and the contacts he could provide made refuge in Japan possible for Sun, who passed for Japanese and learned to make use of the privileges a newly sovereign Japan had won in the international order to pursue his own purposes. Tōten helped make him known in Japan; his only contribution to the Fukuoka newspaper he served as free-lance reporter was a free translation of Sun Yat-sen's *Kidnapped in London*. After 1902 *The Thirty-Three Years' Dream*, which quickly found two Chinese translations, also helped make Sun better known in China.

Tōten was deeply involved in all Sun Yat-sen's affairs for the five years described in this autobiography, and again in the years after the Russo-Japanese War when Sun perfected his organizational network. In 1897 Tōten intervened with government officials to make it possible for Sun to live outside the Yokohama treaty-port community to which foreign

[3] *Zenshū*, Vol. 5, p. 350.

nationals were still restricted under the treaty system. While in Canton, on a secret mission with government instructions to report on revolutionary activities, Tōten met K'ang Yu-wei, who had fled to Hong Kong to escape certain death after the failure of the "Hundred Days" reform effort in 1898, and helped him make his way to Japan. Then and later, until the disastrous effort in Singapore he recounts in his autobiography, Tōten and his fellows did what they could to mediate between Sun's revolutionary partisans and the more highly placed and educated members of K'ang's reform movement. Tōten acted as intelligence agent and political associate for Sun in efforts to combine the Chinese secret societies in south China as prelude for a united revolutionary attempt. Until 1900 his freedom of movement in Singapore and Hong Kong was greater than Sun's, and even thereafter the protection he could receive as a Japanese citizen made it possible for him to take risks that would have been suicidal for Sun himself.

The Asia consciousness that made even China part of a larger cause was one Tōten shared with Sun Yat-sen and other revolutionaries. Together they accepted the logic of trying to help Aguinaldo fight for independence against American imperialism in the Philippines, confident that the islands, once liberated, could serve as a base for revolution in China. After that effort foundered with the overaged ship on which ammunition had been loaded, the conspirators secured the Filipinos' agreement to use the money and arms that remained for revolution in south China, since that in turn would benefit the Philippines. For a moment there was also a glimmer of hope for utilizing the new Japanese base of Taiwan; Japanese imperialism did not, as yet, seem to present a serious road-impediment block to the liberation of surrounding lands. The 1900 effort for revolution in south China also failed, betrayed by a corrupt Japanese businessman-politician who had been entrusted with Filipino money for the purchase of guns and ammunition. Violent disputes about responsibility and retribution for this outrage led to

Tōten's estrangement from his Japanese associates; they are detailed in the apologetic letter to Sun Yat-sen with which his volume closes. Tōten's conclusion that he had wasted his years and failed in his mission led to his final resolution to abandon hope and take up ballad chanting.

The rōnin *Life*

Private participation in international affairs was of considerable interest and occasional use to those on the fringe of the Meiji establishment, but covert purchase and export of arms for the export of revolution was of course illegal, and it became increasingly difficult and even dangerous as Meiji Japan itself was able to join the international establishment in the twentieth century.

This fact did not deter Tōten and his associates. They saw themselves as rebels against established authority and morality in the interests of a higher and a grander vision. They gloried in a frequently unkempt appearance, mocked conventional morality, and claimed for themselves the legacy of the masterless samurai (*rōnin*) of the time of the Meiji Restoration. Tōten contracted an early marriage and had family responsibilities that might have given pause to a more practical man, but he contented himself with occasional laments for his family's unhappy fate of grinding poverty while he followed his own "higher duty." On occasion he responded to emergency needs by attempting to find jobs for his wife, in one case selling coal, in another taking in boarders. More often he tried to provide solace and strength in letters that combined affection with calls to duty. In some memoirs she wrote in 1929 at the time of the dedication of Sun Yat-sen's tomb in Nanking his wife quotes one such letter; Ryūsuke, the oldest boy, was three, Shinsaku had just been born, and she had written to tell her husband of her desperate straits. Tōten assured her that he too suffered because of her plight. He had just read an account of the Restoration martyr Umeda Umpin and had found solace in it. "If we have any hope and faith," he counseled her, "we can find comfort in the midst of poverty. It is not poverty that is our great enemy, but pride that leads us to corruption. The wife that follows me must look through broken windows bravely. Our friends are the poor and the hungry. Our enemies are the aristocrats, landlords, and wealthy. We have to fight against the strongest people in society. I must ask you over and over again to accept poverty as the natural order of things. . . . After all, once you set out to fight the wrong what counts is that you fought bravely, even if the evil overcomes you." Other letters stress the futility of a hermit's retreat to the mountains, and hold up the greatness of Jesus and the Buddha as examples for her.[4] Meanwhile, for his readers Tōten repeatedly describes the way he tried to drown his loneliness by drinking sake and sought solace in liaisons with favorite girls in distant inns. It was a form of romantic and sentimental self-commiseration that spoke for his honesty and endeared him to his Meiji readers.

A *rōnin* was no more dependable as a guest than as a son-in-law, and in occasional rueful backward glances Tōten ruminates on innkeepers, geisha, and benefactors who fell victim to the generosity with which they tolerated his inability to pay his bills. No doubt such creditors had hopes of future greatness for a guest who seemed engrossed in affairs of note; they must have been impressed by the quality of some of his acquaintances, and undoubtedly they were drawn personally to a man of spirit and presence. In this they, too, had precursors in Restoration days when more than one of Japan's future leaders would have met an early end without the protection and benevolence provided by innkeepers and favorite geisha.

For Tōten and his associates the final judgment would depend on the quality of the goals that motivated him. Chivalry, noble generosity, and unselfishness were his measures.

[4] Letter written to his wife shortly before his departure for Siam. In 1967 Heibonsha edition, p. 276; and *Zenshū*, Vol. 5, p. 504.

His countrymen, then and later, as well as the Chinese revolutionaries who were his friends, recognized these qualities in him.

It should be noted in closing that Tōten's career as balladeer, like his early activities on behalf of the Chinese revolution, ended in failure. Fortunately for him, he had the opportunity to resume his career on Sun Yat-sen's behalf. Japan's victory over Russia in 1905 brought thousands of students from China to Tokyo to learn the secrets of successful modernization and national strength. In that setting Sun Yat-sen, who returned to Japan in 1905, was able to forge the new national organization that served as prelude to the revolutionary government of 1911. Tōten and a handful of other Japanese became charter members of the new revolutionary organization, held powers of attorney to act on its behalf, helped organize the publication of the revolutionary journal *Min Pao*, and journeyed to China in triumph when the revolution came in 1911. Sun Yat-sen himself was soon out of power again but Tōten, until his death in 1922, was tireless in travel, writing, and praise of his old friend, becoming himself a venerable example of the intimacy of Sino-Japanese cooperation that was doomed by the aggression of Imperial Japan in China.

The Text

Sanjū-sannen no yume was first published serially in *Ni-roku shinpō* between January 30 1902, and June 14 1902, in 123 installments. *Ni-roku shinpō*, which later became *Yorozu chōhō*, was a reformist, anti-government paper, and Miyazaki's account appeared on the first page in each issue. The work appeared in book form in August of that year and went through ten printings, eight before the year's end. A second edition appeared in 1926 with introduction by the distinguished political scientist and liberal leader Yoshino Sakuzō, and a third during World War II in 1943. The book has enjoyed periods of great popularity. "If someone were to ask me what my favorite ten books are," Yoshino Sakuzō wrote, "I would certainly include this." Takeuchi Yoshimi, a literary critic and Sinologue, ranked Tōten's with the accounts of Fukuzawa Yukichi and Ōsugi Sakae as one of the three great autobiographies of modern Japan.[5] Yet even among these it stands out for its candor, human interest, and color.

We have used the corrected text issued by Heibonsha in 1967 edited by Etō Shinkichi and the late Miyazaki Ryūsuke. This includes Yoshino Sakuzō's introduction to the 1926 edition as well as the full text of Miyazaki Ryūsuke's commentary prepared for the 1943 addition. Miyazaki's recollections of his father incorporate the memoir written by his mother, Tōten's wife, in 1929. This introductory essay has also drawn on several essays appended to materials in the five-volume *Complete Works* (*Miyazaki Tōten zenshū*), published by Heibonsha between 1971 and 1976, with Onogawa Hidemi and Miyazaki Ryūsuke as general editors. Notes for comprehension of the text have been drawn from those provided by Etō Shinkichi for the 1967 edition, pp. 237-252, by Shimada Kenji for the *Works* in Vol. 5, pp. 655-724, and from other sources. The events that are the subject of the book and the nature of Miyazaki's contribution are also discussed in Marius B. Jansen, *The Japanese and Sun Yat-sen* (Cambridge: Harvard University Press, 1954 and 1969; repr. also Stanford University Press, 1970); Etō Shinkichi, "Tōten to Shinkoku kakumei wa dō shite musubitsuita ka": ("What Was It That Drew Tōten to the Chinese revolution?"), *Shisō*, March 1968, pp. 371-382, Nomura Kōichi, "Ajiya e no koseki—Tōten no shisō to kōdō" ("The Sea Route to Asia: Tōten's Thought and Action"), in *Works*, Vol. 3, pp. 561-605, and Onogawa Hidemi, "Miyazaki Tōten to Shingai kakumei no zenya" ("Miyazaki Tōten and the eve of the Revolution of 1911"), *Works*, Vol. 1, pp. 593-611.

[5] From Yoshino's preface to 1926 edition, republished in 1967 Heibonsha edition, p. 255. Takeuchi's evaluation from Takeuchi Yoshimi, ed., *Ajiya shugi* (*Gendai Nihon shisōshi taikei*), Vol. 9 (Tokyo, Chikuma shobō, 1963), p. 48.

MY THIRTY-THREE YEARS' DREAM

Sapporo
Hakodate
Sendai
Yonezawa
Seoul
Nagano
Tokyo
Kyoto
Nagoya
Yokohama
Pusan
Kobe
Osaka
Hiroshima
Moji
Wakamatsu
Fukuoka
Saga
CHEJU I.
Kumamoto
Nagasaki
Yatsushiro
Kagoshima
OKINAWA
(RYUKYU)

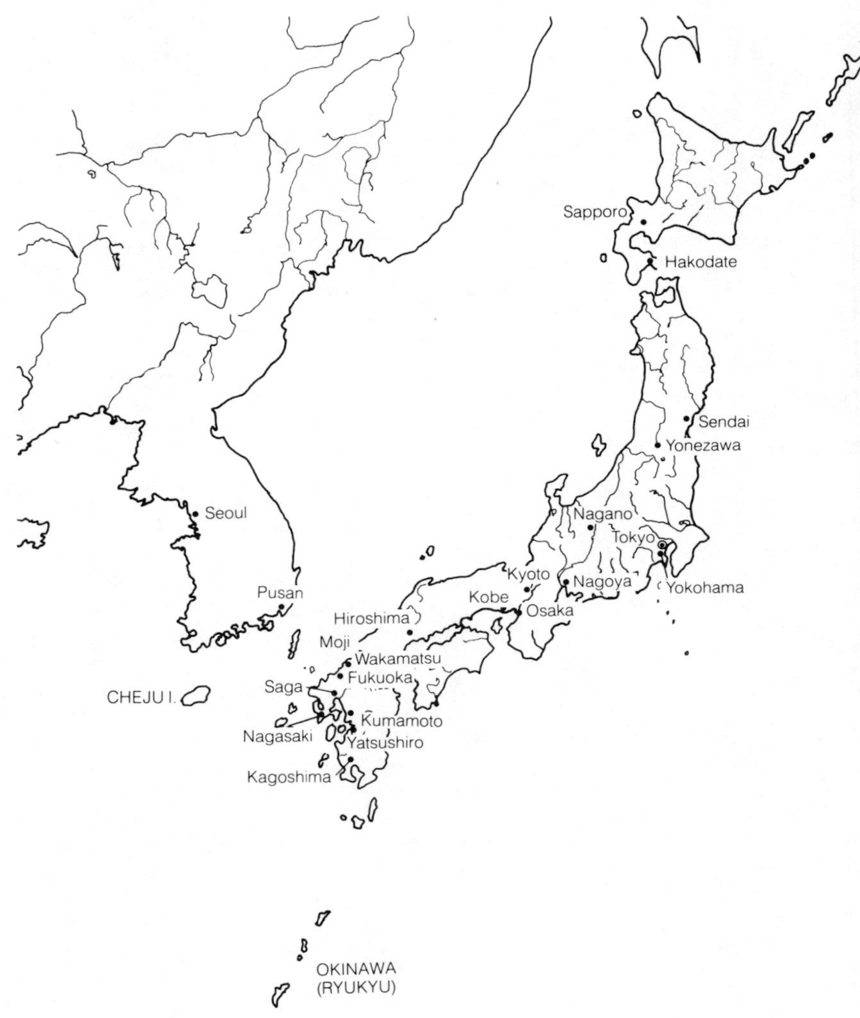

Japan

[1]

HALF MY LIFE A DREAM, I LONG FOR FALLEN BLOSSOMS

"MT. YOSHINO!" THE POEM GOES; "THE booming bell scatters the cherry blossoms." Yet the wind drives petals before it too, and it is wrong to blame the priest alone who sounds the bell. Some rejoice to see a branch heavy with blossoms, laden as though with snow; others delight in the wild blizzard of blossoms before the wind. Ten cases, ten tastes: each of us is stirred according to his spirit. The blossoms themselves, however, are not sensitive to this, but quite indifferent to it. Let me be like those blossoms.

Blossoms are beautiful. They are splendid when they rival fallen snow on cherry branches, and splendid when the wind drives them in a mad swirl of storm. But for me all this is past now, a dream of my life that is over. How should I bring it back? Am I not a blossom that has fallen in the mud?

Alas, half my life is gone, like fallen blossoms. I smile when I see the face in my mirror, and say to it, "You look like someone who might do great things, but the fact is that you lack courage. You look as though you might be a hero, but you haven't been able to achieve a thing. Imposing height and a splendid frame have been wasted on you, for your soul is puny. Your actions have seemed generous and noble, but your spirit is womanlike and timid. What it comes down to is that you're a great non-hero of the realm." Ah, a non-hero of the realm? Only that face and I!

> Then let us sing together of fallen flowers,
> let us act out a play of fallen flowers
> let us gather the flowers of Musashino,
> yes, let's, let's. . .

[2]

MY NATIVE HILLS AND RIVERS

IT HAPPENS THAT MY MOTHER, WHO HAS reached the great age of more than seventy years, still lives in my native village. If my song of fallen blossoms and of failure reaches her ears, what will her emotions be? My wife and children too are there in the same village. Faithful to the dream of their husband and father, they have endured all kinds of hardship. If they hear this song of mine, whatever will they say? And if I should ever go back what would Ichizō and Hyōkichi, our old servants, think of me? Indeed I wonder how the mountains and rivers would greet me if I went back?

There is a little hamlet in Kumamoto prefecture called Arao. It is about ten miles northwest of the Kumamoto castle that stands as reminder of the dream of Katō Kiyomasa,[1] and situated along the Nagasu road that runs like a long thread to the border of the province of Chikugo. The people in Arao are poor, but they are forthright and honest. The soil is barren, but the landscape is splendid. It was in this lonely hamlet that I was born to a well-known local family of the *gōshi*, "country samurai," class. I grew up with calls of "Master! Master!" ringing in my ears. In the morning the eastern sky would brighten

[1] Katō Kiyomasa (1562-1611), a leading daimyo during the sixteenth-century wars, was granted the domain of Kumamoto by the first Tokugawa shogun and constructed a famous castle there.

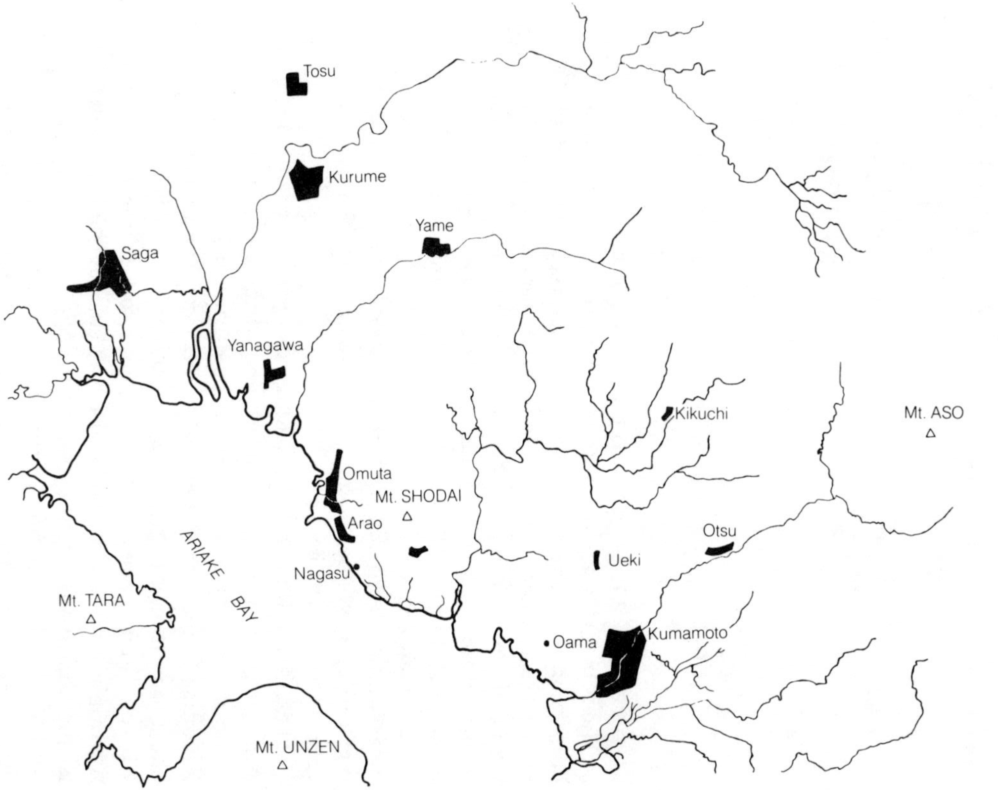

Tōten's native Kumamoto Prefecture

over Shichimenpō, an eminence once crowned by the castle of Lord Yukihira; the evening sun would set on the white caps of the waves that washed Ariake Bay. In the distance I could make out the ridges of Unzen and Tara in Hizen to the west. How often I exclaimed aloud, as I marveled at this setting of mountains and ocean, "Wonderful! This is a landscape to produce heroes!" And yet what of me now? Did it fail me, or was it I who failed? What is a hero, anyway?

[3] MY FAMILY

My father died when I was eleven, so I have only a few memories of him. I do remember that he opened a school in which he taught fencing to the boys of the locality. I also remember that he would sometimes load a horse with watermelons that he had grown himself and go through the village giving them to the aged and the sick. And I remember how frightened I could be sometimes when, after having had too much sake to drink, he would wave his arms around and bellow some tuneless song at the top of his lungs. But what stands out most clearly in my mind is the unforgettable way he had of patting me on the head several times a day and telling me to be sure to become a hero or a great general. Also, whenever money was put in my hand he would tell me sternly that only beggars ever asked for money. My mother reinforced my father's teachings. Hers was a strong spirit. She was forever warning me that nothing was more shameful than for a man to die in bed. And my relatives, and the elderly men and women in the village, all added their voices to urge me to "be like your elder brother!" They meant my oldest brother, Hachirō, who had become an activist in the movement for freedom and people's rights in the early Meiji period. He had traveled all over the country, before losing his life in the Satsuma Rebellion of 1877. I didn't have much of an idea of what it meant to be a great general or a hero, but I did know that I wanted to be one. I didn't know what freedom or people's rights were, but I knew that they were good things, and I was sure that government armies, government officials, in fact anyone involved with government, was a criminal and a thief. A great general or a great hero, I thought, should lead a rebel army or an insurrection. As I look back now, I wonder whether the teaching I received at home was wrong, or whether it was I who failed to measure up to that teaching. At any rate, this is all I have amounted to.

There were eleven children in my family, eight boys and three girls. I was the youngest. In addition, there was for a time an additional adoptive elder brother named Motoeimon, but I never knew him. According to what my mother said, it had been my father's plan to have this adoptive son succeed to the family responsibilities as head, so that his own children would be free to follow their own desires and ambitions after he had provided them with what they needed in the way of education. But in fact the adoptive son had other ideas; instead of accepting his responsibilities he had abandoned our family and household, he had fled the domain to become a *rōnin*, and he was killed fighting with the Chōshū troops at the Hamaguri Gate in Kyoto in 1863.[2] All but two of my elder brothers died early too. At the time of my father's death, only two sisters, two elder brothers, and I were still alive. At that time my sisters had already been married off, my elder brothers were studying in a private school in a nearby county, and I was in a nearby village primary school. During the hours for penmanship and writing I would write the words for freedom and people's rights,[3] although

[2] A high-water mark of the radical loyalist movement leading to the Meiji Restoration, in which regular and irregular forces of the Chōshū domain tried to seize the palace gates and thereby control the imperial court.

[3] *Jiyū* and *minken*, new compounds (and concepts) that designated the movement for democratic rights of the period. Used interchangeably with "liberal movement."

the teachers frequently told me that I should not do so. I was a natural activist for freedom and people's rights, and I wasn't going to let the teachers' warnings change my attitude. After I became fifteen and left primary school for middle school the same obsession continued, even though the school principal and the teachers warned me about it. My fellow-students in particular resented my attitudes, and they trapped me and roughed me up after school at night more than once.

When I was in middle school my oldest brother, Tamizō, was in Tokyo and the other, Yazō, was studying in Osaka. My mother looked after things alone with a faithful maid called Onaka. My father had never paid much attention to household finances. He had taken great delight in giving what he could to the poor and in entertaining guests who came from far away, and as a result the household had fallen on such difficult days that it was almost more than could be managed. My mother, woman though she was, somehow had to manage things and pay for three sons in school. It can be imagined what a difficult time she had. Sometimes when I came home needing additional money for school that we didn't have, my mother would take things like bedding or mosquito nets to the pawn shop. All I could do when I noticed this was stay out of sight and cry quietly. How much I owe my mother for managing to overcome such difficulties and enable us to get a certain amount of schooling! There was also an old farmer, Hirakawa Hikoyomi, in the village who gave her some help in managing things. When the old man died his son, whose name was Senma, succeeded him and continued that help. He continued to help us in looking after our run down place as a substitute father. He was a benefactor of our family, and more: it is remarkable that such a man should have appeared in our degenerate age.

[4]
MIDDLE SCHOOL AND THE ŌE ACADEMY

My classmates in middle school all had the same ambition: they were constantly saying, "I'm going to be an official" or "I'm going to get a job in the government." All they could think of was a government position. But to me officials and administrators were robbers or criminals, and I considered them enemies of the movement for freedom and people's rights. As a result I disliked those students even more than they disliked me; in fact I despised them. The problem was that I was powerless against so many. I was a single rebel, surrounded by a government army. It would be hopeless to try to engage them in battle; on the contrary, I had to retreat into defensive positions. Furthermore, two of the teachers had been members of the old Kumamoto "Divine Wind" reactionary party;[4] they still wore their old samurai topknots. Personally they were in fact estimable gentlemen, but for someone as intent on freedom and people's rights as I was, having to study under such teachers was like having to beg for food in the enemy camp. I found it very unpleasant. Consequently I developed plans of escape from this setting in which I was surrounded by my enemies. I

[4] The *Shimpūren* revolt of 1876, in which anti-foreign, loyalist lower samurai in Kumamoto rebelled against the local government's adherence to the modernizing policies of the new Meiji government. The revolt was precipitated by an order to samurai to stop wearing their swords.

got up an excuse to give my mother, and then planned my getaway. Where was I to go? At that time the prevailing winds were conservative and subservient, and only one school raised the banner of freedom and people's rights for the education of men of ability. This was the Ōe Academy in Takuma, in Kumamoto.

The Ōe Academy had been established by Tokutomi Iichirō,[5] and I became his disciple. At that time Tokutomi was not only a vehement advocate of people's rights; he also ran a remarkably democratic and free school. Our teacher did not allow his students to call him "Sensei," but insisted we call him by his first name. Consequently it was not "Tokutomi Sensei," but "Iichirō-san." The curriculum and schedule were worked out in discussion between Iichirō-san and the other teachers, but they did not lay down any school regulations. These the students worked out by themselves through discussion. In other words, we were a free and autonomous people. As a result everybody supported the regulations enthusiastically and we all worked hard at our studies. On a winter morning there would be some who got up early and practiced fencing with bamboo swords in the morning frost, and others would try to read books under their bedding late at night. On the one hand white-bearded Kisui, Iichirō's old father, would be seated on a shabby floor-mat lecturing on Spencer's *Principles of Ethics*; on the other our Iichirō-san was getting more and more excited talking about the French Revolution. As his lecture reached its climax, the students would involuntarily break into wild approval, jump up and dance around, swing their swords and strike the pillars. Iichirō-san would never make the slightest effort

[5] Tokutomi Iichirō (Sohō) (1853-1957), educated in the Kumamoto Western School of Captain L. L. Janes, and then at Dōshisha in Kyoto, taught for a time before the 1886 publication of his buoyant *Shōrai no Nihon* (The Future Japan). He then moved to Tokyo to take up a remarkable career as journalist and publisher, initially as exponent of liberalism and English thought, and subsequently as a leading voice of Japanese nationalism.

to still this wild confusion. For me, the contrast with the heavy formalism of the school I had left was enough to make me think that I had returned home.

A Speech Club that met every Saturday morning was something that particularly impressed me. This included not just the older students, who might have been expected to belong as a matter of course, but even snot-nosed youngsters of twelve or thirteen who were expected to give speeches too. Now it was one thing for them to be able to speak. But I was really taken aback by their eloquence. And it was another thing for them to be eloquent. But I, a self-defined advocate of freedom and people's rights, was put to shame by the knowledge of these speakers, who went on and on lauding Robespierre and Danton, quoting Washington and Cromwell, and arguing about Cobden and Bright with confident enthusiasm. My advocacy of freedom and people's rights had consisted of little more than the conviction that they were good things, and that they were essential to the success of a great general, a hero, and a revolutionary army. That's all I knew. How was I to know about Cromwell and Robespierre, much less Cobden and Bright? How could I mount the speaker's rostrum? I had nothing to say when I got there. So I tried to get out of it by pleading illness, or taking long walks in the mountains. In this manner I, the born advocate of liberalism and freedom, was driven to desperation.

The Ōe Academy was indeed an ideal home for me. No, more: it was a paradise of progressive liberalism and democracy, and I was truly happy to be there. The only problem was that Saturday Speech Club. I got out of it two or three times by pretending to be ill, but when the count went up to five or six I knew I couldn't very well keep that up. Shouldn't I take a chance and mount the rostrum? But then what if I had nothing to say? I developed a rationalization to conceal my own shortcomings. I argued that anybody could speak well if the occasion called for it, and that to practice speaking as an exercise was to lower oneself to the level of a performer. I built myself up in this manner so that the born advocate of liberalism would not be disgraced. But what began as a rationalization became a firm belief. And then I extended it to practice in writing. I think that is why my writing is poor to this day.

Things thus reached a point at which I scorned practice in speaking and writing as appropriate only for performers. Those who had embarrassed me by their skill could now be dismissed as entertainers. Consequently, all sixty of my fellow students were just showing off. There was no reason whatever to be intimidated by them. The admiration I had for them now turned to contempt. And then another doubt came into my mind. What was that? It concerned sincerity. My fellow students praised freedom and people's rights and wrote essays about their love of people, their love of our country, and their readiness to give their lives for its good. But were they really sincere in this? The doubts I should have directed at myself I now directed to others instead and the questions I should have asked myself I asked of others. Was I concentrating on the shortcomings of others and excusing my own, and pointing out the ugliness of others to conceal my own? I didn't know, wasn't sure. But I was tormented by these doubts and gradually stopped studying. I could not sleep, and I knew only that I was terribly upset by all this.

I finally put my doubts to Matsue Yaichirō. I thought he was probably the most sincere of the students at the academy. I asked him this question: "I recognize your sincerity. When you speak of devoting your life to the country and to the service of our people, do you do this without any thought of self at all, without any idea of bringing honor to your own name? I wish you would reveal your true feelings to me." Matsue laughed aloud and said, "Doesn't everybody think about his own reputation? Isn't that why people do what they do? My reputation means everything to me." That was his reply. On hearing it I was startled: was it that way even with him? "Well," I asked, "what about Iichirō-san?" He was emphatic in his answer: "Why, Iichirō-san is even more concerned with fame than we are." When he saw how disappointed I was, he tried to reassure me. "It's best not to worry too much about unnecessary matters like this," he said. "A man is born in the world, achieves something, and builds a fine reputation; then he dies. That is enough. You shouldn't worry any further." But these reassurances didn't console me in the slightest. I thought to myself that it was elegant and splendid to die for one's country and for one's people. But if you did so just to build up your own fame, wasn't it only another form of egoism?

So-called "idealists" of this sort seemed to me no better than butchers who labeled dog meat as lamb. In fact, if this was really true of Iichirō-san, shouldn't he be exposed too? As a result of all this I became dogmatic and arrogant. I despised not only my fellow students, but even my teacher. And then, by extension, all the great heroes, the men of high purpose of former and present times: they too became objects of my contempt. After a while I began to examine myself as well. How could I be an advocate of freedom and people's rights without knowing what those things were all about? How could I affirm civil rights without understanding them? Then these questions were suddenly solved for me: I was just a slave to the movement for freedom and people's rights. I was even more despicable than my schoolmates who advocated liberalism without sincerity. If I were to despise my fellow students, I had no choice but to go on to despise myself. Right. I too was despicable. As a result I was without hope, deep in melancholy, and unable to sleep or eat. I had thrown my disguise away, but my true self had not yet emerged. My heart was like a kite whose string had broken, fluttering in the sky without being able to return to earth. My body was like a lamb separated from its flock, wandering through the wilderness without knowing where to go. I was in total despair. When I asked myself what could be done in a life of fifty or sixty years, it seemed that all that could be done was to take care of one's immediate wants and desires. My own ugliness had been revealed in the mirror I held up to my associates, and I had myself become entrapped in my own questions about the philosophy of life.

Truly, self-rejection is the most dangerous state that a person can fall into. All hope and desire are lost in such cases. As a result, the barriers against any kind of action go down too. No one in this world can cope with that. When a person is not where he thinks he ought to be, and cannot grasp what he thinks he ought to be able to grasp, he is overcome with misery and unspeakable pain. Suffering follows suffering and produces confusion; confusion and pain merge, become ever more entwined, and finally end in self-abandonment. Emotion then flares up in the heart of such a person. If that emotion meets virtue, he can still attain supreme wisdom. Otherwise he will be scorched and killed by its flame. That is why I say that despair itself is not fatal; rather, it marks a point of life and death. Only the god of fate determines which path will be followed.

I now stood at the crossroads of adventure or of pain, at the brink of self-rejection. What was I to do? I had developed a liking for sake. So I went to town and drank. I had a taste for good food. And so I broke the academy regulations and indulged myself in restaurants that served chicken and beef. I was sixteen, and had begun to think about women. If I had had money and companions I would have gone on to visit brothels. But all I had was three yen a month, and I couldn't even manage chicken, beef, and cheap sake, much less prostitutes. Still, if I had wanted to do so strongly enough I probably could have found some way of doing so. I could have stolen money. Since I had given up all thought of fame and reputation, there were after all no bounds of morality to restrain me. No judgments of good and evil stood in my way, and I was at the point of self-abandonment and rejection. No thought of virtue stayed my hand from theft. But in fact I did not go that far, and I find some consolation when I reflect on that.

Nevertheless the Ōe Academy, which had been a land of freedom for me, now became a land of bondage in which I felt shackled. Its counterfeit exponents of freedom and people's rights were loud in their criticism when they saw me drunk with sake. Those slaves of fame and reputation maligned me when they saw me frequenting chicken and beef restaurants. At the point of self-rejection, I also despised them, and ended by disliking the Academy. So I manufactured an excuse for my mother and my brother Yazō. I said I was going to study German. I left the Ōe Academy and set out for Tokyo.

[5]

I ABANDON MYSELF TO DESPAIR

NOW THAT I HAD QUITE DESPAIRED OF MY OWN worth, I stood at a point of great danger and temptation. How was the god of fate going to deal with me? Upon my arrival in Tokyo, I got in touch with a friend from Kumamoto and arranged to stay in his lodging-house. At a time when everything I saw was new and novel to me, nothing astonished me more than the transformation of my friend. To begin with, I could not get over the change in his outward appearance. He had always been a healthy fellow with cropped hair and shabby clothes, but now his hair was slicked down and combed sideways. Instead of the short gown he used to wear, he now affected a long kimono of softly rustling silk that even hid his toes. A mirror occupied the place of honor on his desk. His face, formerly of a metallic and ruddy complexion, was so pale that he had the look of a ghost that had caught a cold. When we went to the public bath together he would spend about an hour washing his face with soap. I was no less astonished by other changes in him from the way he talked with his friends. He had always been a fervent advocate of freedom and people's rights, his speech full of virtuous filial morality, but now all he could talk about was the comparative merits of prostitutes, geishas, serving-girls at archery stands in amusement centers, and waitresses in fancy restaurants for beef; moreover he seemed to base those evaluations on action. He and his friends of course had no knowledge of the depth of my despair; they were afraid of the news I might send home, and at first they tried to conceal what they were doing. After I was on to them they begged me to keep it to myself and then did their best to drag me into their pattern of dissipation.

I had settled on a position of despair. That being so, might it not have made sense for me to take the course they had taken? Would they not be appropriate guides for action? Should I take another step and fall in with them? I did not do so. I held off, and flatly refused to join them. But even I, however, was not sure why. All I know is that I conceived a dislike for them that I couldn't explain. All I know is that I wanted to vomit when I saw how they looked, how they sounded, and how they acted. Finally it reached the point that I didn't even want to see their faces. So I left that lodging, moved to a private boarding school, and broke off all contact with them.

Saigō Takamori[6] once said that schools are meant to build character and that character is something that should prepare men for action on the world level, and not just on the local village or county level. I felt this way about schools too. Still, my purpose in entering this particular school was an unusual one. I had not resolved to cultivate my determination and prepare my character for a global task. Nor was I seeking to become a scholar by studying languages and reading books. My main purpose was to get away from the offensive mannerisms, talk, and actions of these obnoxious friends I had left behind, and the boarding school simply provided the cheapest way I could do it. To put it most simply, I used a place of learning as an inexpensive hiding place in which to nourish my despair. In

[6] Saigō (1827-77), Satsuma samurai and hero of the Meiji Restoration, regarded then and since as a paragon of personal and moral courage. He died leading the Satsuma Rebellion against the Meiji government in which Miyazaki's elder brother Hachirō met his end. Both loyalist and liberal opponents of the Meiji regime laid claim to his legacy.

this purpose I succeeded. But I failed in the first objective, because I merely exchanged four or five obnoxious companions for forty or fifty who were equally objectionable. I managed to get out of the mud puddle only to end up in the privy. For that school turned out to be not just my individual cut-rate lodging; it was also bargain lodging for a community of sex maniacs. So I often thought of the poet's lament, "What I once deplored now looks attractive in my recollection." The Ōe Academy that I had considered so constricting, the old classmates whose advocacy of freedom and people's rights I had considered insincere, all this now began to take on a more pleasant cast in the recollections of my despair. Ah, wide as the world was, where was I to fit in? And so I changed again, from a child of despair, to a child of complaint, and then once more, becoming a world-weary misanthrope. How often, at night when everyone else was quietly asleep, would I feel that I alone had been left out of things! I would quietly break into sobs.

[6]

I BECOME A CHRISTIAN

AT THAT TIME THERE WAS A STUDENT AT THE school named Araki Mihohiko who had been ahead of me at the Ōe Academy. He took me around to see the famous places in Tokyo every day, and thereby managed to ease the despair in my heart to some degree. One Sunday evening Araki was serving as my guide again on a stroll; when we passed in front of a Christian church on our way back, he suggested that we enter. Accordingly I followed him in without particularly thinking about it. Once we were inside I listened to a hymn, still without giving it much thought. Somehow the organ sounded beautiful. The music of the hymn seemed truly pure. I listened to this for a little while, and then my heart seemed to soar until it was as clear as a serene autumn evening sky. Moreover, when I looked at the members of the congregation who were singing along with the organ I envied their apparent composure and peace of mind. When the sound of the hymn and the organ died away a missionary stood up in the pulpit. He talked about the existence of a supreme being. I don't know whether his sermon was good or bad, and I cannot remember the arguments he used anymore. All I can remember is that because of this it was suddenly as though I was seeing the hope of light in the darkness of the night. All I can remember is that I had the feeling that I should dedicate my life and everything I had to that god. I do remember the selection from the Bible that he read at the end of the sermon. After the reading of the Bible the clear tone of the organ sounded again and another hymn was sung. It was as though I was sad, then happy, yet unable to express a word and somehow close to tears. I left the church as though in a dream when the service had ended. And, still as though in a dream I went to a bookstore to look for a Bible and a hymnbook and purchased them. Still in that same state, I returned to my school and read in them; looked for the passages the missionary had read from the Bible, and read them to myself. "The light of the body is the eye: if therefore thine eye be single, thy whole body shall be full of light. But if thine eye be evil, thy whole body shall be full of darkness. If therefore the light that is in thee be darkness, how great is that darkness! . . . Therefore I say unto you, take no thought for your life, what ye shall eat, or what ye shall drink; nor yet for your body, what ye shall put on. Is not the life more than meat, and the body than raiment? Behold the fowls of the air: for they sow not, neither do they reap, nor gather into barns; yet your heavenly Father feedeth them. Are ye not much better than they? Which of you by taking thought can add one cubit unto his stature? And why take ye thought for raiment? Consider the lilies of the field, how they grow; they toil not, neither do they spin. . . . But seek ye first the kingdom of God, and his righteousness; and all these things shall be added unto you. Take therefore no thought for the morrow: for the morrow shall take thought for the things of itself. Sufficient unto the day is the evil thereof." Those words and phrases pierced my heart like the sharp edges of a sword. Every phrase, every sentence could be a wellspring for my life. Feelings of joy and of sorrow surged in my heart, and finally I wept. Weeping I read, reading I wept; as the night passed I was alone with my feelings of joy and grief and experienced the sensation of an exquisite sorrow. Was it because the god of fate had not yet discarded me?

At one bound the child of despair had become a child of hope. Already I had seen a stream of light. I could not stop without pressing on to the point I had to reach. For the space of a week I hardly slept as I read through my Bible. Its phrases and sentences all struck my spirit like charges of electricity. "But I say unto you, That whosoever looketh on a woman to lust after her hath committed adultery with her already in his heart. And if thy right eye offend thee, pluck it out, and cast it from thee; . . ." When I read these phrases I trembled for my past. But then, as I read phrases like, "Come unto me, all ye that labour and are heavy laden," and "what man is there of you whom, if his son ask bread, will he give him a stone?" I was buoyed up by a joy I had never known.

Of course the fellows who shared my cheap lodgings with me had no understanding of this at all. They laughed at me because I suddenly seemed to be becoming studious. Some of them made fun of me and suggested that I was planning to become a Christian minister. Ah, you poor sex maniacs! Can't you realize that there are standards by which to judge morality and behavior aside from what other people think and say? I have now discovered that there are. Don't you know that man has a soul as well as a body? I am now moving upward to its source. Can't you realize there is a god on high? I am trying to understand that now. You fellows are so obsessed with the smell of women's powder that you are like a lot of flies buzzing around filth, and you cannot see that I am intoxicated with the pure zephyrs of spring. I am no longer the I of yesterday. The I you see before you is a new person. None of their lies and slurs could hurt me anymore. I had become generous and forgiving. I was no longer the whining malcontent of yesterday.

Sunday was the happiest day of the week. Now it was I who invited Araki to go to church with me. We attended the morning service and breathed in the pure air of our new world. And then we attended the longed-for evening service again. As the melodious organ played my spirit was at peace, the pure music of the hymn calmed my heart and I listened to the sermon of the missionary. When the service ended we left the church as though in a trance, full of emotion. One day, as I was returning from church alone, full of emotion, someone suddenly tapped me on the shoulder from behind. When I turned to look it was the missionary who had been standing in the pulpit. I bowed to him without thinking, and then he spoke to me in the kindest terms imaginable, "You are somebody who should receive God's grace. The Lord wants to save you. I live in Tsukiji, house number 4. Just ask for Fisher[7] and you won't have any difficulty finding me. My wife is there too. Please come to visit us any time you wish. I would be delighted to talk about God and about the saving power of Christ with you. Please read this booklet on your return. You will see that there is a Lord God." With that he took a small pamphlet out of his pocket and gave it to me. I was unable to keep the tears from welling up in my eyes. But since I didn't know what I should say I just bowed to him while sobbing. I returned to my school, and as if in a dream read that small pamphlet. It was entitled "The Three Principles of Christianity," and explained the existence of God, the sinfulness of man, and salvation through Christ in simple terms for beginners in the faith.

The next morning I went to the Reverend Mr. Fisher's house after breakfast. He welcomed me warmly, introduced his wife and his children, and treated me like a member of his family. Now I understood the expression about becoming an old friend on first acquaintance. And yet it really was the first time they had met me. What particularly moved me was so warm a response from a

[7] Charles H. D. Fisher (1848-1921), a pioneer Baptist missionary from Illinois who came to Japan in March 1883 from India and worked in Japan for thirty-seven years, returning only three times on sabbatical. A colleague described him as a preacher of such intensity that tears would run down his cheeks, and an orator whose voice was like thunder.

foreigner. What was more, Mr. Fisher then proceeded to teach from the Bible for me, and his wife began to teach me the first steps in English. So I got into the pattern of going from my dormitory in Hongo to house number 4 in Tsukiji every day.

Time went on, and it became mid-summer. The Reverend Fisher took his family off for a summer vacation and my dormitory mates gradually moved on too, until there were only two or three students left with me. However, it never occurred to me to flee the heat or to envy those who had left. After all, I had a source of solace the others did not know.

At this time I heard that my old teacher Iichirō-san had come to Tokyo and that he was staying in Shibaura. I went to see him right away. I had missed him, but it was also my intention to apologize quietly to him for the way in which my attitude and immature outlook had led me to scorn him and criticize him. Yes, I had become such a faint-hearted person that I wanted to do this quietly, though I didn't have the courage to make a full public apology. However, my teacher not only made light of my failings as though I had nothing to apologize for, but drew me to him and wanted to know all about me and what I was doing. When he heard about my fervent interest in Christianity he reassured me and rejoiced. Furthermore, he suggested that I move in with him and then he introduced me to his friend the Reverend Mr. Kozaki Hiromichi.[8] By this means I was able to become a disciple of Kozaki, and every day I went from my teacher's house in Shibaura to see Mr. Kozaki, thus gradually entering the path of Christian faith.

And then the summer vacation came to an end, school opened again, and the students all returned to the capital and resumed their studies. As for me, I had left that

[8] Kozaki (1856–1938), like Tokutomi a member of the "Kumamoto Band" of converts of L. L. Janes, was a leader of modern Japanese Protestant Christianity through his Tokyo Reinanzaka Church and the journal *Rikugo zasshi*.

inexpensive lodging, renewed my determination, and entered Waseda.[9] By this time my teacher Iichirō-san had decided to stay in Tokyo, and sent his faithful student Hitomi Ichitarō to close the Ōe Academy in Kumamoto. Many of the students followed their teacher to Tokyo, and a good many of them ended up in Waseda also. Accordingly, the fellow students whom I had formerly despised now ended up lodging with me in a corner of the capital, and we often enjoyed talking about the past.

At this time the support I got from home came to only 6 yen a month. My expenses each month were 3 yen for food and 1 yen 80 sen for tuition, thus totalling 4 yen, 80 sen. I used the 1 yen 20 sen that remained for supplies and pocket money. I couldn't even afford baked sweet potatoes. That's how poor I was. The same was true of some of my fellow students. After getting a group together, we bargained with a nearby *shiruko* (bean soup) shop and worked out a monthly price of 2 yen and 50 sen for food; combined with lodging, this left us with 50 sen more each month. Fifty sen was a lot of money. We were delighted with this arrangement, but after a month the *shiruko* man called it off: we were eating too much, and he was losing money. Since it couldn't be helped, we shifted our trade to a nearby barber's wife, who agreed to our proposal. But she too called it off at the end of a month, for the same reason as before. Finally, we rented a tiny six-mat house in Toshima, did our own cooking, and carried on our studies more comfortably. There were five of us, all former students of Ōe Academy. People called it the house of the five paupers. However, I myself was not conscious of living in poverty. I had the staff of life in the Bancho Church where the Reverend Mr. Kozaki preached. I went there every Sunday and listened to the sermon, sang the

[9] Waseda University, as it is now known, was founded in 1882 by the political leader Ōkuma Shigenobu after his break with the government. Originally a private academy called Tokyo Senmonkō, it was officially renamed Waseda University in 1903.

hymns, and in listening to the sermon, singing the hymns, and studying the Bible knew a joy beyond comparison. Thanks to that I marched toward a new life.

Fall and winter passed and I entered the spring of my 17th year. One day Mr. Kozaki spoke to me and asked me whether I would not like to be baptized. Of course that was what I wanted. However, I had been introduced to this path by the Reverend Mr. Fisher and for that reason regarded him as my spiritual father. When I explained to the Reverend Kozaki that I thought I should be baptized by Mr. Fisher he agreed, but went on to say, "The Reverend Mr. Fisher is a Baptist. Baptist church governance is on the whole close to ours, but their provisions for baptism are rather complicated. Still, Christianity is ultimately one faith, and you should do what you want to do." I hadn't realized up to now that Christianity had just as many sects and denominations as Buddhism. And now that I found this out, it troubled me greatly. When I asked why this was so, Mr. Kozaki explained the history of the church in simple terms to me. Then for the first time I realized that I stood at a point at which I had to make a choice. In the end, without a great deal of consideration, I chose the Congregational Church, because the governance of that denomination was republican in character and its articles of faith were liberal. Could this have represented a resurgence of the liberal movement whose thought I had previously abandoned? In the last analysis I was a person who could not give up that movement.

I received baptism from the Reverend Mr. Kozaki and joined his congregation, becoming a child of God and a member of the Kingdom of God on earth. What could be happier than this? I went to see the missionary, Mr. Fisher, and told him that I had been baptized by Mr. Kozaki, and that I had joined the body of believers. To my astonishment Mr. Fisher didn't look pleased at all when he heard this. Instead he began arguing about baptism with me. Because of this I was quite upset, not so much for reasons of dogma as because of my personal relationship with Mr. Fisher; I did not see how personal relationships could, in the final analysis, conflict with universal principles. I stated firmly that I was perfectly satisfied with the Congregational Church. But Mr. Fisher became angrier and angrier, and finally raised his voice and warned me that baptism in the Congregational Church would not suffice for my salvation. I had gone to visit this minister in order to share my joy with him; not only had I failed in that purpose but I had been affronted. To be sure this wasn't enough to destroy the peace of mind that I had gained. Still, new as I was to Christianity, a small cloud had formed in my mind. I thought, I would have to study more before I could reach heaven.

Meanwhile, my mother, living in my native village, had reached the advanced age of sixty and had not yet heard these happy gospel tidings. When I thought of this, the warm spring of my heart gave way to a sudden cloud of concern that I could not suppress. And so I hurried back to my rural home and expounded the faith to my mother. I pressed it strongly on her. But although my own faith was strong, I wasn't sufficiently educated in Christianity yet to be able to persuade others. And so I wept and prayed, and prayed and wept, and in the end conquered my mother with prayers and tears. She told me later, "I was amazed by your fervor. I thought if a young fellow is that fervent, there must be something quite extraordinary in Christianity. You raised all sorts of doubts in me, and in the end I entered your faith." My mother is still a believer, and her faith has grown stronger with the years. But I am what I am. How strange life is!

"Now that I have become a believer thanks to you, you can be at ease and go back to Tokyo. Study hard so that you don't fall behind the others," my mother said. Without any hesitation, she had some of the timber on our family land cut down and sold for my benefit. I received travel money and several months of school expenses from my mother with tears in my eyes, and went back to Tokyo a second time. My elder brother Yazō had come to Tokyo from Osaka with his friend Shishido and taken up residence in a house in Kōjimachi.

Soon summer vacation came and I moved into my brother's lodging. Living together with him, I tried to utilize the opportunity to become an evangelist for Christianity. For some reason they seemed unprepared to listen, and constantly tried to avoid my eyes and whisper quietly together. I was deeply puzzled by this, but didn't comment on it, and simply continued to preach my way of faith to them. One day, as I was preaching in my usual manner to my brother, he replied with some irritation "Religion is very important, to be sure. But at the moment I have more important things in sight, and I really don't have time to talk about religion with you." I answered that there were of course many important things in human life, but what could be more important than eternity? I took out my Bible and read the phrase "What shall it profit a man, if he gain the whole world and lose his own soul?" "Shouldn't this phrase make you stop and think?" I asked. Yazō read it through again and again and seemed deeply moved by this, then turning to me said, "You've succeeded in cooling my fervor and ambition. I've lost the courage to reject your warnings and pursue my own ambition." He then went on to reveal his own secret intentions to me.

"Every man must have some major direction in his life. I have been devoting my thought to this for many years, and recently I've come to think that I have found a solution. The present situation of the world is a battlefield in which the strong devour the weak. The strong use force as it pleases them and the rights and freedoms of the weak are being devoured and overrun day by day and month by month. How can we overlook this state of affairs? Surely those who prize human rights and revere freedom have to develop a plan to overturn this state of affairs. If we do not work out some defense, I believe that the yellow race will be oppressed by the white race for years to come. The upshot of this, the way this destiny plays itself out, will depend entirely upon the rise or fall of China. Although China is now in decline, its territory is vast and its people are numerous. If its institutions are reformed and its unity restored, it will be in a position to restore the rights of yellow people and, what is more, to control the world and extend the way of morality to all countries. All that is needed is for a great man to rise and implement this program. Because of this, I have decided to go to China and look for this hero, and if I can find him and persuade him, I shall serve him in any way I can. If I cannot find such a person, I myself will be that hero. For that reason I have already arranged with a friend to make preparations secretly to enter Manchu China. I didn't want to tell you anything about this. But now my heart is not at peace because of your preaching. I want to give up this ambition of mine, but I cannot do it. I want to go forward, but I cannot. You have brought me to a point at which I am unable to advance or retreat, and I am lost in a dense fog."

After this my brother began going out alone every day to the countryside with his rice bowl and his Bible. He would go out in the morning and return in the evening. He was seeking eternity, and in the end he became a convert to Kozaki's teaching and gave up his plans to enter China. On the other hand, that "China" of his had now left an impression on my heart that did not fade.

[7]

CHANGES IN MY IDEAS, AND MY FIRST LOVE

AT THAT TIME TAMIZŌ, MY OLDEST BROTHER, was home in Kumamoto and ill. He wrote me that I should come home. Because of a bad crop the family finances were strained, and they would be unable to send me money for schooling for some time. So Yazō and I came home; we three brothers were together again for the first time in many months, and we gathered around our mother to help and serve her.

Our house now unexpectedly became a center for the study of religion and philosophy. Yazō and I tried to persuade Tamizō of the truth of Christianity, but he just listened and responded with rationalism. My mother was there listening and once in a while she would join in and try to help us by referring to her own experience. Gradually a number of the young men of the neighborhood also came to join in these discussions, and in time the young daughters and sons of neighboring houses, and even the servants in our house, joined in, gave up their vulgar songs, sang hymns, and happily turned to their work. I also organized Sunday services, and invariably gave the sermon myself. As a result I, who had so disliked the requirement of public speaking in school, was now beguiled into becoming an orator.

Even my mother now stopped fretting about the decline in the family fortunes, and seemed quite at peace with the view that "sufficient unto the day is the evil thereof"; she took the lead in inviting our maids and servants and neighborhood youths to join these study groups. As a result, it was soon as if warm zephyrs of spring filled our house. However, once we stepped outside the house, the landscape of the whole village was that of an autumn wind driving the leaves before it. The bad crops that had now extended over several years had wiped out the savings of the villagers and made it impossible for them to have even a poor meal of rice and potatoes three times a day. Furthermore, when the time for the land-tax payment came on, the tenants had to have their rice ready. Money lenders confiscated without mercy, and farmers even had to sell the horses that were their only form of wealth. I can still remember how several dozen tenants would gather in our house and stress the difficulty of their circumstances. They would entreat my mother with tears for an adjustment of their rent-rice that was due, and some who had had something to drink would even become quite vehement in their appeals. My mother would show no anger, however: instead she would argue persuasively with them about a solution to the problem. What made a particularly deep impression on me was something my brother Tamizō said to them. "Look," he said, "of course it's not right that one man should hold a lot of land and eat the tenant's rice that you deliver. Actually, I would like nothing better than to be able to divide it up among you now, but remain patient for a little longer and pay your rent. Once we have carried out our study we will certainly do our best to destroy this unjust system, and try to restore the rights tenants should have. This is a time of preparation. Without preparation, we cannot begin the war. Please understand this." Tamizō spoke with deep sincerity. They were unable to answer him, but bowed amid tears and left. Truly they were pure of heart, and one had to have compassion for them in their position.

There was a peasant woman in my village whose name was Onaka. She could work harder and better than a man and she was a natural orator. Once I listened to her story and could not sleep that night. She said, "They say that if you work hard you won't be poor, but no matter how hard tenants work they remain poor. I too was once a girl of eighteen. Then I married this man. We loved each other and started our household with one cooking pot, two bowls, and two pairs of chopsticks. That's all we had. So, with those poor possessions we rented land from your family and worked and worked and really did our best. As your old mother knows, after three years of marriage, we had saved up forty or fifty bags of rice, and we never failed to pay our rent. But, we loved each other, and since we just couldn't control ourselves, the babies started coming. Somebody had to watch them. The mouths in my family became more numerous, and I wasn't able to do half the work that I had done before. The children would get sick, and then we needed doctors. Then we would need clothes. Meanwhile, I'd be having another child. I began to wish it would be stillborn, but once I heard its cries I couldn't end its life. Soon I couldn't do one-third the work I used to do. The bags of rice we had saved up became fewer and fewer, and then there weren't any left at all. You could go crazy worrying about it, but it wouldn't do any good. Becoming wiser, we tried to control ourselves, but try as we would, the first thing we knew a baby would come along. Some of them would die. That took a funeral. Then the guests would come to mourn with us and eat the rice we had saved. Then we had to borrow money and got stuck with the interest charges. There wasn't a thing we could do about it. There is no hope for it, we cannot escape this lifelong poverty." Ah, does the provision of bread come first? Does the Gospel come first? Bit by bit, doubts began to rise in my breast again. How would Tamizō's plan for restoring the rights to land fit into this?[10]

Tamizō, said, "It's not enough to calm the ravages of

[10] Tamizō (1865-1928) became a prominent exponent of Henry George's thought and the author of *Tochi heikinron* (On Land Equalization).

poverty with the consolation of religion. Benevolence provides only temporary alleviation with inexpensive morality. What we have to do is work out a plan to restore basic human rights." He also said, "Land is something that is held in common by mankind. Although an individual has the right to cultivate it and profit from it, he does not have the right to monopolize it and use it to indulge his private greed." Tamizō was judging society by a so-called natural law of reason, proving its immediate defects, and trying to set them right by this same law. He went on to say, "The nature of land and of human rights as they bear on land: these are great problems that our society has not confronted. Up to this point no completely rational explanation or interpretation has been put forth. If only a truly rational solution to this great problem could be provided, we would be in a position to change not only the condition of the world's poverty-stricken people, but we would also be able to change the nature of our society and establish a true basis for peace and happiness." I also heard an explanation of European and American socialism and the methods of those movements from him. I heard the name of Henry George, and that of Kropotkin.

How much I owe him! After all, Gautama the Buddha was a great person; on seeing a single corpse he was stirred to speculate deeply on the distinction between life and death. But I, who am without greatness, had seen I don't know how many hundreds of thousands of poor people; yet on seeing them I had shed only a tiny tear, and given them a coin or two, thereby trying to alleviate my feelings of guilt. I had not really dealt with the problem of "poverty" in the bottom of my heart. Heaven had granted me this misfortune and made me return to my village, where I heard and saw the true condition of the poor. Thanks particularly to my brother who expounded the teaching of reason to me, I was finally made conscious of this significance of "poverty."

After I had been home for little more than a half a year, I

went to Kumamoto and entered the care of the Reverend Ebina;[11] then I moved again and went to Nagasaki where I entered the Cobleigh School.[12] The Cobleigh School was American Methodist Episcopal, and it was a so-called mission school. At the time, my fellow students numbered about one hundred. Some of them were scholarship students, and others worked to meet part of their expenses. In this school I saw something I hadn't ever seen before: students who pretended to be believers in order to get their school expenses paid. The missionaries discriminated between the baptized and the non-baptized. They would have mysterious things called revivals at regular intervals, and I saw these too. However, I was tolerant now, and unlike the rigid person I had been earlier. So I kept my distance and went about my work quietly. Although my denomination was different, I was still firm in my faith. It goes without saying that I was quite different from those who pretended to be believers. I was treated well by the missionary teachers and their converts; several times I was invited to transfer my membership, but I did not do it. It seemed to me that if I left the Congregational Church I would be abandoning the creed of liberalism and people's rights, and that I could not do.

Before this, when I had been under the Reverend Mr. Ebina's care in Kumamoto, I had rejoiced at the opportunity to develop my thought in listening to his

[11] Ebina Danjō (1856-1937), like Kozaki a member of the "Kumamoto Band" and one of the leaders of modern Protestant Christianity in Japan, through pulpit and the journal *Shinjin* (The New Man).

[12] Founded in 1881 by a Methodist Episcopal missionary, Carroll Summerfield Long of Tennessee, and named for the former president of his alma mater at Athens, Tennessee, whose widow presented Long and his wife with two dollars at the farewell service held for them at the University of Tennessee chapel with the hope that they could find some use for it. With this as initial contribution Long collected several hundred dollars before leaving, and named the school for its first benefactor. It was known in English as Cobleigh Seminary, and in Japanese as Kaburi Eiwa Gakkō (Cobleigh School of English). In 1906 it became Chinzei (Kyushu) Academy.

sermons. I had done my best to improve my understanding and accumulate knowledge, and I regretted the shallowness of my study and of my knowledge. When I arrived in Nagasaki I worked hard to discipline and develop myself, and in order to develop my theology and philosophy I studied things by myself that were not even required. I also studied an introduction to the field of sociology that my brother Tamizō introduced me to. How could I know that by so doing I was entering a path that would lead to great changes in my faith?

In my search for knowledge I would read a book; then the ideas it conveyed would lead to doubts. I often meditated in order to move forward in my path of faith. When I came up with one idea, it would lead to another, and that would be followed by skepticism. I strove mightily to dispel the clouds of doubts and fogs of skepticism. But in the end I was led by reason to deny the divinity of Christ. I wanted to maintain his divinity to the very end on grounds of emotion. Should I follow the rule of reason and deny Christ's divinity? If so, I would have to leave the church and break off contact with believers; I would have to give up prayer, rely upon myself, and advance alone. I would have to give up my dependence on outside assistance, and I would have to become a self-sufficient person who advanced on the road under his own power. If I were to make a firm decision for this course a sensation of inexpressible loneliness would fill my heart. I would have to march through 10,000 leagues of desolation alone. On the other hand, should I affirm Christ's divinity? Then I would have to abandon the education I had gained and return to my earlier state of ignorance. How could I do that? I had already learned that prayer could not change the laws of the world. How could I have prayed to our father in heaven? I had already learned that human nature had to be disciplined in order to march toward the path. How could I rely on the atonement of Jesus Christ? In this way reason and sentiment battled within me. In my soul the warm spring color soon faded and gave way to the harsh winds of autumn. Once again I became a man of gloom and agony. I would give up reading books for a time and climb the mountain of prayer again, weepingly call on heaven, only to ridicule myself and laugh at such foolishness; then, meditating by myself again, once more call, weeping, upon Christ's help. After spending a week in this way I finally reached a decision. Truth existed in the world, and reason existed in me. Moreover, what was there to deplore? Relying upon myself, I descended from the mountain and returned to my school. Yet the doubts in my soul were still not laid to rest entirely.

Just at that time I received a letter from my brother Yazō. When I opened it I found that he was telling me that he had changed his beliefs and was hoping to help me reconsider mine. Yazō described in detail the way in which he had come to change and explained his new views. What it came down to was that he had begun by doubting the divinity of Christ, and then went on to reject him completely. He now took the entire world of phenomenal objects as scriptures of revelation, believed that he was the master of his fate by his own powers of reasoning, and proposed to continue his studies and work out his own path. It was almost the same pattern that I had been working toward. But in addition Yazō enclosed another letter, from a friend of ours named Fujishima, telling us that he too had changed his beliefs. Fujishima wrote that, now that heaven had graciously granted him leisure to study and reflect, he had had the opportunity really to familiarize himself with the sages of antiquity. In quiet sitting and reflection he had been able to come to an appreciation of Wang Yang-ming and his teachings on knowledge and action. He had resolved to leave Christ's gate and to enter the path of enlightenment through his own efforts, and he was writing to ask what we thought about this. Our friend, Fujishima was from Chikuzen, and used the literary pen name of Gōtotsu.[13] He was very tall, unusually powerfully built, and his insight was also above average. He was sensitive and quickly moved to fervor or indignation. He grieved for the fate of East Asia. He and I had been students together at Waseda, and together with Yazō he had also studied with and received instruction from Mr. Kozaki. We had all become Christians. How strange that the three of us should now change at the same time! Fujishima wrote that he had been imprisoned because of his involvement in secret publications; that was the context in which he spoke of heaven's granting him the leisure to study. He has died now, and is no longer with us. My brother Yazō too has passed on and is numbered among the spirits. Yet I alone remain in this world and write this story of my dream. That too is a dream, is it not?

I had already decided I had to reject the doctrine of the Trinity, and yet hesitated to do so finally. When I read the letters from Fujishima and my brother, however, it was as though I had suddenly been reinforced by a mighty host, and my final decision was made. What a weak, dependent creature I was! Is this because I alone was irresolute and weak, or is it the human condition? I do not know. Whatever the case what I want to say is that in moving through this world of change one should not rely on God or on Christ, but rather look to true friends within the human race. That being so, it remains a regrettable fact that it is so difficult to find real friends.

But just then it happened that I made a new friend. This was an old beggar who had been born in the West. Everyone called him the crazy beggar, because his attitudes were extreme and he seemed very eccentric. He regarded himself as unique in the universe, and he was convinced that everybody else was insane. He affirmed a pantheist view and held an extreme naturalist position. Consequently

[13] Lit. "surpassing elegance."

he opposed Christian supernaturalism; he also deplored modern culture. His ultimate desire was to destroy modern society and create a world without government in which private property would have no place. He wanted to establish a collectivist pattern, abolish currency and outlaw commerce, and return to the simple barter system of antiquity; all mankind would be one family with free love, and agriculture would be the way of life everywhere as it had once been. Such a society would need no laws except a simple book of physiology. Moreover, my friend did not stop with advocacy of such a society; he was determined to make it come about as far as he could. Because he was a vegetarian he absolutely refused to eat meat, and because he was a confirmed naturalist he would not sleep on *tatami* mats and instead slept on the ground. Since he believed in sharing mates he sometimes drew women to him and tried to argue the point with them. I was more impressed by his determination to act on these beliefs than I was by the way he argued for them. Most people, seeing him suit action to words, dismissed him as crazy. We do not have adequate definitions of insanity. Should we not wait one hundred generations before deciding whether men like this are crazy or not?[14]

I owe him a great deal. He helped me to free myself from my mistaken notions about Christianity. He explained the facts about poverty in Europe and America to me, and showed how differences of poverty and wealth accompanied the progress of modern civilization. My espousal of the movement for people's rights, which I had inherited at home and which had deepened in connection

[14] Tōten returns to this individual in a context of religiosity and madness later in *Kyōjintan* (Tales of Madmen), published serially in 1900. (*Zenshū*, Vol. 3, 21-90). It begins, "It is a weakness of mine that I am exceedingly fond of so-called crazy people, perhaps because I'm close to those I like, but more because I'm carried away by the fact that their spirit is so close to original human nature; whatever the case, it is certain that I have been close to and have become fond of a good many."

with my adherence to Christianity, became more broadly based and more real. I envied him the virtue and the courage he showed in acting on his beliefs.

At that time there was also an organization in Nagasaki calling itself the Seifunsha.[15] Nobody knew where it got that name, but it was headed by Satō Ryūzō, and the people behind it were Ichiki Seitarō, Suzuki Tsutomu, Norimoto Yoshitsune, and Honjō Yasutarō. They were quite eccentric in the way they carried on; they created a mock peerage with Count Rice, Baron Horsebone, and so on; those without aristocratic rank were just as strange. They met every day at the head-man's house and argued about their crazy theories and eccentric ideas. Since I was young I kept a back seat but I could make some sense out of what went on and saw some truth in their arguments, and this helped me in my own thinking. It happened that one evening I told the group about the old beggar. They thought he sounded remarkable, and asked me to bring him around. Thereafter they wanted to cooperate with him and set up a school. Consequently we decided to try to get a comrade from my native area, Maeda Kagaku,[16] to put up some money. He agreed, and came to Nagasaki to meet the old beggar-teacher; I was the interpreter. Next, I took the old fellow to Maeda's place. After several months of talk, preparations for the school were still incomplete, and the police became concerned. They thought the old beggar-teacher was a disciple of Bakunin, and ordered him to go back to Nagasaki. The plans came to nothing. When the old beggar got back to Nagasaki the police once again ordered him to move on, and after that I lost track of him. It is a decade and more ago, and I haven't heard about him at all since then. He called himself Isaac Abraham. He was

[15] Lit. "Excrement Manufacturing Association."

[16] Maeda Kagaku (1859-1933), was born in a landlord family in Oama, Kumamoto Prefecture. A sister married Tōten, and a younger brother accompanied Tōten to Siam. The father, Maeda Takashi, was a friend of the author Natsume Sōseki.

born in Sweden, but was really a man without a country. I wonder where he is dreaming his dreams now?

This beggar-teacher was truly a spiritual benefactor of mine. Indeed I am obligated to him for more than spiritual guidance, for he was also a corporeal benefactor who endowed me with an animate creature, my wife. While I was interpreting for him at the Maeda house, I became engaged to a daughter of the family. He not only was a disinterested go-between creating the opportunity for us, but also served as a kind of animate telephone. Turning to me he would tell me that the daughter was in love with me, while to her he praised me as a rare prize and urged her to try for a betrothal right away. That is how we met, and now we have brought three children into the world. But in the life of man the road is dangerous and the traveler frequently loses his way. Waves are high in the sea of emotion and the boat is driven off its course. I wonder whether it can be said that happiness lies in being born, becoming a husband, a wife, or a child? That is a problem to which there is no ready answer as yet, but in any case it is a bright memory of life that I experienced such joy for a short period at the beginning of our marriage. The joys of that short period balance out the distress of my later life. Yes, for a brief period I was unconscious of birth, life, everything. Why should I now talk about distress?

Certainly I had never encountered so strong an adversary as love. At that time I still had no fixed purpose in life. I had narrowly succeeded in extricating myself from Christianity; I had concluded that it was impossible to save oneself or others by evangelism, and now believed that one should place great emphasis on self-cultivation in order to read and study, and thus could get some understanding of how to embark upon that path, but tenant farmers like Ichizō, Hyōkichi, and Onaka could not do this. In view of this I came to realize that the most urgent matter in life was to possess an education. Yet people like them worked long days and despite that didn't have enough to eat; how could they be expected to pay for an education? And from this I came to realize that even education required time and money. To be sure, there were charitable schools and schools for the poor. But these practiced what my brother Tamizō termed the sale of virtue; those who established them strode the earth as benefactors, while the pupils were made into beggars' children. Was I to be satisfied with this? It seemed to me that the first problem for me was to provide people with enough to eat. But how was I to see to it that Ichizō and Hyōkichi, once they had enough clothing and food, would get an education? In truth, the ideals I have received at home, and the knowledge I had received from Christianity, had combined to acquaint me with the needs of all mankind. Moreover, crazy old Isaac Abraham had taught me that even in the civilized countries of Europe and America[17] there were many people whose circumstances were no different from those of Ichizō and Hyōkichi. So it should become my mission to work to change the poverty of the masses in all the countries of the world. But I still had no scheme for doing this. Not only this, my brother Yazō had gone on to tell me about the state of other countries, the struggle of competition between the races, and the truth about the condition of the world under arms. What I needed was a plan to make a total change in the contemporary world, one based upon the great principles of human rights, in order to bring peace to all people on the basis of a united world. But I didn't have a plan for this as yet. Alas, what an enormous task! It would not be easy to make such a plan, would it? But I was determined to devote my life to the search for such a plan; therefore I pursued it. I had not yet been able to work it out, and there were all sorts of difficulties along the way. I had made up my mind to struggle with these difficulties the rest of my life. And yet, however firm my

[17] *Bunmei shokoku*, the standard Meiji term for advanced countries.

resolution, my path was blocked by a stronger adversary than I expected. What was it? Nothing other than love.

When I entered into the betrothal arrangement with the daughter of the Maeda family, I first tried to break it off by considering its pros and cons for my future. But that didn't work out. Then I tried to break it off so that I wouldn't ruin her future happiness. Again it didn't work out. Next, I tried to forget all about future pain and gain, put aside thoughts of her future or mine, and just follow my emotions. I discussed this with my mother and my brother Tamizō; they approved, but Yazō did not. So I went against his wishes. My friends also tried to warn me any number of times about how harmful an early marriage could be for a man of high purposes such as those I had set for myself, but I paid no attention to them. As I look back on this now I still break out in a cold sweat, but at that time I was not myself. I was the embodiment of "love." What could come up against that? In actual fact, all this was the work of old Isaac Abraham, who preached free love. Ah, I wonder where that old fellow is praising the beauty of nature now?

Love leads to the satisfaction of sexual desire. But when I reached that satisfaction, I was suddenly overcome with repugnance and revulsion. I thought it was the end of me, and felt as though I had committed some great crime or as though I had fallen into some deep ravine. It was as though I had fallen from the heights of heaven into the depths of hell. The noble ambitions so long in my breast now seemed to rise and strike my head with the force of a fierce wave. Now the warnings of Yazō and the friends who had disapproved of my marriage plans seemed to dance in front of my face like so many laughing spirits. Overcome by these feelings, I said I was breaking off the engagement. Yes, weeping and with head held low, I tried to explain. I was conquered by her tears. I tried to combat those tears several times, but always without result. For the first time I understood how a woman's tears have power that even guardian deities respect.

But meanwhile I had time to reflect. I was no longer the embodiment of love that I had been at the outset. I realized now that love and ambition could not co-exist on equal terms. So now I tried to see if I could hate the girl by thinking of her as the enemy of my ambition. That didn't work out either. Was I then to forget all my hopes and instead become a slave to love? Surely this was impossible? The strife between reason and emotion had passed, only to return now in new form as a conflict between ambition and human emotion. I experienced real suffering. Then I took a page from the writings of the military strategists and prepared a subterfuge; I would escape from the bonds of sentiment and love by fleeing abroad. And so I explained to her the struggle that was in my breast, what the future held of loss and gain, and got her to agree with my plan that I go on a long journey alone. But it was a very special kind of journey to the West that I had in mind.

First I proposed to go to Hawaii as a laborer. By diligence and thrift it would be possible for me to go on to the United States as a student. But the difficulty in implementing this plan was that I couldn't afford the trip. Try as I would, I couldn't come up with a solution. Finally I decided to take some Buddhist images that had been in our family for many years and sell them to a rich man in our neighborhood. I got thirty yen for them, and with this I made my way to Nagasaki, where I waited for a coal ship owned by Mr. Miyakawa Tatsuzō to arrive. He and I planned to set out together with the proceeds raised by selling what we had. I had been in Nagasaki about ten days, and Miyakawa still hadn't arrived, when an urgent telegram came from my brother Yazō in Tokyo. Don't go anywhere, he said, but wait for me to get there. And so he came.

"I hear you're going to Hawaii," he said, "Is this true?" Yes, I answered, it was. "The reason I rushed down here when I heard this," he said, "was to be able to talk with you. I believe that although there are a fair number of men of ability in the world, the number of those who are idealists and stand for sincerity is very small indeed. I wish you would combine your actions, your determination, with mine, and devote your life in the way that I shall commit mine. I respect you as I do our brother Tamizō. I have reached a decision recently, and I want to share it with you. I want you to base yourself on these ideas. Let us make plans together and establish a grand design for our life work." And so there, in that narrow alley in Nagasaki, while the world slept around us as we talked under a bright moon, Yazō poured the tea while I trimmed the lamp wick, and we talked till dawn. Truly, that one night became the one that set the course for half my life.

[8] I SET MY COURSE

MY BROTHER YAZŌ WAS NOT ONLY A BEACON of light in the dark for me: he also provided the compass whereby I could steer my life's course. His views on religion were the same as mine, and so were his ideas about society. That is, we had come to the same view on the priority of a solution to the problem of hunger. There was the difference, of course, that though I had wandered off the track by entering the byway of love instead of concentrating on the problem, Yazō had not allowed anything to take priority over the problem of providing food and had come directly to the point with a plan of action. As he saw it, wise men of the past had already worked out solutions for the problem of hunger. Theories for the reform of society and for the equal division of land were already at hand. What was needed was a way of putting them into action. He argued that there was no alternative to the use of power in bringing these plans to fruition. Moreover, it seemed to Yazō that when he looked at the condition of the world it was Russia that threatened to violate human rights and trample on the way of humanity by barbaric force. Consequently he saw no alternative to reliance on counter force in order to protect and nurture such rights. And for that reason he thought it extremely urgent to establish a base for such force if one were to try to establish the way of humanity throughout the universe, or at least to defend human rights where they still existed. And where was such a base to be established? For this he revived his cherished dream of many years that centered on the problem of China. As he put it, "People say that the Chinese worship the past, and that they are therefore against progress. But that is an unbelievably mistaken view. What the Chinese have done is to take the three dynasties of antiquity as their ideal of good government, but they consider them as norms and not as exact patterns to be followed. Those norms are actually not very different from our own ideals of government. They may seem to idolize the past, but in actuality they are trying for progress in the future. The problem is that the present dynasty has ruled for three hundred years and that it maintains order by keeping the people stupid. As a result the people are weary and the country is in grave condition; they are at the point where they cannot bear any additional evils. Isn't this a good time then to overturn the mandate and realize the ideal norms? Talk and discussion won't do any good. What we should do is to devote our lives to a project of getting into the Chinese interior. We must show a determination that will be unshakable for a hundred centuries, make our spirit Chinese, find a true hero, and thus establish a basis upon which to work heaven's will. Let China once revive and base itself upon its true morality, then India will rise, Siam and Annam too will revive, and the Philippines and Egypt can be saved. Countries like France and the United States, where there are still people who respect ideals and revere morality, will by no means become our enemies. In my opinion there is no other way to revive human rights, and to establish a new reign of justice throughout the universe." When I heard this, I got up and danced for joy. My long-standing doubts suddenly melted away under the influence of this vision. Truly, I had found my life work. We went on to discuss the details of these plans. I was to go on ahead to China to familiarize myself with its language and customs, and Yazō could follow after he had made additional preparations. Again, since we wanted to discuss these plans with Tamizō, I left Nagasaki for our home.

However, when I returned home and told Tamizō about the plans that Yazō and I had worked out and what we intended to do, he disapproved. He of course approved of the spirit in which we had made our plans, but not of our methods. "There is no way you will be able to explain your high motivation to the Chinese," he said; "if you were going to go ahead with this plan you would have to wear a pigtail, assume Chinese dress, conceal your name and your nationality; you would be using trickery for the sake of morality. I'm absolutely opposed to such schemes." "If you want to establish justice and morality throughout the world," he went on, "your methods have to be open and above board. If you can't carry out your resolves without resort to trickery, you'll do better to give them up." To this I answered, "These goals of ours are not for ourselves, but for all people. If our plans succeed, future generations will benefit; if they fail, the only cost will be that we ourselves lose our lives. It doesn't bother me if people see this as trickery." Tamizō answered, "Work openly; even if you don't succeed in one generation, if you proclaim your cause abroad others will take it up for future generations. I would prefer to place my confidence in this." I rejected this: "There is enough talk abroad already. We need action to carry out our intentions. Otherwise it's like waiting for a hundred years, or waiting for the Yellow River to flow clear of silt." So we were unable to resolve our different arguments. I sent a letter to Yazō to tell him; he too came home. He and Tamizō argued vigorously, but in the end they could not agree. The three of us now entered two separate paths, each determined to act on his beliefs.

Inevitably, Yazō and I were downcast because of the disagreement. Still, he consoled me by saying, "Our plan is something of a gamble. If we succeed, we will establish the basis for ten thousand generations in one generation's work; if we fail, all that happens is that we die like dogs or horses. Tamizō's attitude is more appropriate for establishing a school or a sect. But even if you and I do not live to see our plans succeed with our own eyes, the ideas we advance will take root and grow. So even if we should lose our lives uselessly, our spirit will live on thanks to Tamizō. It will be as though we had one heart and two bodies. If we do our best, things will surely work out." On hearing this I was reassured and enthusiastic again. I was eager to set out. Accordingly, Yazō and I wanted to get things underway as soon as we possibly could. Unfortunately, there was the prior requirement of money, and neither of us had any way of getting any. We had no choice but to turn to Tamizō, so we asked his help. He agreed, saying, "I can't provide the money you need right now, but I promise to get it for you within a few months." Since I was supposedly so eager to be on my way, the phrase "few months" should not have been agreeable to me. Then why did part of me rejoice secretly? Ah, was it love? I wanted to give in to you. But when you tried to trap me and hold me against my better judgment, I had no choice but to treat you like an enemy.

I sat down with Yazō one night to discuss the steps that lay ahead. In the course of the discussion, he said "Strategists warn that brothers should not go into battle together because of the way emotion and human weakness can affect their judgment. I don't think we will make such mistakes, since we are entering upon the kingly way based on righteousness. Still, it might be a good idea to travel with close friends rather than together, in order to avoid any such errors." I agreed with him, and asked his opinion of my friend Kiyofuji Kōshichirō.[18] He clapped his hands,

[18] Kiyofuji (1872-1931), a Kumamoto stalwart who will appear frequently in this narrative, later edited a *Kokuryūkai* (Amur, "Black Dragon" Society) periodical and collaborated in the publication of a Chinese-Japanese dictionary. Miyazaki hereafter refers to him by his *gō*, or pseudonym, *Don'u*.

and said, "He's just the one! Given his cleverness and ability if he agrees to work with us he will provide just what we lack and really make a difference in our larger plans. You must talk with him and try to get him to come with us." Kiyofuji was in Tokyo at that time. I went to talk with him and revealed our secret plans. He slapped his knee in pleasure and agreed immediately. We then returned home separately and agreed that we would head for Shanghai together after the money had come through.

Kiyofuji was an impulsive fellow. Once he had made up his mind to go to China he was so worked up that it was more than he could do to sit quietly waiting for the money. He went ahead, alone, to Nagasaki to begin the study of Chinese. Meanwhile the arrival of the money for my passage was delayed longer and longer because it just couldn't be put together. As day followed day I became ill and had to be hospitalized. My future wife arrived secretly and began to take care of me. That I should have become weak and ill at a time when I cherished such high hopes and resolves was a source of frustration for me. But there were also nights when I hoped that my illness would last longer. The impatience shown by Kiyofuji, who had not fallen in love, contrasted strikingly with my patience.

[9] I ENTER THE COUNTRY OF MY DREAMS

MY FRIEND KIYOFUJI SUDDENLY CAME BACK from Nagasaki. "I've changed my mind about going to China," he said. "I want you two to release me from the agreement I made with you." When I asked him the reason he said that he had changed his whole outlook and couldn't work together with us any more. He detailed the reasons for his change of heart with great eloquence. He now asserted the inanity of spiritual theories and argued that only materialism made any sense. In an overnight reversal of his previous positions he held forth on materialism, the survival of the fittest, and total hedonism. I was too narrow-minded to listen very generously, but I did not make great efforts to argue with him either. I put it to the changeable nature of man, took the travel money Tamizō had now provided for me, and headed for Nagasaki alone.

In Nagasaki I waited three days for a boat. Two days before it was to come, I ran into "Count" Rice of the Seifunsha quite by chance. "My honor is endangered," he said, "all for the lack of a little money. Could you let me borrow your travel money for a day?" I agreed. Came the day, and he was unable to keep his promise to repay me. I waited another week. Another boat came, and again I missed it. My spirit had taken wing and flown to the skies of the neighboring land of China, and yet there wasn't a thing I could do about it. I had to cool my heels another week in my lodgings. At this point the "Count" paid up barely a third of what he owed me and suggested that I go ahead to Shanghai on that. He promised to wire me the rest. He also gave me a letter for a friend of his, Munekata Kotarō,[19] who lived in Shanghai. I took him at his word and boarded the Saikyō Maru for Shanghai.

After two days' trip I saw the approach to Wusung. Water, sky; sky and water, clouds; these gave way to land, seemingly floating in the water; this was the mainland of China. This was to be my second homeland, one that had appeared so often in my dreams. The closer the boat approached, the clearer the landscape of the continent was to my sight, and the higher my emotions rose. Standing in the prow, and walking around the deck, I wept. I do not know why. The ship arrived in Shanghai. I put up at the Tokiwakan. It was May, 1891, the spring of my twenty-second year.

I had planned to avoid the Japanese settlement as much as possible and live quietly in the countryside near Shanghai by myself, so I waited eagerly for the money "Count" Rice was to send me. But there was no word from him. In order to economize while waiting I moved to a smaller inn, hired a Chinese tutor with the help of Mr. Munekata, and began to study. Meanwhile I sent letter after letter dunning Rice, but without getting any response from him. One day Munekata came to visit me. "In that letter you brought me from Rice," he said, "he told me that he had spent all the money you lent him. You must be about out of money by now. Why don't you come to my school and board with me? Rice more or less hinted that he'd like me to do this." The school in question was the Sino-Japanese Trade

[19] Munekata (1864-1923) was a Kumamoto samurai who first went to Shanghai in 1884 and spent most of the rest of his career there as investigator of political conditions, then as employee of the *Dōbun Shoin* (Common Culture Institute; see fn. 87) and, at the last, founder of the East Asia News Agency (Tōhō Tsūshinsha).

Research Center;[20] Munekata was an instructor there. I had been cheated by Rice.

The revelation of this dishonesty came as a great shock to me. I clearly had no course preferable to boarding at the school, as Munekata kindly suggested. But at that time I thought that the head of the school, Arao Sei, and his group were bent on the occupation of China, and I thought our philosophies would be quite different. I had no desire to eat their food. I thanked Mr. Munekata for his kindness and declined his offer. On the other hand, I was almost out of money. I couldn't make it alone. I decided to return to Nagasaki and put pressure on Rice. I boarded a ship for Nagasaki, put up at an inn there, and headed for Rice's place. To my astonishment, no Rice. The people there told me, "He left for Tokyo just after you sailed for Shanghai." Clearly, he had completely taken me in. Now I went to the store operated by Miyakawa Tatsuzō,[21] put up there, and sent telegram after telegram to Rice in Tokyo. The responses were pleasant, but they brought no money. This went on for more than fifty days. I finally returned home thoroughly discouraged. After a few days I had word from my Nagasaki host: "Your money came from Tokyo, but I've spent it." My great hopes had come to nothing in this farcical manner.

[20] The Center was founded in 1890 by Arao Kiyoshi (Sei) (1859-1896), who was first sent to China at the orders of the Army General Staff in 1886. Arao coordinated training and reporting activities with commercial establishments.

[21] Miyakawa was from Tōten's village of Arao, and later helped provide a job for his wife.

[10] FOUR WASTED YEARS

Soon after I returned home, I was married to Miss Maeda. Everybody thought that that was why I had returned; I suspect that the only one who knew that that wasn't the case was "Count" Rice. Nevertheless I was a long time getting over the resentment I had for him for having forced me to exchange the sights of the continent for the pleasures of home. My old friends, however, were all concerned for me. They were afraid that I had become softened with love for my new bride that my resolve had been dulled, and I was no longer of any use to the world. I was even more worried than they were. When I went to bed there was someone to help me with the covers; when I got up she was there to help me wash; when I stood she handed me my clogs, when I sat down she was there to hand me a pillow. When I compared myself now with the way I had been I feared for my will-power. And so I warned myself. In the end I managed to drive myself into resisting love and emotion. But this battle within me went on night and day. What joy was there in that? Then why did I remain in such a joyless position? Alas, was it love? I wanted to give in to you. But when you tried to hold me too closely, I once again had no choice but to treat you like an enemy.

It's true. It is not necessarily one's duty to take a wife and build a family, nor is it necessarily conducive to one's happiness to do so. On the other hand, a man's emotions are constantly pushing him in this direction. Consequently, however poor, he becomes the head of a family, and without particularly planning or wanting to he becomes somebody's parent. That is how couples like Eiza and Onaka end up spending entire lives in poverty and many gifted people end up as whitened bones, without having accomplished a thing. My family's resources had been divided into three, one third of them mine, and with that I constructed a house close to the main house. At that time I paid little heed to warnings not to let my spirit flag, and unwittingly intoxicated in the spring of family life, I felt as though I had achieved the aim of a lifetime. Then came the problem of household management. Next a child raised its cries in this world. Somehow I felt as if heavy responsibilities had fallen upon me. And that somehow seemed dreadful to me. I thought to myself, isn't this the time to seek danger? Isn't it time to show how different heroes are from the ordinary run of people? So pleasure and worry came together, and became a kind of pain. It's true: a wife and family constitute a milestone in one's life.

At that time my brother Yazō was in Kumamoto suffering from prolonged stomach trouble, and he was studying English and French while recuperating. I, however, was spending that time fighting with love and struggling with household management, and meanwhile three years went by like a dream. Finally I was able to rouse myself. I went off to Kumamoto to meet Yazō and put a plan before him. What I said was this: "There is no point in sitting with folded arms waiting for something to happen. I think I should go ahead on my own. By good luck, I know about a refugee from Korea named Kim Ok-kiun.[22] He is almost a man without a family and without a

[22] Kim (1851-1894) was a reformist Korean literatus who first visited Japan in 1881, where he was befriended by many Japanese leaders. He fled to Japan after the failure of a Korean coup d'état against conservatives in 1884.

country. Homesick as he is, he nevertheless has a clear insight into world affairs. If we talk to him about issues of major importance, and show him that what really matters is the China problem, we should be able to get him to look beyond Korean affairs, turn his thought to the fate of China, and devote his full strength to our plans. I would like to try this by talking with him." Yazō enthusiastically agreed with this, and I left for Tokyo right away.

In the southern part of the capital there is a bathing beach near Shinagawa where fresh breezes cleanse the dust of the city. I heard that Mr. Kim was staying there in order to avoid troublesome visitors, and went there to see him. Kim was glad to see me and showed me into a room. There were two or three other guests in the room, and we spent a relaxed and happy time in drink and conversation. But I had come for more than wine and talk, and had made this trip of more than three hundred miles for a reason. Therefore, when the chance came I asked him if we couldn't talk privately a little. Kim nodded his head quietly without saying anything. When the other visitors took their leave he ordered his maid to rent us a fishing boat; then we walked down to the shore, got in, and rowed off in the moonlight.

Kim had created a perfect setting for secret conversation; if we let the opportunity go, it was not likely to come again. While we rowed along trailing a fishing net, we got down to serious talk. With that I straightened out my seat cushion and first of all told him that I had decided to go to China. I went on to say that I intended to observe the state of affairs in China, explained my commitment and purpose, told him about my agreement with Yazō; I described the way matters had gone up to this point, and in the end threw myself on his mercy and asked for his help. Kim agreed immediately with what I had said: "You are

---

His brutal murder in Shanghai in 1894 inflamed Japanese public opinion on the eve of the Sino-Japanese War.

absolutely correct in saying that China is what matters in the future. Countries like Korea are just small problems on China's periphery and for their fate we will have to see how the China problem is resolved. China is not just the linch pin of all of East Asia in the future; it is probably the place where the fate of the entire world will be settled. Your approach strikes a responsive chord in my heart." Then he lowered his voice, and went on: "I too plan to visit China. My preparations are almost complete. I plan to set out before very long. Because of the way things are I have to keep this secret, but it won't be very long before I go. I won't stay very long, and I will probably be back within three weeks. I would like you to go back home and wait quietly for word from me. Let's work out a long-range plan for work in China when I get back. But I hope you won't tell this to anybody else." Kim's words and his manner were serious. I had achieved part of the purpose I had come for. I bowed my head in thanks and raised a cup of sake to Mr. Kim. He took it and drank it. Then he raised his voice and sang a Korean song, after which he asked me to recite a Chinese poem. Just then a fish happened to flip into our boat. Kim was delighted and pronounced this a good sign. We seized it, blessed it, and tossed it back in the water. As the hour grew late a wind came up, the moon began to set, and we returned to land reciting poems about the moon. Ah, I wonder how that moon in the heavens felt as it looked down on mortals ignorant of the fate that lay ahead?

I returned home full of optimism, and told Yazō everything. He too was delighted that our long-held hopes were to be realized at last, and we waited eagerly for word from Kim Ok-kiun. Instead a newspaper came with terrible news, news that was like a nightmare for us. The story said the Kim Ok-kiun had been murdered by Hong Chong-u. The public was astonished by this news, but Yazō and I were especially struck by it and unable to believe it for a time. We sent a telegram to Mr. Kim's closest associate in

Tokyo to ask him whether it was true, only to have his reply echo the news we had seen in the newspapers. Even so, we still hoped that it was a false report. The next day a telegram came from Kim's manservant in Nagasaki. It read, "Aboji dead letter follows." Aboji means great teacher; it was an honorary title for Mr. Kim. I wanted to continue doubting, but now it was impossible to doubt. Next a letter came. It was very explicit, and told us that our sole hope had been destroyed by an extraordinary tragedy. Ah, spring dreams had gone without a trace! To whom could we tell the secrets that were in our hearts? After careful discussion, we decided that Yazō should stay to sell the family land; I would go alone to Tokyo, attend the Kim funeral services, join the procession, and attend the burial.

There must have been a thousand mourners at the memorial service for Mr. Kim. Some were well-known people. I was impressed by one gentleman I happened to see; he was short and fat but I did not know who he was. Afterward we went to the Aoyama Cemetery. As we were sipping tea later I asked a friend who that might be, and the more I heard about his activities and career the more impressed I was. Finally, I asked my friend to introduce us. It turned out to be Watanabe Gen, an unsung hero who was living in seclusion in Nagasaki. Though we did not realize it then, this man was later to become a secret benefactor of ours. After the funeral I was also able to meet a little known chivalrous woman named Tama, from Hakodate. The story was that she had come to Tokyo to follow Mr. Kim and that she had sold all her possessions to help him with his travel needs when he was to go to Shanghai. A friend and I extended our sympathy to her and accompanied her to her residence after the funeral. She said, "As I'm only a woman I naturally cannot fully appreciate Mr. Kim's great aspirations, and I would not presume to judge the right and wrongs of the situation. I am sure that he discussed all that with you gentlemen, and I shall leave it to you to continue his efforts in the future. May it go well with you . . . if there should be anything at all I can do, I hope you will not hesitate to call upon me at any time. As for me, all I can do is resign myself to a geisha's life again." Ah, how could we have known that in the future that chivalrous woman would be such a help to us?

After the Kim funeral I went back home to our village. I found that Yazō's plan to sell off the family land had not gone smoothly and that he was waiting for me to get back so that we could discuss our plans. Then, however, the general political situation seemed to change. In Korea the Tonghak Rebellion[23] was flaring up, and it would soon become the occasion for a clash between China and Japan. A military expedition was sent to Korea; they were recruiting interpreters, and people were being examined for military service. Among the people there was a good deal of enthusiasm for volunteering for the army, and in the general excitement everybody thought that war was at hand. Since Yazō and I had been to China once, the officials called us in and wanted us to serve as interpreters. But we did not agree, giving the reason that our Chinese was not good. One evening when we three brothers were sitting around the *hibachi* speculating on what the future might hold for us, I said to my brothers, "If I stay on here like this I'll be drafted by the army, sooner or later. I wonder if it wouldn't be a good idea to avoid that by going abroad for a while?" I hardly had these words out of my mouth when Mother, her face flushed and trembling with rage, shouted "Get out of here! I despise my sons! Get out! Don't you realize that even peasant sons are eager to go join this glorious war? Are you going to be a slacker? You can't stay in this house any longer. Get out, all three

[23] Upon the outbreak of the Tonghak rebellion the Korean government requested assistance from China, and Japan insisted on dispatching troops also under terms of its 1885 agreement with China. Chinese and Japanese troops clashed after the Japanese insisted on a joint demand for Korean reforms.

of you! How could I ever explain it to your father? I'm too ashamed to hold my head up in front of people. If you don't leave right away, I'll die!" Tamizō tried to calm Mother, explaining that it wasn't that we were afraid of losing our lives in battle: rather, the point of our argument was that instead of fighting as ordinary soldiers we thought we should wait for the chance to do something really important for our country and our people. Surely she could understand this? With this comment she finally calmed down. But what a noble soul she was, and how mean I seemed!

If we had told Mother of the secret plans we had, she would not have become so agitated; instead she would have wept tears of joy. But my brothers and I did not share, even with her, our secret plans. In fact, Yazō and I kept our intentions from Tamizō as well as from our mother. Not only did we keep them secret, but we even manufactured subterfuges to mislead them and throw them off the track. We let them think that our reason for selling the family land was for me to be able to go to the United States, when actually it was to provide travel money for the trip to China. The reason we were so close-mouthed and secretive about this was that we were determined that nothing was going to keep us from going Chinese.

Unfortunately, the plans to sell the family land did not go the way we expected them to. The best we could do was to raise several hundred yen by putting the land in pawn. With this Yazō headed for Tokyo while I settled my family affairs before following him there. We agreed that we would meet in Tokyo and then, with our bridges burned behind us, sit down to make firm plans for the future.

Once Yazō left for Tokyo, I went about settling my family affairs, but this proved to be very difficult. There is an old saying, "There's never so much that you can't use it up." How much truer for a petty landholder with an income of 50 bales! And even more so for the likes of me, who squanders money so quickly! The debts I had piled up in three years had become a mountain. I would have had to straighten things out even if I had not had ambitious plans to carry out. I really scarcely knew which way to turn. Finally I followed my wife's advice that we sell our place, move to Kumamoto City and rent a house there, and then try to make ends meet by renting out rooms. My old friends laughed at the thought of my prospering as a manager of a hero's hostel, and as a matter of fact my lodging-house became a conspirators' lair (*ryōzanpaku*) for the Ten'yūkyō[24] people.

When I had more or less managed to take care of my family affairs I headed for Tokyo. On the way I stopped in Kobe to talk to a Mr. Iwamoto Chitsuna, who was enthusiastic about activities in Siam. Himae Sutejirō, a Kumamoto friend, had worked together with him and provided the introduction for my talk with Mr. Iwamoto. As Iwamoto explained the state of affairs in Siam and especially the great influence exercised by Chinese there, I suddenly had a fine idea. Why couldn't I use Siam as a springboard for my larger plans? I kept this to myself and went on to Tokyo, where I took a room in Yazō's boarding house, above a green grocer's at Yūrakuchō. As we were together all the time we were able to talk quietly about our future plans.

I was usually the one who worked out general plans, but it was Yazō who developed the specific courses of action. In this case I came up with three possible lines of action. The first was that we look up the nameless hero I had met at Mr. Kim's funeral, explain our secret plans to him, and ask for his virtuous cooperation. The second plan was to accept the hospitality of that chivalrous woman at the funeral; she was now in Hakodate. We would cut all our

[24] The name taken by a group of Japanese adventurers who worked with Tonghak rebels in Korea to hasten the confrontation with China. Tōten's friend Matono Hansuke (1858-1917), a Fukuoka nationalist, publisher, and parliamentarian, played a leading role in organizing them.

outside contacts, devote ourselves fully to the study of Chinese, and, when we had mastered the language, spend our several hundred yen to defray the costs of a second trip to the Chinese interior. A third was to go to Siam; living was cheap there, and we had heard that over half the population was Chinese. We could steep ourselves in Chinese language and customs there, establish a base among the resident Chinese, and wait for the opportunity to enter the Chinese mainland. The way things worked out, we ended up having to try all three methods.

We were anxious to get the help of some of our senior acquaintances, and wanted to tell them what was in our hearts and ask their assistance. Surely, we thought, there must be at least one man of virtue we can recruit. But we had no faith in the so-called idealists we knew. All they were interested in was profit and fame. Our plans were too big and important for that. We were afraid that if we revealed our secrets we would endanger our success, and so we resolved to keep silent.

My brother said, "Before you came to join me in Tokyo I was unable to work out a line of action. When I was at my wit's end and couldn't contain my desperation any longer, I rented a rickshaw and went to see Count Soejima Taneomi.[25] He has a wonderful reputation for integrity and virtue, and I went to ask him his views about the outlook for China. The old count answered sadly, 'That is entirely up to the Chinese. If a strong leader develops, things could change almost overnight, but if not the country is headed for ruin. Unfortunately there is no such leader in sight at this time, and that is extremely regrettable.' Then he went on to talk about so-called great men: 'Right now, Li Hung-chang is the outstanding minister of the Ch'ing court, but he is already well along in years and not on a par with

[25] Soejima (1828-1905), an important Meiji government leader from Saga (near Kumamoto).

Tseng Kuo-fan.[26] Tseng was the one really great figure of recent times, and it was he who worked out the plans for a restoration. But in the end not even he was able to achieve his purpose. I'm afraid that the crisis of present-day China requires somebody with a genius greater even than that of Han Kao-tsu, the first emperor of the Han dynasty; it has to be a Kao-tsu with Western skills. What if there isn't such a person? Unfortunately, I too am getting old, and all I can do is sit and wait for our neighboring country to go to ruin.' I said that I should sympathize with his emotions, and asked whether I might be presumptuous enough to make a comment of my own. 'Unworthy as I am, I would like to become a hero, greater than Han Kao-tsu. Please do not be too despondent.' With that I went on to tell him in general terms about the secret plan in our hearts. The old count clapped his hands and said, 'Really? Get to it and don't tell anybody what you are up to! If you tell the present brand of idealist about it, it will hurt your plans and not do you any good at all. There just aren't any patriots with real insight around today!' That's the way the old count felt about the activists of the present day. He agreed with our view. However, it's different where women are concerned, because their feelings are stronger. If you show great sincerity in talking with them, they are likely to respond with full sincerity. And as a matter of fact, there is the case of the woman you met at the service for Kim Ok-kiun. I think you probably should try going to talk with her." I followed Yazō's instructions and took the night train from Ueno for Hakodate. We had decided to rely on a Hakodate geisha, instead of on well-known activists.

When I arrived in Hakodate I registered at the inn and sent the woman a letter asking to see her. She herself came to my inn and asked why I had come. I explained why, in

[26] Tseng (1811-1872) was the principal architect of the Ch'ing rally against Taiping and other rebellions in the nineteenth century.

a very serious manner, and she immediately and willingly accepted our request, "There must surely be something behind your request. That you should come to so ordinary a woman!—my house is very small, but it does have two stories, and since I live alone here with my aged mother it would probably be a quiet place for your studies. I earn enough to pay for your food. Please be assured it will work out." I was so moved at that I wanted to cry.

The next morning I got up and looked around the town to find a Chinese language-teacher. Because Japan was at war with China, however, all the Chinese had returned home so that they would not be in an enemy country. The only ones who had stayed behind were people who were unable to raise the travel money, and they were not qualified as teachers. The woman also did her best to look for a teacher, but without success; all her hospitality was in vain and I finally had to go back to Tokyo. The woman felt badly that her efforts to help me had failed; she came to my inn to say goodbye, and brought a box of cakes as a farewell gift. When I opened this on board the boat, I found Pirate brand cigarettes, the variety that Kim Ok-kiun had smoked. There was also something wrapped in paper, and this turned out to be some money. Truly, how considerate! Ah, chivalrous lady, how are you at the present? I have to say that I owe much to my friends.

[11]
I GO TO SIAM

When I returned to Tokyo and reported all this to Yazō, he too rejoiced on hearing about the chivalry of that woman. He stood and said to me, "If our determination is firm we can storm the heavens and conquer the oceans. Let us continue. Let us now try to persuade the nameless hero." And with that we left the greengrocer's where we lived.

Our "unsung hero" stayed temporarily in a back room on the second floor of a small Western clothing-store named Isekō in Ginza. Despite the noise, horse-carts, and crowds, it looked like a haven from the dusty area in which it was located. What did the host and his guests discuss? It was Yazō, speaking softly, who discussed the matters of great importance. It was the unsung hero who listened gravely and quietly. And it was I who prayed for success and feared and trembled for the failure of the outcome. When the exposition was over, we made our great request of him. Our host spoke deliberately and carefully: "The intentions you two have are admirable indeed. Unfortunately, however, it is still early for me to help you. If you could give me a certain amount of time, I am confident that I would be able to assist you. But in any case the two of you first have to perfect yourselves in studies of Chinese language and customs. I think the best thing for you to do would be to get yourself placed in a Chinese firm, cut all your contacts with Japanese, and become Chinese clerks, waiting until I can help you enter the country of your desire so that you can achieve your purpose. If the two of you are willing, I could help arrange the introductions you will need for this." His bearing as he said this was righteous and sincere. We thanked him for his great consideration, and withdrew after asking for another day's reflection before deciding on the matter.

Yazō and I needed less than an hour to make up our minds. That is, Yazō would follow this good advice and enter a Chinese firm, while I would sail for Siam and prepare a base for us there. The two of us would follow separate paths and separate tasks, but eventually we would combine forces and follow the direction that had proved to be most promising. We then returned to the unsung hero's place and told him of our decisions. He highly approved. Right away he called a Yokohama Chinese merchant and made the necessary arrangements. He then selected the name Hakuyū (Pai Hsiung) for Yazō, fitted him out with pigtail and Chinese clothing, and got him placed in a Chinese firm. This done, Yazō cut off all contact with his old friends and didn't even let our close relatives know where he'd gone. The only four people who knew his whereabouts were Yazō himself, our nameless benefactor, the woman who owned the Isekō clothing shop, and I. Several times friends asked me where Yazō was but I told them all that I didn't know where he was. I felt guilty about this, of course, but I think those friends would have forgiven me if they had known that I deceived even our own relatives.

I then left Tokyo and headed for Kobe to meet Mr. Iwamoto and make arrangements for going to Siam. He told me that since he was on the point of taking a group of settlers to Siam I should not lose this chance and come as soon as possible. So I hurried back to Kumamoto to make preparations and once again returned to Kobe to visit Mr.

Southeast Asia

Iwamoto. My dismay at finding that he was seriously ill and at the point of death can well be imagined.

Close to a hundred settlers were waiting to leave the port, but Iwamoto was essential and became more and more gravely ill, with the result that a date of departure could not be set. Furthermore the hospital announced that his condition was critical, and as a result the organizing agency, the Hiroshima Immigration Company, was at a standstill. To make it worse, a number of newspapers began attacking Mr. Iwamoto personally, endangering the enterprise by charging that he was a swindler; the immigration company, concerned for its future course and alarmed by these circumstances, began making plans to transfer the immigrants to Hawaii. Then there was a clash between the Iwamoto faction and the immigration company, and next an argument between the immigrants themselves and the immigration company. A confused struggle raged with no solution in sight. Since I saw no prospect of leaving for Siam that way, I decided to go ahead by myself instead. Having made this decision, I visited Mr. Iwamoto in his hospital room to tell him so.

Mr. Iwamoto had looked tough as steel, but now he lay in bed looking frail as a thread. When he saw me he greeted me without a word, used hand signals to order the nurse to bring cold water so that he could wet his lips, and then spoke in a very weak voice: "Look what I've come to. I don't know whether I will recover or not. I am so distressed that I cannot keep my promises to the Minister of Agriculture and Commerce of Siam." With this his voice failed and he was unable to go on. Then he drank a little more water and struggled on: "I hear that over half of the settlers are changing direction to go to Hawaii, and that only about twenty of those who remain still intend to go to Siam. I think that Heaven has not yet destroyed my work. What I want to ask you to do is to take my place and lead these people to Siam, and there plan with the Minister of Agriculture and Commerce, Prince Surasakmontri, and our immigration company officials and build a base for future immigration.[27] If that proves possible the outcome will be not only gratification for me, but true happiness in the future for both Japan and Siam." This was all I needed to be sent into action. Up to this time I had had some doubts about him, but now I immediately agreed to his request without any further discussion of the enterprise. Can anything be as persuasive as speech?

When I agreed to take Mr. Iwamoto's place and to lead the company of immigrants going to Siam the immigration company agreed, as they were obligated by law to designate a representative. For them it was just a convenient and inexpensive way of discharging their responsibility. And for me, since I had only a steamship ticket, it was a fine way to make a little money. I signed a contract that provided for a monthly salary of 40 yen and a travel allowance of 100 yen. This is the only job with a salary I ever held in my life. And so the conflict was finally settled and my sailing date was set. The people who ran the immigration company were extremely pleased and their top executives took me with them to a first-class geisha house in Fukuhara. This was my first experience in the gay quarters.

Our party was served by a geisha who danced and sang; we all became pleasantly tipsy, and as the hour grew late people prepared to go to bed. Then one of the members of the party said to me, "Thanks to your assistance the

[27] Chao Phya Surasakmontri (1851-1933) was a member by marriage of the Bunnag family; he served the modernizing Thai monarch Rama V as a military bureaucrat responsible for the king's security. After he was denounced in 1883 he resigned from the royal guard, but was soon appointed commander of expeditions against rebellions in Northern Thailand, reaching the rank of major general and being granted the title Chao Phya, equivalent to the Japanese *Kōshaku* (Prince). He resigned from the army in 1892 and was then appointed Minister of Agriculture, a post in which he served until 1896. Rama VI appointed him to his privy council, and granted him the surname Saeng-Xuto, and Rama VII named him Field Marshal. Miyazaki, here and later, refers to him as Prince Surisaku.

problem our company faced has been solved, and we are delighted that the worries we have faced the past few days are finally at an end. If you go home alone now it will spoil the fun for the others. Won't you change your mind and spend the night here?" I agreed. But then he went on to say, "We came here to give you a send-off, and not to bring you to a brothel. You are about to embark on a long journey with high purpose and if you should contract a disease now the hopes of ten years would come to nothing in one night. So for your sake I propose to spend the night alone. Won't you make the same sacrifice for the same reason?" I agreed with him and promised not to have a woman, and went to bed. But I was so inflamed by desire that I was awake all night. The next morning, when I went to the room where the party had been held, the man to whom I had made my promise was there before me. He looked at me and smiled sheepishly and said, "I gave in after all. I'm sorry about that." Everybody there burst out laughing. On the other hand I was able to brag about my will power. But what a shameful thing to forfeit those boasts only a day later!

I had not forgotten the circumstances of our boarding-house in Kumamoto. I worried about that and about the circumstances in which my wife and child might be finding themselves there; it created, in fact, worry and agony that I could hardly stand. I did what I could to comfort my wife and ease my own concern for them; I copied out Umeda Unpin's Kannondō,[28] and sent it to her, and I also wrote my friend Matono Hansuke to ask him to look after my family. That was my state of mind at that time. Nevertheless, on returning from that geisha house I also found myself uneasy and unfulfilled. I had a restless feeling,

[28] The emotional account of a year's refuge spent in the Kannondō outside Kyoto by Umeda Unpin (1815-1859), a Restoration loyalist famed for a poem describing his sacrifice of his beloved wife's health to his higher duty of loyalism and expulsion of the barbarians. Umeda was executed in the Ansei Purge.

as though I had forgotten something there. I did my best to counter these feelings, but I just didn't have the strength to overcome them. In the end I drank some sake, got a friend to go with me, and went back there again, and this time, plucked a blossom from the branch. And I couldn't stop with one visit; I went back there two or three times. Why wasn't I overcome with remorse? What had become of my morality and conviction?

The night before the ship was to sail, I went to the place where the immigrants were staying and called together the twenty people who were going, to make sure they knew what they were getting into. I said to them, "I have never been to Siam, and I don't know much about it. You can't place much confidence in what people say about it. We will not know whether our efforts will succeed or fail until after we get there. However, I suspect that for you people the principal motivation in going is probably that of profit: that is, that you want to get some wealth together as quickly as you can, return to Japan as quickly as you can, and then lead a life of ease with your parents, wives, and children. Don't you think you might prefer a place that is better known and less dangerous, instead of entering a dangerous and uncivilized area where success and failure are so uncertain? My purpose in going to Siam is quite different from yours. I think you should think about this carefully once more, lest you regret it in the future. If you decide you want to change your minds and go to Hawaii, I will state your case to the immigration company myself. Please make up your minds about this tonight." But they all said that they had made up their minds and wanted to follow me. "Whatever hardships we meet, we will have no regrets. If we fail to make any money, we will think of our trip as a pilgrimage to Ise."[29] I put another question to

[29] Pilgrimages to the great shrine at Ise were favorite trips for commoners in Tokugawa Japan. Large-scale pilgrimages became cyclical phenomena first taking place at sixty-year intervals and later with increasing frequency. Hundreds of thousands of pilgrims would throng the roads and throw them-

them: "It's all very well to regard this as a pilgrimage to Ise if you don't make any money. But what if you lose your life? What then?" "No matter," they answered. "This is what we have struggled for with the immigration company. Live or die, we intend to follow your instructions." One has to admire simple honesty and determination. My spirits were raised by this; I bought some sake and drank to their determination. Then, carried along by the liquor and moving unsteadily, I sang a farewell song softly and let my feet lead me once more to the Fukuhara geisha house to enjoy a fleeting evening of spring. Was my love for my wife giving way to love for someone else? Not at all. But how could I square such behavior with my original resolve to restore humanity?

Sexual desire can really throw a man off his course. If you give in to it it comes more and more frequently, and if you try to control it you just generate more desire. Since this is a fact of human nature, shouldn't one just accept it? Yet I should not try to explain this. For me to do so would be like having a thief try to justify his robbery as a loan from the unwitting victim. There is no need to try to justify it. Although I had rejected the restraint of Christianity, I had not gone so far as to accept old Isaac Abraham's espousal of free love or Mormon polygamy. And in fact not even they would have approved of buying prostitutes. Nor did I. Although I could no longer commit myself to traditional ethics, I was certainly not proud of myself for having done this. It was sexual desire that had brought me to this point. I should probably be judged as some kind of thief for having let ordinary lust lead me into such unprincipled opportunism.

High ambition is something that is hard to suppress. Check it on the right and it emerges on the left; restrain it in front and it comes out in back. This is natural to human

---

selves on the generosity of the inhabitants of the districts through which they passed.

nature. Shouldn't it be allowed to grow? But I shouldn't try to explain this either. If I tried to justify this, it would be like having a murderer blame his sword. So I will not try to argue it. At that time I had made the move from thought to action. My determination, as before, lay with the survival of humanity, and I was determined to work out a solution to the problem of hunger. Was I not to be allowed any private desire? Yet my spirit was far removed from my basic principles; my body was ready to go to Siam, but my spirit lagged behind. When I dreamed about the outcome of my activities in Siam, I imagined myself entering the Chinese continent in front of a host of Chinese, a general mounted on a white horse in white raiment. When I thought about this I would cry for joy and fortify myself with sake. At other times, when I dreamed of the trials of the Chinese revolution, the white-robed general would fall victim to the enemy assassin's dagger. And when I dreamed of tragedy I would end up heading for the geisha house singing a gambler's song. Ah, that white-robed general on his white horse, he was not the real me but a phantom of my high ambition, a make-believe figure. I couldn't get away from such illusion; I was not yet a stable, mature individual single-mindedly pursuing my purposes. Instead, at that point I was the make-believe figure, the phantom. Certainly I had high ideals, but I lacked the morality appropriate to them. Consequently spirit did not match with morality, and will wandered apart from resolve so that they could not proceed in tandem. I hadn't come to realize that half my life was made up of sake and sex.

The boat left Kobe and reached Hong Kong after five days and nights. In Hong Kong we changed ships and headed for Siam, finding ourselves together with several hundred Chinese laborers. These were so-called coolies, people who are despised as though they were birds or animals. They seemed so filthy even the farmers of our party didn't want to get very close to them. But I could not help loving them. I regarded them as Chinese people on whom I was basing my life. I thought of them as people I was going to use for my work of restoring humanity. Since I felt no hostility toward them, were they not all my friends? How quickly they took to me! How honest their speech! They all asked me what country I was from. Since I was tall and had long hair, some of them thought I must be Korean, and others that I must be Okinawan. They argued among themselves without settling the matter, but when I told them I was Japanese, they were a little startled. Some of them asked if we were going to conquer Siam, and others wondered if we were running away from the war with China. But the one who seemed best-informed of the lot tried to mediate between us and talked in pidgin English: "Last month China and Japan fight all right. Yes now finish. Japan king say, I spend money so and so. China king say, I am poor, cannot pay money. Japan king say, then I will take Taiwan. China king say, all right! all right! You take Taiwan. You and me brother, no like more fight. Japan king say, all right! all right! I will stop fight. Now finish, all finish!"[30] He explained about the treaty of peace, and quietly urged the coolies not to take offense. And this was spoken by a coolie who some would despise as a bird or animal. Thanks to them I felt no hardships during the long eight-days' journey that took us to Siam.

Ah, then scenery of the continent again! Land, giving way to water, as far as the eye could see. The sluggish current of the Menam extended the smooth surface of the ocean; green grass and trees stretched on forever and gave color to the yellow mud. Truly, it looked just the way Shanghai had looked when I was there some years before. The setting brought to mind old stories about Yamada

[30] Verbatim from Tōten's text. Grammar aside, it constitutes a remarkably accurate account of the discussions between Li Hung-chang and Itō Hirobumi, which have since been published. English was the official language used at the Shimonoseki Peace Conference.

Nagamasa in earlier times.[31] Even our immigrants, tired as they were by the long journey, raised their eyes, cried for joy, and seemed to be genuinely moved.

After the boat went up the Menam for two or three hours, we reached Bangkok, the capital of Siam. I disembarked alone first and went to the home of Ishibashi Usaburō, presented him with the letter of introduction that Iwamoto had given me, and reported our arrival. He said, "That fellow Iwamoto is an incredibly insolent rascal! He went back to Japan with important business for the immigration company, but it is already more than six months and he hasn't returned. Meanwhile not one of the promises that were made has been kept. Because of this we have lost the confidence of Prince Surasakmontri. I had to pay merchants penalties for broken contracts and having lost both trust and money on this there isn't anything I can do. Finally last month I had to dissolve the immigration company. Consequently, I can't do anything for you in an official capacity for the company, but I'll do what I can as an individual." He was decisive in manner and speech and looked like an old-fashioned warrior. He poured me a beer and toasted our safe arrival, and then, taking two or three subordinates along, went to the ship with me. We boarded a smaller ship with the settlers and went down a tributary of the Menam and ended up at a pavilion called Dawn Bell Hermitage (*Gyōshōan*), which was set under palms and bananas.

The Gyōshōan was an old estate of the Minister of Agriculture and Commerce, Prince Surasakmontri, and had been made available to the Japanese immigration company. It was dilapidated, but not disintegrating. It was a big place, and could take as many as a thousand people. The

[31] Yamada, whose dates are uncertain, was a seventeenth-century adventurer who made his way to Thailand, came to head the Japanese community in Ayuthia, married into the royal family, and became a leading minister of state until a coup brought him down. Japan's seclusion system doomed the Japanese community there to extinction.

prince's servants who met us there expressed their sincere appreciation to us. That showed how deeply the prince respected the Japanese. The people of our party were now in much better spirits and more optimistic; some of them offered to go to the market, where they looked for vegetables and meat, bought some Chinese wine, and then invited Mr. Ishibashi and his men to a party to celebrate our arrival in Siam. I can still remember how Mr. Ishibashi got up, sang with a strong voice, and did a sword dance. Alas, now he is dead.

Since the immigration company had been dissolved it could no longer take care of things, and the immigrants could not be placed in agriculture as had been planned, but Mr. Ishibashi and some others who had formerly been connected with the immigration company managed to get the twenty settlers placed in a shipyard at first so they would not lack for food. While I was serving as supervisor and interpreter in these matters, I was also busy investigating immigration matters and thoroughly familiarizing myself with them. I thought the immigration enterprise was an important one and I wanted to meet Prince Surasakmontri with a view to getting it under way again.

The prince was an aristocrat who had been an army officer and gained reknown in a war with Laos. Subsequently he had been promoted to the office of Minister of War. It was said that when he traveled to Europe he had plotted to smuggle dynamite into Siam. When the matter was discovered he had been denounced and almost lost his life, but as he enjoyed the good-will and confidence of the king he had received a special pardon and been appointed to the little-regarded post of Minister of Commerce and Agriculture. The prince was a hot-blooded man of courage, and although he was now in a post of little importance he could not forget the humiliation his country had suffered at the hands of England and France. He regretted his own compatriots' inability to deal with this, and used his own resources to establish the immigration company with the purpose of importing Japanese settlers to Siam in the hope of reviving his country. When things did not work out in line with these plans he had dissolved the immigration company. Should not one think this tragic? And yet his determination had not been crushed by this one failure.

When I met Prince Surasakmontri in his villa in Saladaeng he welcomed me warmly and took me into an inner room. First of all he thanked me for coming such a long distance. Then he went on in a more melancholy manner: "The friendly relations between your country and mine have a long history, and they are not something that has just begun. Today, however, your country's condition is truly that of a rising sun in eastern skies, while my country's condition is one of decline in autumn winds, forlorn and helpless. The fate of my country will be settled very soon, and I worry about it day and night. Let me therefore be so bold as to ask this question: How far will your country go in extending to other countries the spirit with which you defended Korea?" When we talked about the affairs of the immigration company he did not express any resentment at Mr. Iwamoto's trickery, but instead said that those failures would have useful lessons for the future. Then he went on to say, "If people in your country would provide the means to start up an immigration operation again, we would greet it with full enthusiasm and cooperation. I am poor, but I do own this residence. If I sold it, it would not be hard to put together several hundred thousand yen. All in all it would provide the needs of the immigrants." Ah, honest officials are always poor. The prince really was the poorest among the ministers of state in Siam, but his enthusiasm was of this order. That was the reason I decided to go back home. I was determined to revive the Hiroshima Immigration Company and its settlement project, to take advantage of the prince's backing to make a success of things.

But the heart of man changes easily. The twenty immigrants who had sworn to go through fire and water with me were now persuaded by a certain Japanese doctor to accept employment on a Tha Rua railroad project. It was because the wages were high. But the wages were high because the area was extremely unhealthful and full of disease; even the natives fled it. Consequently all the Japanese who went there fell ill and died. I was determined to do what I could to block this and used every argument I could think of, but in vain. When I reminded them of the promises they had made in Kobe and charged them with breaking their word they just bowed their heads and apologized, but in the end there wasn't one who followed me. I really had to feel sorry for these poor dirt-farmers. They were so intent upon quick profits that they had no thought for mortal danger. When I saw that all my words would have no effect I finally said, "I have had your welfare in mind with the stern advice I have been giving you, but you people show no inclination to change. I have shown you all the good-will I possibly could. But now, as representative of the immigration company, I have to make this statement. Do not do this thing. If you do not follow my instructions you will have to break connections with me and with the immigration company." When I revealed that I was going to go back to Japan to start the immigration company up again over half of them changed their minds and decided against the railroad jobs, but six refused to budge. Those six prepared a document that read, "We are going to Tha Rua against your orders. We will not hold you or the immigration company responsible for whatever misfortunes may befall us there," after which they broke off relations with me.

They had cut connections with me, but they had not lost their respect for me. And I, since I had their interests at heart, did not hold a grudge against them. So we prepared sake and had a farewell party, at which I gave them a final warning and wished them well: "The document you have just signed clears me of responsibility as an official of the immigration company, but it does not affect the relations between us as individuals. If any of you find yourself in trouble or sick, I hope that you will come back to my office right away. I will certainly do anything I can to help you. If I go back to Japan, I will ask Mr. Yanagida Ryōmin to act in my place, and he will do whatever he can to help you." When they heard this they shed tears of gratitude. They bowed to me. Then why didn't they change their minds? It would be wrong to say they were devoid of a sense of morality. Had they not apologized over and over again? Nor were they devoid of affection. Had they not wept and bowed to me? All of them knew these things very well. But knowing them, they suppressed them, and furthermore went off to a pest-hole in the interior. All for money. No, you cannot even say it was for money alone. Without money they would not have been able to take care of their parents, or to live with their wives and children. This was their life. Alas, they could not help it.

Yanagida was the most knowledgeable among the settlers. When I first met him in Kobe I mistook him for an agitator who got the settlers worked up for his own advantage, and I bitterly reproached him with this to his face. But we became good friends, and I came to realize that he was an unusual person. He once explained himself to me in these terms: "I used to be a priest, and when I read the biography of Shaku Genkyō,[32] I was moved by it. That is how I joined this enterprise." I regretted my earlier misunderstandings deeply, and we became extremely fond of each other. That is how I came to entrust the follow-up to him while I myself went back to Japan to try to revive the immigration company.

[32] A romantic and perhaps legendary figure, supposedly born in 1867, who was credited with travels in every part of China, and was the subject of several "biographies" during the enthusiasm for stories about China that accompanied the Sino-Japanese War.

[12]
THREE MONTHS IN JAPAN AGAIN

As I wanted to propose reviving the Siam immigration project to the Hiroshima Immigration Company, I went straight from Moji to Hiroshima. I had never been to Hiroshima before. As had often been the case, my strange appearance and air roused suspicion; I was often denied a room at inns where they did not know me. Since I was worried about this, and thought I wouldn't fit a high-class place, I asked the rickshaw man to pick out an inexpensive inn for me. He moved along in high spirits, and brought me to a small inn. "A guest" he called with a loud voice. A maid came running; she took one look at me and ran away again without saying a word. Since there might still be some chance, I just stood there and didn't leave. After a bit I noticed another woman who was peeking at me from behind a screen; she now had my fate in her hands. Good or bad? The maid came out again. Her expression indicated that things would be all right. Sure enough: she bowed courteously and said, "Please come in." Soon I was given a room and treated like a special guest. Never had I had such luck. Who was it who had determined my fate? Don't ask me now. This was the prelude to later repentance on my part.

That same day I went to the immigration company to advocate sending settlers to Siam. The company representative showed some interest, and told me that they would make their decision in an executive meeting; I was to wait for their decision. I did not feel bored, for I had friends to drink with and, thanks to the warm hospitality of the inn hostess, was well treated.

Takeda Hanshi and Ōsaki Shōkichi were old friends of mine. They were involved in the assassination of the Korean queen,[33] and had been jailed in Hiroshima during the trial that followed. By now they had been set free, however, and they came to my inn every day to drink sake with me. We rambled on swapping old and new stories and experiences; declaimed with high spirits and our songs were lubricated with sake. Ōsaki's favorite was an old Sendai folk chant (*sendai-bushi*); how far off pitch he was! Takeda's specialty was a Kumamoto chant, "Kin-kira-kin." How sour his tone was! These discordant tunes and sour notes remain with me as unforgettable memories that I still carry with me. They are more than songs, and more than melodies; they are quite special. On one occasion, when we were well along in our drinking, Takeda picked up a brush and picked out a posthumous Buddhist name for me. It was Tōkūan.[34] I could not understand the reasons for it, and asked him to explain. He took up the brush again and wrote this Chinese poem:

> On, on, time moves onward from past to present
> days.
> Empty, empty, all the universe is empty
> Go alone, and find enlightenment
> Beyond the universe.

I still could not get its full meaning, and pressed him for a further explanation. He laughed and said, "All men attain

[33] On October 8, 1895, a group of Korean and Japanese strong-arm men dashed into the Korean royal residence in Seoul and murdered Queen Min because she was obstructing pro-Japanese politics of reform.

[34] Lit. "onward and empty hermitage." The first two elements also can be used in combination to indicate ascension. Takeda Hanshi also provided one of the prefaces for the book. See Appendix.

enlightenment a second before their death. Don't worry about it!" We raised our eyes and toasted each other. The inn hostess was the one who always waited on us and poured our sake. Her hospitality and kindness were quite out of the ordinary. My two friends teased me by saying. "This young widow has developed a liking for you!" I myself was suspicious that she might be a police informant, and warned my friends not to talk much in her presence. They accepted my misgivings uncritically and we all became very watchful of her. And so despite the fact that that woman was the one who was to determine my fate, we repaid her extraordinary kindness by acting as though we were going to determine hers. How dangerous one's life course is!

I had written to my brother Yazō in Yokohama when I first arrived in Hiroshima to report my return from Siam. He replied asking me to come to see him as soon as I had finished my work in Hiroshima. But before that was finished, I received a telegram from him: "Come right away!" I had no money then, and borrowed some from the inn hostess. With this I hurried to Yokohama immediately and found Yazō lying down and very sick. His eyes were sunken and his cheeks hollow: he seemed an entirely different person. He said his problems were chronic intestinal catarrh and depression. He raised himself when he saw me come. "It's good to see you here," he said, "I feel better already." He went on, "Since we parted, I have been studying English, French, and Chinese besides holding down my job. I guess I studied and worked too hard, and this is what happened to me. There is a saying, haste makes waste; I guess that's what it means, don't you suppose?" Beef was brought in and sake was warmed; Yazō offered me some, filled his own cup, and took a few pieces of meat for himself. As we talked, his spirits rose and he forgot his illness; we paid no attention to the time and talked until dawn, when we lay down on his bed and slept side by side. The next day I went to Tokyo to see some people I thought I might be able to interest in the Siam enterprise, but to my disappointment all they wanted to talk about was Korea, and no one paid any attention to me. I came back to Yokohama alone and spent the night with Yazō again. When I was preparing to say good-bye to him after breakfast the next morning, he looked very upset, and sighed as he said, "Ah, I don't want you to leave. We've about finished our business but still I don't want to let you go. Why don't you stay until this afternoon?" Then, with tears in his eyes, he went on, "I sound a little bit like a weak woman, don't I? Maybe the decline of my physical strength has affected my spirit as well. But you could stay a half day longer, couldn't you?" I agreed immediately. We devoted the fleeting hours that remained to a discussion that ranged through philosophy and religion, government policy, and human nature. Time passed quickly as we talked and laughed, and when it became time for me to leave, Yazō straightened out his clothing, stood up, looked at me and said, "Now, let's go to the Western-style restaurant near the park and have lunch together. Then I'll say good-bye to you." I tried to dissuade him, but he wouldn't listen to me and said, "You have cured my illness. Don't worry about it anymore." He picked up his stick and led the way through the gate. Alas, little did we realize, as we sat drinking Masamune sake and eating beef in a second-floor room of that Western restaurant, that it would be our last farewell. We wished each other good luck and parted. It was exactly the last day of the last month of the year.[35]

I took the train to Kobe and boarded a ship for Hiroshima there, arriving on New Year's Day. I got together with my friends right away, and we drank and talked the night away. Quite by chance, my friend Matono

[35] That is, 1895. Attention in Japan was on events in Korea, where the Japanese participation in the assassination of Queen Min had brought international criticism.

came along. "I have a friend named Suenaga Setsu,"[36] he said, "who wants to go to Siam with you. Why don't you stop by at my house on your way home and talk to him about it?" In the meantime, the decision about establishing a new immigration project had been made. A senior executive of the Hiroshima Immigration Company came and informed me, "It is too soon. We plan to wait a little longer." Then he handed me several hundred yen for my travel expenses. I saw that there was nothing I could do, and I did not try to argue with him. I decided to leave Hiroshima for Wakamatsu as soon as possible; both Matono and Suenaga lived there. The night before I left, the inn hostess came to my room with two maids, and ended up spending the night with me. Could I never stop compromising myself?

When I arrived in Wakamatsu I met Mr. Suenaga, and told him what Matono had told me. He seemed direct and forthcoming in manner; he talked freely, and we soon found ourselves in agreement. We more or less agreed on a day of departure; he promised to meet me in Nagasaki, and I headed for my native village of Arao alone.

Since I had left my family in the city in Kumamoto, where my wife was running a boardinghouse, only my brother Tamizō and his family and my mother were in our village. If my spirit had not been burdened by Yazō's illness, how happy this trip would have been! In my impatience the train seemed to plod along as slowly as a water ox. And yet my spirit was not in any rush to arrive; I knew they would be pleased to be able to hear my stories about strange customs and matters in Siam, but what was I to say when they asked me about Yazō? When I thought about that I felt like jumping out of the train. But the train ran mindlessly without understanding my feelings, carrying

[36] Suenaga (1869-1965), a Fukuoka adventurer who figures frequently in the pages that follow. He accompanied Japanese armies in the war against China, affiliated with the expansionist Kokuryūkai society, and dreamed of a great "East Asian Free Empire."

my spirits, which were half happy and half sad, until it got to the place it was going.

It happened that my mother was not home, as she had gone to Kumamoto to see how my wife was managing. Tamizō, his wife, and their children were the only ones there. Tamizō asked about things in Siam and then, as I had expected, asked about Yazō. But when he asked that question he looked very hesitant. Was that because he knew there was a secret agreement between Yazō and me? I did my best to evade the question, but I cannot describe the distress that was in my heart. I felt even worse because he didn't press me for more details. I drank away at the sake his wife brought me, concentrated on stories about Siam, and then took my leave and headed for Kumamoto and my wife's boardinghouse.

At the boardinghouse I found my mother, wife, and sons. They were, of course, glad to see me back from a trip of a thousand miles to foreign countries, and they put their concern of recent years behind them and celebrated. But it is only human to respond to joy by trying to make it complete. When my mother saw her youngest son before her in good health, it was natural for her to be reminded of her other son. "Where is your older brother, and how is he? Haven't you heard from him, haven't you met him up around Tokyo on this trip?" Those were her words. Ah, sake! I needed your strength to hoodwink my mother. Parents are likely to believe what their children say, but how could I have made up such lies without the reinforcement of sake? Ah, sake! When I wanted to lie but hesitated to do so, it was sake that helped me become an accomplished liar. When thoughts of gain and loss arose in me, it was you who gave me the courage to put aside gain and choose righteousness. When thoughts of ease began to rise in me, it was sake that moved me courageously along the proper path. When I was plunged into despair and disillusion, it was sake that breathed new courage into me.

Without sake this dream of mine would have come to nothing. Truly, my dream and sake were inseparable.

That's right. Sake was my best friend. With it I could fool my mother, and create a cheerful atmosphere at home. But then suddenly something began to torture me. It was a rumor that my wife had a lover. The warm atmosphere in my home and the pleasures of sake disappeared at once, and I felt as if I wanted to die. With my spirit close to death it was natural that my reason and my ambition seemed destroyed. I did my best to get hold of myself and get the facts of the matter to be sure, but I could not. And so I couldn't make up my mind about the matter; I half believed, half doubted. How was I to make up my mind? I thought I was going mad. When I thought that she had dishonored me, that she had dishonored our sons, and that she had dishonored my mother and my brothers, my blood boiled. I was so outraged that my fury would not be satisfied by sucking her blood and tearing her flesh. In truth, the flames of my anger consumed her any number of times. But then when my anger reached its height, a touch of compassion would come welling up in me. For the first time I realized the truth of the saying that excessive love can turn to bitter hate. But I also realized the fact that great love can be hidden within extreme hatred. Both love and hatred tend to be extreme, and they were at war within me. Because of this the soul loses its rightness, man drifts in darkness, becomes foolish and then insane, and at the last life almost comes to an end. That is how it was with me; at that time my spirit had almost come to such a pass. Unable to see any way of resolving the matter, I finally proposed a divorce. Meanwhile I had forgotten all about the larger matters that had engrossed me. All I thought about was taking my two youngsters off into the mountains and spending the rest of my life there. But when my wife protested her innocence in tears before me, I too raised my voice and wept. And then when I tried to restore the feelings of earlier days in my heart, fresh waves of resentment would come over me. Things went on and on in this manner. In my imagination I killed her any number of times and then let her live again. And so my heart became confused as a tangled thread, my spirit would glisten like a rainbow. I crossed the border of strain and agony, and seemed likely to enter the realm of the possessed. Warnings from my mother and advice from Tamizō did little to console me. But then, suddenly, a telegram came from Nagasaki. It turned out to be from the woman who had been hostess at the Hiroshima inn, telling me that it was urgent that I come to Nagasaki immediately. Now, it was this telegram that was responsible for my reconciliation with my wife. When I saw it I realized that I was the one who should repent, for it reminded me of the night I had spent with the woman who sent it. Who was I to insist that she alone be faithful? What if we changed places? For sure, even if my wife had not been faithful, I was in no position to reproach her. And in fact the truth of the matter was still not clear anyway. So that was my final decision and the result is that our marriage has lasted to the present.

Actually marriage is a kind of hazardous enterprise that depends upon lifelong fidelity. And I had already endangered that hazardous enterprise. It was impossible to return to the warm affection of earlier times. Instead I drank more heavily and became trapped in the pleasures of the red-light districts. That's how it was: if I wanted to destroy the jealousy that was in my heart, I had to make light of the love that bound me to my wife. But do that as I might, I found no peace, and in the end I turned again to sake and to the licensed quarter. Were my emotions never to come to rest? What is the essence of jealousy? The continuation of love? Then what principle is to determine its breadth and limits? If I could only understand this, would I be able to return to true standards of humanity, or would I be able to restore our former affection?

Before this a friend named Hirayama Shū,[37] who had agreed to go to Siam with me, came to see me at my house. I had discussed what I should do about our boardinghouse with Tamizō, and had decided to close it down and move my family back to my native village of Arao. I left it for Tamizō to take care of the details, and headed for Nagasaki together with Hirayama. We put up at the Fukushimaya and waited for Suenaga Setsu to join us. He soon came. In addition my wife's younger brother, Maeda Kunishirō, had made up his mind to go with us and came too. The four of us were in a little four-and-a-half-mat room on the second floor, where we waited for the mail ship. Meanwhile, the matter immediately at hand was the problem of the woman who owned the Hiroshima inn.

Why had she come? Although I had had the pleasure of a night with her, I retained the doubts I had about her. Moreover, my friends distrusted her too. One said, "She's come to follow you." Another said, "She's a police dog." And I myself could not get over a feeling of some apprehension about her. She herself, however, was perfectly composed and took part in all our talk and laughter and fun. That made my companions even more uneasy. One day she said to me, "I'd like to talk to you about something alone." We went into another room and sat facing each other. "This is a matter of life and death," she said, "and I want you to promise me that even if you do not agree you will keep it secret." I promised. Then she posed the question: "You do not seem to be embarrassed for money but, on the other hand, if you are to do the things you propose, money is surely a prerequisite. Isn't it true that the more you have, the more easily, the faster, and better you can do what you want to do? I don't fully understand what it is you're planning to do, and when I say this you may think I'm out of order, but the truth is

[37] Hirayama (1870-1940), a Fukuoka-born China hand and adventurer, became Miyazaki's closest collaborator in the events of which the book speaks.

that I am extremely impressed by you: not by your face or appearance, but by the fact that you want to do something in the world—and I would like to see you do it—that's what I think, out of order or not. However it is of course impossible for a woman, especially a foolish woman like me, to provide real assistance for aspirations like yours. But if it's possible that money would help, then I wonder whether a woman might not be able to help there? If you agree with me, I know how I can get you twenty or thirty thousand yen within a month. I'm sure of it—there may be some problems for me afterwards—but I'm sure I can raise twenty or thirty thousand yen, though it will take some unusual methods. I'd like to talk about what lies ahead for me in that case—yes, I know that you have a wife, and I know that we can never be married, but won't you take me overseas with you? I promise I will never get in your way. Once we set out, I could always support myself, even if I had to do it through prostitution. Won't you do this for me?"

I did not know how to respond to her. When I asked her how she proposed to get the money, she once again swore me to secrecy. Then, when she revealed her secret, I refused flatly saying, "Although I am eager to achieve my objectives, I am not prepared to stoop to improper methods of funding. I thank you for your generous offer, but I am unable to accept it." She replied, "I understand you." She said no more, and after spending a night in that little room left me. Ah, that heroic woman; I wonder where she is today?

Nagasaki was the place where the "unsung hero," Watanabe Gen, to whom Yazō and I were obligated, lived. While my friends and I waited for the arrival of the mail ship, we talked together at our inn about our future course, dreamed about the things we were going to do, and argued about philosophy and religion. Once we even took all the comforters out of the closet, crawled in and sat there in Zen contemplation. Everybody thought we were crazy.

While Hirayama and I were drinking sake together Suenaga and Maeda were competing in consuming bean jam (*yōkan*) confectionery; the Fukushima maids were astonished by the amount we consumed in that four-and-a-half-mat room. Suenaga startled people by intoning Buddhist verses with a voice that boomed like a cracked bell and Hirayama made people sad by the way he sang his Chinese poems. The halls resounded with the sound of smacking lips as the *yōkan* faction competed with the sake faction. Was it not natural that people referred to our four-and-a-half-mat room as a conspirators' lair (*ryōzanpaku*)?[38] I myself often called on Mr. Watanabe, the "unsung benefactor" who was so good to us, visited with his mother, who rather resembled my plump mother; I would also play with his two carefree boys, and almost forgot the worries that swirled around me.

After this had gone on for several weeks, Mr. Watanabe one day sent someone to call me to his house. When I went there, he handed me a letter. It turned out to be from Yazō in Yokohama. Nothing could have made me happier at that time. Yazō wrote to report that he had met a member of the Chinese revolutionary party. He described the details in his letter. It amounted to the following news:

> After you left my illness became worse, so that I had to rest again. One day a missionary I know, accompanied by a Chinese, dropped in to visit me. At the time it was impossible to talk, but as soon as I was well enough I paid a visit of thanks to the missionary and asked him more about the Chinese. The missionary was not very well informed, but just said the man was a member of a revolutionary group in South China. After I managed to find out where he lived, I went to the home of the Chinese and asked to see him. He greeted me cordially and invited me into

[38] *Ryozanpaku*, meeting place for chivalrous comrades, a term made standard in Chinese romances like the *Water Margin*.

his living room. I began by thanking him for coming to see me. He said that he had heard about me from the missionary and that he had come to respect me. After this exchange of compliments our talk turned to the China problem. He tried to get me to say what I thought, but I said that I was only a simple merchant, really did not know much about world affairs, thereby trying to evade his questions. With that he spoke eloquently about the corruption of the Ch'ing government, described the hopes of people outside the government, and predicted that a revolution against the government was inevitable. I wanted to leap for joy, but thought I should protect my anonymity; so I restrained myself and listened coldly. Next he asked about my opinions about political thought; I answered as briefly as possible. I said that I accepted the position that within the four seas all men were brothers. He seemed to find my response satisfactory and welcomed it; he then went on to explain his interpretation of the significance of that brotherhood. "The wisdom of all the sages of east and west is contained in this single phrase," he said. "Unfortunately it is very far from being realized at present. There has to be a revolution to bring it into being. That revolution has already begun in China. Would that you would work with it!" On hearing this I realized that he was a member of a revolutionary party. I really longed to tell him of my aspirations and determination, but I restrained myself. While I maintained my composure and continued to listen coldly, he became more and more worked up and wanted me to reveal my thoughts. It was all I could do to keep from doing so. Just then two other Chinese came. He excused himself for a moment and went into the next room with them. At the entrance of the room was a sign in English that said "Private Room"; from this I knew that it was their secret meeting-room. Just then his Chinese servant came to

> serve me tea, and I asked the boy about his master. The boy was big-eyed and gestured with his hands as he said, "He is a great man. He tried to overthrow the Chinese king, but failed, and recently took refuge in Japan." I speculated on whether this might not be the party of Sun Yat-sen. Soon the three men came back in, and I thought it best to excuse myself. What matters is that this provides evidence that the things we thought would happen in China in fact are taking place there. As a matter of fact, things are farther along than we thought. This is no time to go down a side alley. You should finish up the Siam business and come back home at the earliest possible moment. There are many things I want to talk to you about. In view of the present state of affairs, the sooner the better.

Yazō's letter was a roll more than six feet in length; every character, every clause was alive. As I read about the construction of the house and the description of the room interiors, and again the descriptions of the host and his visitors, I felt as if I had been there myself. It was clear how excited Yazō had become. It can be imagined how moved I was on reading that letter. Mr. Watanabe waited quietly for me to finish reading it, and then added a quiet word of advice: "Now that you have read that, it might be a good idea to burn it." I followed his instructions and did so immediately. He also urged me to write a response right away. So I took brush in hand and wrote a letter along the following lines:

> When I read your letter I leaped for joy. I can imagine how pleased and moved you were to meet that revolutionary personally. However, when I think about it carefully, this man seems rather rash to reveal all his thoughts to someone he had just met, and to want to discuss all this with you. He must be in a tremendous rush to find some Japanese friends to help

> him. If so, it is easy to see what will happen to him; if Mr. A doesn't help him, Mr. B will. He's likely to fall into the hands of so-called rebel helpers. The danger is that his elaborate undertakings will end up as publicity stunts for Japanese adventurers. As a result, although I feel sorry for him and sympathize with him, I would suggest some caution; I suspect that he and his group are too rash to be willing to wait quietly for the right occasion. I think we should not get involved in their movement just yet, but watch their activities for a while. So far we have been successful in keeping our high purpose to ourselves; if we were to collaborate with these so-called revolutionary agents and throw away our lives in an abortive uprising, wouldn't we always regret it? I may be somewhat off in this prediction but probably not far. Nor is this just my own opinion; Mr. Watanabe agrees with it too. If you agree with us, won't you keep some distance between yourself and these unfortunate Chinese martyrs and prepare for the future? My thoughts have flown to Yokohama: I wish I could go. I have gone too far with the Siamese affair to give it up now. But I will hurry to wind it up and will want to discuss ways of accelerating our work with you. I do hope you will recover soon.

Ah, it was Hirayama who encouraged me and took me from my boardinghouse in Kumamoto, where I had been desperately discouraged, to Nagasaki. It was Suenaga who shed tears of sympathy for me and who restored my enthusiasm with his affirmation of our high goals. In our four-and-a-half-mat conspirators' lair, the atmosphere was so animated that I did not have the chance to be reminded of my own tragic worries. It was my benefactor Watanabe who kept me from going through the gate of despair and disillusion and who watched my progress. These four were the reason I was able to survive. But it was Yazō's letter that provided the final encouragement and a resurgence of enthusiasm. Yes, I was really revived by his letter. But on the other hand, is it possible that my reply may have led to Yazō's untimely death? If he had been able to communicate freely with the Chinese he had dreamed about so long, if he had revealed ideas long kept secret in his heart, might he have eased his mind, and might he have been able to avoid such a tragic death? In fact, however, Yazō was completely faithful to my letter to the day of his death. Alas, I myself and the high purpose we shared, bear the responsibility for his death. Yazō himself never blamed me.

Meanwhile, I still loved my wife, whether or not I was supposed to. I tried to trust her, unfaithful as she might be. The situation was enough for me to have less interest in going to Siam. And then there was Yazō's letter. My spirit had been regenerated by that letter, but at the same time my interest in going to Siam disappeared. If I had not had my cheerful friends with me I might very well have given the plan up. Moreover, we had waited for a ship for thirty days; the delay of our departure brought us all close to despair.

It was true: everybody was bored. Our room became less animated. A mail boat did come in but it would not accept steerage-class passengers, and that was all we could afford. So we had to wait for another ship. Consequently boredom turned to discontent, and from discontent came Chinese and Japanese poems. With this our cramped headquarters changed again. For instance, Suenaga, the Zen master, wrote some Zen couplets of complaint:

> The enlightened man stands above the dusty world,
> My twenty-eight years were spent in elegant pursuit of
>   books and swords,
> I smile to think I have been poor for a lifetime,
> I reached enlightenment and so destroyed my
>   discontent.

At that time Mr. Yamazaki of the Sakuragi Trading Company in Siam returned to Japan and was in Nagasaki. We became friends with him and drank together every day. He, in turn, introduced his friend Yato, and had him join us too. Finally, a ship came and our departure was set. Now our party was in high spirits; and everybody selected an alias that would include the word "south." Suenaga's was Nan-Tosei (Southern Star), Hirayama's Nan-Banri (Southern Distance), Maeda's Nan-Tenshi (Southern Son of Heaven), and Yato's Nan-Ōsei (Southern Cherry), and mine was Nan-Bantetsu (Southern Barbarian Steel). All of us were men of high purpose, our hearts full of fervor, and we gave longevity little thought. Our spirits truly rose. In this atmosphere of high spirits, I too began my journey without any of the depression that had beset me. Harada wrote a long farewell poem in Chinese for our departure, and Suenaga and Hirayama responded in kind. I have forgotten them all, and cannot re-create them. We now boarded the American mail ship Garrick and headed for Hong Kong.

[13] MY SECOND TRIP TO SIAM

WHEN OUR SHIP ARRIVED IN HONG KONG WE found that plague was raging and no ships could leave port with passengers. Nobody knew when we would be able to leave. We looked at each other with consternation at this new setback.

Still, we had to be ready for setbacks like this. Except for Yato, who was a banker and trader between Siam and Japan, all of us were poor fellows. If we had to stay in Hong Kong for even ten days, we would run out of money for room and board. It was as clear as fire before our eyes that we were facing a crisis. Talkative Suenaga, the saliva running out of his mouth, was full of enthusiasm. "Let's take the overland route to Siam via Kwangtung, Kwangsi, and Annam! Isn't that what courageous men like us should do?" Hirayama agreed with him, and Maeda, impressed by the difficulties of going by ship, agreed too. I myself, though, still responsible for the twenty immigrants in Siam, was afraid that the overland route might delay us, making it impossible for me to do my duty as representative of the immigration company. Consequently I proposed putting Suenaga's idea aside until we had been able to talk to the captain directly. My friends were persuaded and agreed, leaving the negotiations to Yato and to me. The two of us hired a sampan and headed for a ship named Kungming.

We were able to see the captain and asked him to take us. He finally agreed, provided that we did not mind a circuitous route to Bangkok by way of Swatow and Singapore; he also warned us that the police were not to know. When we went back to the hotel to report this to our friends, they agreed that there was no real choice and that we should not let this opportunity go. We agreed immediately that we should hesitate no longer. Once it was dark we boarded the ship quietly.

We had to travel as cheaply as possible, so we were in the hold. Our fare for the trip by way of Swatow and Singapore was only twelve yen, and it can be imagined what things were like. When the ship left Hong Kong for Swatow it was stormy and the skies were covered by black clouds; a warning signal of red balls was hoisted at the Kowloon harbor. As soon as the anchor was raised and the ship left Hong Kong, we were hit by a storm. It was indescribable. Our spirits plummeted; Yato soon looked half dead, and Maeda looked far gone too. Hirayama, who was proud of his past experience of going after whales in small boats through choppy seas whithout getting seasick, now turned a ghastly color and was unable to move. Suenaga, who considered himself a professional because he had worked as a sailor, shook his head and couldn't eat. I was the only one who could eat and walk around as usual, so my four friends lost face. The ship finally hove to and drifted for a night and a day. After the wind died down and the waves subsided, we got underway again and arrived in Swatow.

But we still had a long way to go, and more trouble lay ahead. No sooner would we get out of one difficulty than we got into another. When I think of what happened on the way from Swatow to Singapore I still tremble with fear.

At Swatow our trip was enlivened by having more than a thousand coolies board our ship. They fought for space in the hold, beating and hitting each other. Suenaga enjoyed the sight and applauded, shouting "We can use these fellows in days to come, can't we?" We all agreed. But then the Chinese began to encroach on our space, and we tried to hold our ground. Suenaga, who had been clapping his hands and shouting for joy, now snarled, "You dirty Chinks!" and reached for his sword. It was amusing to see Hirayama's dismay as he called, "Hey! Wait! Wait!" And it was exciting to have the captain pull off a coolie who was coming after me with a stick more than six feet long. But after a while the space problem was settled. As I looked around at the coolies, crouched down with their things in front of them, I thought they looked like so many pigs. Yato said in a low voice, "Only the adventurer knows what adventurers have to go through." I couldn't help agreeing with him.

The first hardship that now developed was that we were so crowded that we couldn't move. The next was the smell of opium. That was followed by the assaults of bedbugs, and then the foul air. In no time Yato looked half dead again; and Maeda screamed "I can't stand it! I can't stand it!" The sea was choppy because of the previous day's storm, and without a wind the ship just bobbed around. The sounds of people vomiting resounded all over the ship like bugles on the battlefield. The coolies who had gorged themselves before now disgorged equally freely, and the colorless stalls of a moment before were transformed into a greengrocer's marketplace. Those who had had the courage of fierce tigers were now meek and submissive. Next they had to urinate, and after that they pulled up their clothes and tried to hit bamboo pipes that were provided for urine with their feces. Then the pipes fell over and the contents mixed with vomit to become waves that lapped across the hold. Add to this the foul air and smell of opium, and then add the equatorial heat that brought this mixture to steaming point. The distress was indescribable. Maeda whimpered "Unbearable, unbearable." Suenaga held some pungent pills to his nostrils, and only his eyes flickered;

Yato looked half-dead as before. But I climbed up on deck with Hirayama. The night was dark and it was drizzling. The coolies who lay exposed to the rain looked like corpses on the battlefield, and we could hardly step over them. We stood by the door looking for some water to drink, but couldn't locate any. Then by chance we saw a basket full of big fresh radishes. Ah, a gift from heaven, we thought; it would be wrong not to receive it. We looked around and quickly took some. We bit into them as quietly as possible and enjoyed the fresh taste. Hirayama and I breathed a sigh of relief together. What a relief! How could anybody who had not gone through what we had just gone through appreciate that taste? Truly, there is a Buddha in the very depths of hell.

Three days after we had left Swatow, when we were off the coast of Annam, the captain set aside a special cabin for our party, and kept the Chinese out. At this we felt renewed. Suenaga made some tea and served it, and we all took it with sighs of relief. How good it was! Hirayama stood at the side of the ship chanting a song of his own:

> A limitless universe is forever the same
> Standing alone in the gunwale emotions rise
> Clouds without limit appear in the ocean
> The tide rising in the sea is even more endless.
> The moon shining in a serene sky lights my collar,
> The wind blowing over the water stirs my long hair
> I do not know where I will be tomorrow morning
> Like a fabled bird alone on a journey of ten thousand
> miles.

That certainly fit the circumstances and our emotions at the time. The words were Hirayama's alone, but we shared his feelings.

Truly, man's emotions change with circumstances. But this is natural for corporeal beings. How quickly Yato, who was half-dead, awoke to expressions of pleasure! And how quickly Maeda, from holding his nose, regained his cockiness! So, too, Suenaga's eloquence and Hirayama's recitations seemed to undergo lightning change. Consequently we were able to reestablish the mood of our crowded conspirators' lair in Nagasaki on shipboard, thanks to the captain's generosity, and Hachinoe was easily able to peddle the canned foods that he had brought along, though he didn't get any money from us for them.

When we got to Singapore the coolies all got off, and we did too. We went to visit Ōi Kentarō[39] at his residence, and he then accompanied us to the Fusōkan, where he treated us to sake and food. He had a great beauty with him, or at least he considered her so; she stroked his wispy beard as he drank beer, sucked eggs, and held forth on the proper policies for the revival of East Asia, all in great good humor. He discussed the development of Sumatra, and quite shamed the younger men with his vigor. It was one of the pleasant interludes of our journey. I wonder if Ōi still has the vigor he did then?

From Singapore to Bangkok we were the only passengers. We enjoyed calm sea and clear weather. After four days we got to Bangkok with songs of gladness. Heaven, however, had many more trials in store for us. When we disembarked and I went to my company offices, I found seventeen of the twenty Japanese immigrants lying there ill. They told me that after I had left they followed the six who had chosen to break off with me, and went to work on the railway construction. There they found themselves in a situation that was so miserable that they were lucky to escape with their lives. Several of them very nearly died. Therefore I got some assistants to put the most seriously ill in the Jikei Hospital, and let the others use the

[39] Ōi (1843-1918), a student of French law and leading figure in the Meiji movement for representative government, was involved in trade ventures with Korea, and arrested for organizing a filibustering expedition to Korea in 1885 (the "Osaka Incident"). Pardoned in 1889., he served briefly in the Diet before returning to trade ventures with Singapore and Dairen. He was a leading "Asianist" among the Meiji political figures.

company premises and provided medicine for them. Then some of them came down with cholera as well. I took them to the hospital, interpreted for them, and served as nurse for them. I could hardly bear the agony of it all. To make it worse, I was almost out of money. Three of them died within two days; yet not even that was the end of the misery.

Who was it that said "life is like a morning dew"? Whenever I think of Yato's death, I realize its truth. I still remember it clearly. The evening of the third day after we got to Siam, Yato invited our little group for a party of congratulation. As we drank away Isonaga Kaishū[40] came up with a traveler's song. Tsuge Donkai obliged us with Hōkai *bushi*, Suenaga with a Chinese chant, and Hirayama with a mimicry; everybody got into the spirit of things and sang. I too chanted my best Naniwa song and everybody laughed at me. Our genial host, the conventional banker and straightforward trader, laughed for joy as his face turned red and he beamed all over. "That's the way! That's the way!" I thought. We forgot all about the time and babbled on, chanting and singing. I too forgot our hardship and had a fine time. By the time we took our leave and headed for home it was after midnight. Who would have thought that our host would not be of this world the next day?

Early the next morning an employee of the Sakuragi Trading Company brought me a letter that proved to be from Donkai. It said that Yato had begun to vomit at three o'clock that morning, and that he was much weakened in body and spirit and in critical condition. He wanted me to come to him right away; he begged me to do so. When I got there Donkai was in the kitchen, tearing up papers and throwing them into the stove to burn them. When I asked him why he said "Yato asked me to burn these papers. I

[40] Isonaga Kaishū, photographer, was head of the Japanese Residents' Association in Bangkok.

think he sees it as preparation for his death." I hurried up to his bedroom on the second floor. It was hard to recognize the face of the man of the night before; his eyes had fallen, his cheeks were hollow, and he looked like a man about to die. That first look astounded and dismayed me. I thought that it must be cholera. I struggled to control myself and asked him how he was; he opened his eyes, wet his lips, and slowly moved his tongue to answer. "I think this is the end. You were kind to bring me here with you, but it's no good. When you go back, won't you please take my ashes . . . that's what I wanted to talk about. . . ." Who would not have wept on hearing that? Somehow I controlled myself and encouraged him in a firm voice. "You're not going to give up that easily, are you? It's normal to get sick and vomit in Siam. If you make too much of a little puking people will laugh at you." He shook his head in answer, "No, say what you will. There's no pulse. Since there's no pulse there's no chance." I felt for his pulse and saw he was right. His hands were as cold as ice and the skin felt clammy to the touch. I said cheerfully, "It's still beating, isn't it!" but in my heart I knew that it was all over. Then I quietly indicated to Donkai that he should send for the doctor again, and sent for our traveling companions to tell them; I myself sat by his pillow, wiped his forehead, took a fan and fanned his face. Suddenly he looked at me and said, "Would you hand me the letter on the desk?" There was a letter there, and when I picked it up and saw that "Mother" was written on it in pencil, with his name below, I realized this was a farewell letter and last testament. "Is this it?" I said as I handed it to him; he nodded, took it, picked up a pencil again and added something. Then he closed the envelope for the second time, handed it back to me, and asked me to mail it immediately when he was dead. I could hardly bear to sit there any longer. At this time the doctor arrived. He said, "He's not going to last till the evening." Now our three traveling companions came. They sat around the head of his bed and looked after him. Since I had been replaced I took a moment to go to the hospital to look in on the six settlers. When I came back a second time, he had already passed on to the other world.

That night we all kept vigil over the body, and Kaishū too came and joined our wake. When dawn broke we took the body to the temple and had it cremated; the next day we went to claim the ashes. Ah, the man who had joined in the joy of our party the night before was now just a wisp of smoke in a graveyard. How were we who had traveled with him and partied with him to control our emotions?

And still my misery continued. Of the settlers who were ill, six died at about the same time as Yato. We ran low on money for medicine and food. Suenaga and Maeda came down with diarrhea. Hirayama went off to the interior to survey matters, and he did not come back when he was supposed to. The immigration company did not answer my request for help. And finally my body too began to show signs of cholera.

Up to this point I had had as my ideal to see heaven's will in all things. It was only an ideal, of course, as I had not been able to live up to that in actuality. My heart was ill at ease because I had not been able to live up to it. When I saw how the settlers fled from me because of their fear of my illness I could not control my wretchedness. When I thought of the death of the settlers and Yato, I could not help but be disconsolate. Everything sharpened my sense of misery: the distant bark of a dog, a human voice, all kinds of things nearby. So I resented fate and felt sorry for myself, and could not help feeling desolate.

The feelings of loneliness and desolation next gave way to fantasies of resentment. Was I going to die like this? If I could only die in China—Yazō in Yokahama—my wife and children at home—my mother and brother Tamizō—or my benefactor Mr. Watanabe—and similar fantasies without number. Complaint followed compaint and fantasy fed on fantasy. Body and soul alike were brought low. Should I cry? That would be like a woman. Should I go mad? What if other people laughed? Yes, a sense of honor resisted, even at the point of death. Try as I might to conquer the weakness of passion and attachment, it would not depart from me. I would try to reject that sense of honor and end the sense of attachment; exhausted I would doze fitfully and wake up again; tire again and sleep; alternating thought and fevered sleep until I floated on a sea of fantasy. In short, I could not end my pain and anguish, and finally even thought of killing myself in order to put an end to it. But this never got beyond thought. That is, I was too intelligent to become mad and not wise enough to reach an enlightened view of life and death. In the final analysis, pain and anguish are inescapable.

At that time I had only ten yen left to my name. If I paid the doctor's bill of five yen the six settlers and my sick friend would hardly be able to survive. As for my disease, ten Japanese had had it and not one had survived. On the basis of statistics I was already dead. Since my chances were so slim, I decided there was no use in consulting a doctor. But still my spirit was eager to live. Kaishū came tip-toeing into the room and tip-toed out again right away, and I bitterly dismissed him as an unfeeling and superficial friend. But when he came back within ten minutes leading a doctor to examine me, I revised my opinion of him. When Yanagida, while he was taking care of me, became tired and started snoring, I thought him without feeling and was angry with him, but when he woke up, quietly felt my pulse, pinched the skin of my feet, and clucked in disappointment, I was sorrowfully grateful. When I had taken the medicine three days without any result, I decided to follow Yanagida's advice to drink a final farewell toast; it was a cup of chilled black beer, and even today I cannot forget how good it tasted. Now for the first time I began to feel less agony. I began to relax. Then I could sleep soundly. When I woke up I felt a spiritual solace. Yanagida said, "Your color is suddenly much better." And I didn't die. Two days later I began to walk with a stick and visited Kaishū, and startled him and his wife. I followed their advice and ate some bread and meat, the first food I had eaten since I became ill. Truly, I should regard Kaishū and Yanagida as the mothers of my second life.

And so my sickness passed. Meanwhile a letter had come from Yazō in Yokahama asking me to come back to Japan. My health had not yet recovered sufficiently, however, and moreover Hirayama and Masuda[41] had not yet come back from their survey of the interior. People said that they must have been killed by fierce animals or poisonous snakes. Meanwhile the majority of the settlers had left and gone to Singapore, and only four or five remained, waiting until they were well enough to leave. If I let the matter rest at this point people would conclude without further investigation that the whole of Siam was unsuitable for immigration, and the entire enterprise would be dropped for a long time to come. Although I had Yazō's request, I was not yet ready to go back. My spirit was already in Yokohama, but I was still inextricably ensnarled in the claims of human relations and obligations. Meanwhile Hirayama and Masuda returned. Then Suenaga's diarrhea was also cured. So we sat down one day to decide what we should do next. Suenaga said, "If we quit now, it goes without saying that not just the immigration project but Prince Surasakmontri's hopes will be destroyed; don't we risk long-standing resentment that way? The trouble is that in the last analysis we cannot depend on farmers. How would it be if the four of us started something here, tilled the fields ourselves and developed a pilot farm for one harvest as a base for settlers, setting up a model community?" We all clapped our hands, and cried, "Great!" That settled it.

[41] Masuda Saburō (1863-1932), was a Fukuoka samurai whose predilection for drink cost him an army career. He joined Arao Sei's Trade Institute, visited Siam, China, and Korea.

But the immediate problems we had to solve were food, land for our pilot farm, and farm tools. For the food we decided to rely on Kaishū's chivalry and generosity. Suenaga and I visited him and solicited his help, which he promised without hesitation. As for land and farm tools, we did not find any alternative to asking Prince Surasakmontri's help. I, then, went to his residence together with an interpreter and explained our resolute plan and the help we wanted to ask. He not only promised to do his part but even offered to lend a farmhouse. You can imagine how pleased we were. Our vigor was renewed; we took off our Western clothes and shoes and wore undershirts and straw sandals; some of us led the water buffalo and the others guided the plows. We looked like farmers in an old Chinese painting. We moved into the farm house and toasted each other with wine. The prince's estate became our new conspirators' lair. Suenaga wrote a Chinese poem:

A thatched hut near the outer city wall,
Tilling and plowing, our purpose is high,
Rain comes through decayed walls,
Stars glitter through a ruined roof,
Spirit of gallantry based on righteousness.
Vigorous men out to rescue the world,
Deep into the night, we look at the entire universe,
The light of the Big Dipper shows the glitter of a
    sword.

His other poem he called "Window of Wind and Moon,"

After long training with books and sword,
A great and high spirit stirs the breast;
Purpose lies in rectifying the globe,
Duty lies in rescuing the aged country,
No gold can buy him,
The incomparable man of high purpose
Who waits in quiet relaxation,
Retired to a hut with wind and moon for windows.

The immigrants who were still in Bangkok also moved into our thatched hut. But they were so depressed that they were of little use, and their courage was limited to competition in eating beef. Of the group Yanagida was the only one who worked hard with us. For planting rice you have to wait for the rainy season, and we had some time to go for that. But Kaishū had not had his business for very long and with the best will in the world he could not continue to feed us very long. Consequently I decided to return home alone, leaving my friends there, in order to find funds for food. How could I foresee it? This resulted in a change of my course.

Previously, Hirayama and Masuda had gone to survey the interior mainly to investigate the prospects of a lumber enterprise. Although their reports were very different—Hirayama said there were twenty or thirty red sandalwood trees in every quarter-acre, and Masuda estimated three hundred such trees in the same area—they agreed that it looked very promising because the wood was supposed to be free. We decided to collaborate on this enterprise too, and Masuda decided to return home with me. Also, Iwamoto, who had come to Siam after he recovered from illness, wanted to join us in returning home. Kaishū provided travel money to Hong Kong, and the three of us set out on the road home.

[14]

ALAS, YAZŌ DEAD!

THE THREE OF US WERE EQUALLY HEAVY drinkers. As we could not afford liquor on board the ship, we tried to fight boredom with chants and story telling as a ludicrous substitute. When we got to Hong Kong we broke our agreement not to drink and argued stubbornly over who was to blame. Then came negotiations with the Japanese consulate to borrow money, a promissory note for our lodging and locating a coal ship that would take us as passengers: all in good order; we took care of these things in Hong Kong. It was already seven years since my dream had begun with our arrival in Moji and my hurried trip to Wakamatsu.

The reason I went to Wakamatsu and visited Matono was that I wanted to fulfill my duty for my late friend. I had brought Yato's ashes with me and wanted to be faithful to his last wishes. I planned to borrow travel money from Matono and then to go back to Nagasaki to transfer Yato's ashes to his survivors. How could I know that I would first hear my own sad news there?

Matono looked at me with astonishment, and said, "You knew and returned home, didn't you?" I did not understand what he meant at all but noticed that his attitude was very special. So I asked why. He said, "They say your brother Yazō has been hospitalized." I was surprised, for I knew that Yazō intended to remain in hiding, and yet his whereabouts were known; his illness must be serious. I asked him to help me get to Yokohama right away. Matono responded, "Wait a little. It may not be too serious. I hear he is to leave the hospital soon. Why don't you wire him first?" After some thought he went on, "Incidentally, I have heard that your mother is ill, too, isn't she? She is said to be in a hospital in Kumamoto, and to be almost recovered. Both of them, you need not worry about." Although the tone of his words seemed encouraging, their import was very serious. I hesitated for a while, uncertain which way to go, and finally decided to go home to Kumamoto.

When I returned to my home I found Tamizō, his wife and children, and my wife and sons. My mother was in a hospital accompanied by one of my sisters. All the family expressed pleasure at my safe return, told me about my old mother's illness, and then told what they knew about Yazō. "Mother will leave the hospital within two or three days, and Yazō is getting better every day." My sister-in-law showed me two letters from Yazō and said, "This letter arrived about ten days ago, and the brush strokes look feeble. But look at the one we received two days ago. The writing is strong and reflects his vigor. He wrote in this letter that he would come back home a week later. My husband Tamizō will send a check for travel money to him tomorrow. Look at this." She handed me the second letter. As I looked at it, the brush strokes were so strong that it did not look like the writing of an invalid; it seemed to show that he would recover soon.

But I was worried by a sentence that read, "As I am not healthy and cannot achieve anything of note, I plan to return home and retire to the mountain home in Ōtani (our late father's second home) to spend the rest of my life in farming." How were we to know that this was his subterfuge, that by retirement to the Ōtani mountain house he meant his passing to another world, and that his request for travel money was to pay for his funeral! How could we, mortal creatures that we were, know what he meant? Therefore I was very happy to believe firmly what he wrote. I spent a night in my home village, and the next morning I went to the Kumamoto hospital with Tamizō.

There is nothing more childish than the behavior of a man who cannot see the fate that lies in front of him. It can be imagined how pleased I was when I was able to see my mother in the hospital. The agony and pain of the past provide joy for the present. My mother showed me the scar of her operation and explained the course of her illness. She was also pleased to talk about Yazō's apparent recovery, and expected his return home within four or five days. In turn I told her in detail about my experiences after leaving home and how I had narrowly escaped from the jaws of death. She was startled by my story and couldn't hear it often enough. As she reflected on our misfortunes, she was also consoled and happy because of the expected reunion of our family in the near future, and said, "Good! Good! We will have no more hardship, for we have already had our full share." Explaining her ideas and warning us about the future, she went on, "I was very afraid that Yazō would not appear before me again. Now I know he is coming back home in a few days. The three of you brothers have not been together for three years, have you? Be patient this time, Torazō. Get some rest and resume work gradually. Each of you has only two brothers. Why don't you consult and cooperate with each other in any work you want to do? That's the best way. After Yazō comes back, let's invite our fellow villagers to a big banquet to celebrate our recovery."

Meanwhile, Tamizō finished the necessary procedure for mother's leaving the hospital. I told her about my late friend Yato's final instructions and asked her permission for me to go to Nagasaki directly from Kumamoto. She agreed unhesitatingly and was full of sympathy. She suggested to Tamizō and me that we extend thanks to those who had come to see her in the hospital and then returned to our village accompanied by our sister, leaving Tamizō and me behind. All this time not one of us knew that Yazō was nearing the end of his life.

Tamizō and I saw our mother off at the railroad station and then stopped to visit a relative at his house. No sooner had we finished a cup of tea than a friend from our village hurried in. When he saw us he handed a slip to us without a word. It was a cable from Nozaki, a friend in Yokohama: Yazō was in critical condition. This was a bolt from the blue for us. Tamizō and I called rickshaws and hurried to the station at once. We returned to our village immediately after our mother.

The next morning we left home for Ōmuta before it was light and took the train for Yokohama. We were so depressed that we exchanged hardly a word during the two days and nights of travel. When we arrived in Yokohama Tamizō asked me, "Shall we go to the hospital or to our friend's house?" I had an intuitive feeling that we were too late, and replied, "Let's go to the friend's first." We hurried to Nozaki's by rickshaw and saw his sister standing at the gate. As soon as she saw us coming she hurried into the house. I tried to interpret that as a sign, and thought that we were perhaps not too late. We entered the house and were met by his wife, who seemed very calm. Nozaki's sister was sitting next to his wife and smiling. I still thought that there was hope. Tea was served. The wife still did not say anything about Yazō. I didn't dare ask, and neither did Tamizō. Suddenly the wife began to cry. She lowered her head and said very softly, "I'm so very sorry. The day before yesterday, in the morning—at last—according to his request, at the Tōkai temple in Shinagawa—people are waiting for you there—right away." Tamizō and I were taken to rickshaws and went to the station. We took a train to Shinagawa.

Tamizō and I were met by four or five friends at the Shinagawa station. We followed them as if we were sheep going to be butchered, and entered the Shun'u an, a separate building of the Tōkai Temple. There were dozens of relatives and friends there. I found an unpainted coffin in a corner of the room: needless to say it contained the corpse of my brother Yazō. Nozaki led us to the coffin and we saw Yazō through its glass window. A long, black pigtail hung behind him; the hair around it had grown about an inch long, the eyes were closed, his hands together on his chest, snow-white front teeth peeped out through compressed lips; he looked alive. That was Yazō's body. Tamizō turned to me and asked "Why did he shave around his head?" I did not know how to answer, and remained silent. Of course, Yazō was now without words too.

Nozaki handed a letter to Tamizō that he said had been found under the pillow after Yazō's death. On the envelope it said "To Mother and Tamizō," and below it was his signature. We opened it and found only a Japanese poem.

> A gallant sincere man's bow!
> How unfortunate to die unused.

Ah, what did Yazō want to use the bow for? Probably Watanabe, our "unsung benefactor" and I were the only ones who knew. Then Nozaki showed us another letter. It was Yazō's letter to Nozaki. I still remember every word: "If I die, I would appreciate your burying me near the grave of my late brother[42] in the precincts of the Tōkai Temple in Shinagawa. The required sum will be sent from my home soon. But if it should be late, I would appreciate your borrowing money from my relative Tachibana or Isekō. If funds permit, please have a Zen priest chant part of a sutra to mourn me. This is my last request."

Together with our relatives and friends we held a wake beside Yazō's body that night. The next day we had a Buddhist funeral and buried him by Banzō's side as he had requested.

[42] Banzō, who died in 1875.

After the funeral, Tamizō and I went back to the Nozakis in Yokohama. Nozaki had taken care of Yazō from the beginning of his illness to his death, with a kindness that would be rare even among relatives. All Yazō's last effects had been brought to his house. Tamizō was startled when he looked at them, because most of Yazō's clothes and other things were Chinese. I thought that there must be a letter for me somewhere, and stealthily looked for it between the pages of his books and among the other things. But not only was there no letter; all the documents Yazō had kept in his bag were gone. Nozaki said that because Yazō knew our old mother was ill at home he did his best not to worry her and wrote confidently about getting better in his letters. I was the one he had waited for, and he would repeat several times a day, "Hasn't he come yet? He'll come today, won't he?" I asked Nozaki whether he knew anything about Yazō's encounter with a Chinese man of high ambition, but he was not very well-informed. He said, "All I know is that a Chinese in Western dress visited your brother once. When I asked him who it was, he said it was a Chinese student. The man didn't look very unusual." So Yazō had kept his secret, even from Nozaki. Then I went to the hospital and talked to the nurse. "He got his papers together and burned them a few days before he died," she said. How careful Yazō had been! But I now felt like a blind man without a cane.

I returned home together with Tamizō. I found it a vale of tears and a world of lamentation. Within that vale of tears and world of lamentation, I felt myself more and more diminished and increasingly responsible. I too shed tears often, and reproached myself for the fact that Yazō might not have met such a tragic end if he had not kept our secret so tenaciously.

I had encountered so many trials, I had met so many misfortunes, and I had been so regularly disappointed and depressed, that in my extreme distress I wanted to retire to the mountains and live there the rest of my life. Yes, I even thought of seeking peace by killing myself. The only thing that saved me in that predicament was my aspiration. And it was my brother Yazō who had implanted that aspiration in me. It was he who had nurtured it, and when I was depressed and discouraged it was his letters that had revived that aspiration and given me new courage. Yes: quite aside from my aspiration, Yazō's letters, each time I received one, had provided encouragement for the fervor in my heart. In sum: Yazō had been the wellspring of my activities.

[15]

A NEW LIFE OPENS FOR ME

ALAS, THE WELLSPRING OF MY ACTIVITIES HAD run dry. I had now returned to the vale of tears and was in the world of lamentation. I was distraught and had no idea of what I should do. My friends in Siam must have become angry and must have thought I was irresponsible. They must certainly have been in extreme difficulty. I could not put this out of my mind, and yet I did not have the will-power to go back there. At times I tried to force myself to do so, but I couldn't. Then word came from a friend in Siam that one of the settlers had committed suicide and that a payment was due on Prince Surasakmontri's estate. In response to this I was able to send only one hundred yen as an emergency tide-over. Then Maeda came back and, after him, Hirayama. They told me all about the conditions at our project, and now I couldn't put things off any longer. Accordingly I went up to Tokyo with Hirayama.

The reason for coming to Tokyo was to discuss a plan for saving the Siam venture, and at the same time to help Masuda set up a lumber enterprise. But an explosive development destroyed this plan and made us turn directly to the China problem. The one who brought this about was none other than my friend Kani Chōkyō.

Kani was from my home province. He had become acquainted with Inukai Bokudō[43] and lived in his house.

[43] Inukai Tsuyoshi (or Ki); Bokudō was his *gō* (1855-1932) was a major

Now he came to see us and strongly praised Inukai's character and urged us to meet him. I had always despised the Progressive Party (*Kaishintō*);[44] so did all of us, instinctively. One reason may have been that we worshiped the characters for *jiyū* (liberty), and despised those for *kaishin* (progress). Another reason may have been that when I was still a child I had picked up rumors current that Ōkuma,[45] as Finance Minister, had embezzled funds to build his own residence. Whatever the case, I hated the Progressive Party. And since Inukai was now a member of that party, it followed that I didn't want to meet him, so I resisted my friend's advice for a while. But my friend was emphatic in his praise for Inukai's character, and he had set his heart on persuading me to meet him. In the end I gave in. I took Hirayama with me to visit Inukai at his residence. Fateful meeting! It produced a decisive change in my course.

Man has an instinctive tendency to make judgments. When you first meet a person, you tend to judge him right away; the first time you lay eyes on him you tend to decide whether he is a scoundrel or a good fellow and make an impressionistic judgment. Now most people considered Inukai to be a crafty man, and a crafty man has to be objectionable. But when I first met him, I didn't react negatively at all. He was holding a tobacco tray in his left

---

figure in modern politics from the time of his entry into the field as a lieutenant of Ōkuma Shigenobu to his death as prime minister at the hands of mutinous young navy officers. He stood out among other political leaders for his assistance to exiled revolutionaries from other Asian countries and maintained close relations with many individual zealots and enthusiasts like Tōten.

44 Abbreviation for *Rikken Kaishintō*, Ōkuma Shigenobu's Progressive Party founded in 1882. As the more urban and "moderate" wing of the party movement it fought bitterly for leadership with the Jiyūtō, thereby incurring the enmity of self-styled Jiyūtō partisans.

45 Ōkuma Shigenobu (1838-1922), Meiji Period statesman from Saga, founder of Waseda, and head of *Kaishintō*.

hand and a tobacco pouch in his right. He came forward very casually, for all the world like a mountain hermit. He nodded slightly, said "Hello," plopped down quickly, and blew out some smoke with an easy sophistication. I formed a good impression immediately. He laughed knowingly. "How were things in Siam? Anything of interest there?" His manner seemed somewhat sarcastic, but I didn't take offense. I told him about the immigration and the lumber enterprises. He dismissed them laconically: "It won't work." I tried to explain things, drawing on my own experience, but he wouldn't listen. He just shook his head, and said, "No good, no good." I began to get angry, and then he smiled and started to talk. "This enterprise of yours may have looked good on paper, but you're dreaming. I know something about immigration. After all, didn't our scheme to settle Hokkaido from the main islands fail? It might be different if you had a slave trade going, but it's impossible for you or me to make money with settlers. It's probably a good thing you gave it up. And whatever made you think of the lumber enterprise? Where did you get the idea you could do that? Even if you have plans on paper, you haven't got anybody to work with. You haven't got any money, have you? Then you have to persuade lumber merchants to put up the capital. But you can't do that! Somebody like you isn't even ready to work out the figures. Anybody you approach will beg off after taking one look at you." He laughed loudly as he said this, but he was so appealing that I couldn't get angry even though I wanted to. I was going to explain the availability of sandalwood and ebony at no cost, but he didn't want to listen to me. He cocked his head for a minute, and said "There isn't a lumber merchant who will be willing to talk with you. The best we can do is probably Nakamura Miroku.[46] Very well, I'll introduce you; why don't you see

[46] Nakamura Miroku (1854-1929) (also Haisui, and Haizan), a samurai son

him?" With that he took out his brush and wrote a note of introduction to Nakamura.

That same day I went to see Nakamura with Hirayama. When he appeared I saw a rather foppish gentleman: tall, smooth-faced, dressed in silk, with gold-framed glasses. I brought up the Siam lumber project. He listened to me with the appraising manner of a businessman, questioned me closely, and then indicated that in view of the trickery common among lumber dealers, of which he told me some examples from his experience, a matter like this could not be handled by amateurs like us. Hirayama and I were rather annoyed because his manner was very affected. But since there was nothing more to be done, we left.

The next day Hirayama and I visited Inukai again. First-off he asked, "How did it go with Nakamura?" We answered, "He made us listen to him for a long time, but in the end we didn't get anywhere." He laughed: "That's like him; he's part business, part gentleman. A one hundred percent businessman wouldn't have listened to you at all." Then he suddenly asked me "Why are you letting your hair grow so long? Don't you find it inconvenient?" "Just for the fun of it," I answered. But he acted as though there must be some other reason. I couldn't decide what to do; should I open my mouth and tell him my real purpose? No, better to wait; don't give in now. While I was agonizing about that within myself, Inukai said something quite extraordinary: "You know, you can never raise any money looking like that. Why don't you give it up?" I answered, "I can't do what I have to do without raising money, and no matter how poor I may be at it I have to keep at it. That's unfortunately the way the world is, sir."

---

from Nagano who entered the Diet as *Kaishintō* member. By the date of this action, he was a member of the same political group as Inukai, appointed to a Justice Ministry post in the Ōkuma government, named to survey boards for national forests and marine products, and engaged in the lumber business himself, seemingly able to combine political regularity, Asian interests, and business acumen.

He pressed a little harder: "Making money is a lifework too. You think you want to get money first and then turn to world affairs. That sequence looks good, but it doesn't work out that way very easily. You're not cut out for that kind of work; forget it. Give it up and start on your mission right away. World affairs are run on the basis of a division of labor, you know! Get money from those who have already collected it and use it." Ah, did he know of my hopes? Kani was nudging me. I told him that my aspiration was centered on China, and asked him whether he would provide some help. He agreed, and asked me to hold off for a bit. Ah, that word was more precious than gold. My resolve, which had been extinguished since the death of Yazō, quickly revived. I was able to leave the valley of despond and emerge onto the plain of hope again. Inukai was the author of my spiritual rebirth.

Prior to this I had been at a certain Nihonbashi inn with Hirayama. Our pockets were empty, and of course we couldn't pay for even part of our lodging and food. Now they threw us out, and we moved to a little place in Uchisaiwai-chō. We hung around for several months, and gradually began to get bored. We fought our frustration by drinking sake every day. Naturally the god of wine invited us; we went south to Shinagawa, and north to Yoshiwara to roister; the retribution of karma came shortly afterward, and I came down with venereal disease. Hirayama got a doctor he knew to come to examine me, and he said that I would have to enter his hospital for treatment. This was as untimely as the disease was unwelcome. I was mortified. Finally I made up my mind, wrote the details to Tōyama Mitsuru,[47] and asked for his help. He sent me forty yen, so

[47] Tōyama (1855-1944), Fukuoka samurai, took an active role in early nationalist and liberal causes before concentrating on nationalism through the *Genyōsha* (founded 1881) and *Kokuryūkai* (founded 1901) patriotic societies, organizations which spawned virtually all other patriotic and ultranationalist groups in Imperial Japan. He enjoyed access to virtually all ranks of Meiji society and utilized this freedom to patronize refugee revolutionaries and idealist activists.

that I was able to enter the Sakuragi Hospital in Ueno. I kept this from Inukai; I was afraid of having him think ill of me. Was I being a coward? or cunning? Certainly my motives were not of the purest.

About that time Kiyofuji Kōshichirō had come to Tokyo. One evening we opened our hearts and resumed our earlier friendship.[48] After I got sick, he looked after me day and night. Still, although my main disease was not too hard to control, a number of additional ailments combined with it so that for a time my very life seemed in danger. Inukai and his wife found out about it, and they were generous with help and support. If at that time I hadn't had the help of two or three friends, and the benefactions of Inukai and Tōyama, my life might have ended there.

[48] Kiyofuji had earlier agreed to go to China with Miyazaki and then changed his mind.

[16]

I ENTER THE COUNTRY OF MY DREAMS A SECOND TIME

I GRADUALLY RECOVERED FROM MY ILLNESS. Meanwhile Inukai lived up to his promise. Hirayama, Kani, and I received orders from the Foreign Ministry to investigate the state of secret societies in China. I was still in the hospital. When I got the order I persuaded the hospital head to release me. I went to the Foreign Ministry and met a certain high official, made arrangements, and was about to set out on the journey when my illness flared up again and I wasn't able to leave as planned. Hirayama and Kani left for China, and I stayed on in my second-floor room alone. Afterward, warned by the doctor, I moved to Ōmori, avoided all guests, and waited quietly for my illness to run its course.

Finally, my health restored, I set the date and made preparations for my journey. I visited two or three friends, and then went to see Kobayashi Kusuo.[49] He had a visitor with him. When he saw me come into his room, the man's whole face lit up, and he started a monologue: "My, he certainly looks just like his brother. Isn't it wonderful!" The man seemed to be about fifty years old. His grey hair was cut short, his stature was short, but he looked quick. I

[49] Kobayashi (1856-1920), Okayama activist educated in French and law in early Meiji, joined with Ōi Kentarō in the Osaka Incident, and was imprisoned and pardoned with him on the promulgation of the constitution in 1889. Thereafter he agitated for a strong foreign policy.

didn't know who it was. Then I was introduced to him by Kobayashi: "This is Sone Toshitora. He was close to your late brother Hachirō; in fact, they were almost like brothers. He has heard about your activities and said he wanted to meet you; today it just happened to work out." I had heard about Mr. Sone too,[50] and I greeted him appropriately. He seemed delighted and reminisced about the past and argued about the present in high spirits. I felt as if I were close to my late brother, and spent half the day in exchanging questions and answers with him. As I was leaving, Sone looked at me and said, "I have an aged mother who has already reached the age of eighty. The day after tomorrow I'm celebrating with a party; please come with Kobayashi. My old mother will be delighted to meet you too. Also, there will be a Chinese there I'd like you to meet. It would be a good idea for you to meet him before you leave Japan." I promised to come. Now, who do you suppose that Chinese was?

Truly, nothing is more remarkable than man's fate. When I went to Sone's house in Ōmori on the appointed day the first thing I saw was a pair of scrolls hanging in the alcove. They turned out to be written by my oldest brother Hachirō, who had died in the war in 1877. Moreover, Sone also took out an old letter and showed it to me. It too was in my brother's hand, and dated from 1873. Addressed to Sone, who was then in China, at a time when bandits had revolted in north China,[51] it went, "Word has recently come that bandits have risen; I wish you would send me full details on how it goes right away; depending on that I would like to give up what I am doing and come to the continent. As for our island country of Japan, there is

[50] Sone (1847-1910), son of a Yonezawa samurai, educated in Chinese and Western learning, entered the navy, only to resign in protest against his government's seeming indifference to the Franco-Chinese war of 1884; thereafter he was consistently close to the China activists and their refugee friends.

[51] Moslem Rebellions in Shensi and Kansu provinces.

nothing to report. I would like to breathe the air of the continent at the earliest possible moment, and I am waiting for that pleasure."

I read this and compared my own poor efforts, and thoughts of past and present came flooding in on me. When the time came Sone took us to the party, and when we had drunk enough and I was getting ready to leave, he took me to another room and lowered his voice: "The Chinese I wanted to introduce you to did not come today. When you have time, go to this address to meet this man." With that he took out a calling card and handed it to me. It said "Mr. Ch'en Pai." On the back was an address in Yokohama. It was a person I had never heard of before. In my heart, however, I was always looking for the Chinese man my brother Yazō had reported meeting. Therefore the thought immediately arose that it might be he. So I thanked Sone for his kindness and took my leave.

In the meanwhile news came that Hirayama and Kani had traveled along the South China coast and arrived in Hong Kong; they were staying there for some time to investigate things in the Canton area, and they were waiting for me there. Because of this I wanted to get to Hong Kong as soon as possible, and left Tokyo for Yokohama. In order to meet the Chinese that Sone had introduced me to, I stopped at an inn just long enough to leave my bag before proceeding to the address I had been given, where I presented my card. The man who greeted me at the entrance was a fine-looking gentleman. When he saw me he seemed astonished, took my hands in a very friendly manner, and exclaimed, "What a pleasant surprise!" Right away, I knew in my heart that this was the man. Then he looked at me a little strangely. When I noticed this, I said, "Didn't you know my brother?" He looked at the card I had given him a second time, and then, as if he had just understood, clapped his hands and said, "I see! Only one character of your name was different. It resembled his so closely I thought the card was your brother's. So, you're his younger brother?" Then he asked for Yazō, and I told him what had happened. He raised his eyes to heaven and said sadly, "Is that so? He promised to come again, but he never did. I thought I would like to meet him again, and looked for him, but never found his residence. I wondered what had happened." He looked as if he did not know how to continue. I explained a little about the reasons my brother had not come again, and then went on to reveal the pledge that Yazō and I had made to each other. My host was greatly moved and struck the table as he said it was heaven's will. Gradually we moved on to the problem of the future.

Mr. Ch'en Shao-pai[52] and I soon became like old friends. This was entirely due to my brother Yazō and Mr. Sone, who had been my oldest brother Hachirō's old friend. However, Mr. Ch'en did not go as far as to tell me the inside details of his party, but just told me that the party head was Sun Yat-sen, and showed me a small volume that he said was by that man. This was entitled SUN YAT-SEN, KIDNAPPED IN LONDON. It was a full account by Sun Yat-sen himself of his imprisonment in the Chinese legation in London.[53] From this I learned that he was a member of the Rise China (*Hsing-Chung hui*) Society. I surmised that he had been one of those who fled with Sun Yat-sen after the failure of an attempted rebellion in south China at the time of the Shimonoseki Treaty in 1895, and

[52] Tōten uses Ch'en Shao-pai and Ch'en Pai almost interchangeably. Ch'en (1869-1934) a native of Kwangtung, was one of Sun Yat-sen's most trusted followers in the early stages of the nationalist revolution. After the failure of his first revolutionary plan in 1895 Sun Yat-sen went to Hawaii, Cheng Shih-liang to Hong Kong, and Ch'en to Yokohama, where he was helped by Sone Toshitora, above, and Sugawara Dẹn, who had known Sun in Hawaii earlier.

[53] In October 1896 Sun Yat-sen was lured into the Chinese legation in London and detained there, slated for return to China and certain execution as a rebel. He was able to get a message out to an Englishman he had known earlier, who prevailed upon his own government to demand his release and safety. The book made Sun famous all over the world.

this proved to be so, as he revealed in the course of our conversation. He thought that it was a good idea for me to travel to south China, and provided me with an introduction to his friend Ho Shu-ling. It was time for me to leave long before we had said everything we wanted to say to each other. After we had promised to meet again, I took my leave, and then boarded ship for Hong Kong.

When I got to Hong Kong, Kani had already left for Japan. Hirayama too, although he had tried to wait for my arrival, had also boarded a ship and was at the point of returning home. When I heard this at my inn I hurried to his ship and persuaded him to come back to the inn with me; over cups of sake, we brought each other up to date on what had happened since our parting, discussed what we should do, and agreed to go to Macao the next day in order to look for the man to whom Mr. Ch'en had provided an introduction.

Hirayama had been to Macao before I came, and had become acquainted with a man named Chang Yü-t'ao, so the first thing we did when we arrived there was to get in touch with him to find out where Mr. Ho lived. Mr. Chang was cordial and warm, and called his friends together to welcome us with a party. But he also told us how bad things were, with details that would stir the blood of men of high purpose. When the talk turned to secret societies, however, he suddenly became very secretive and close-mouthed. When we pressed him for details he took up a brush and just jotted down a few names; inside China there was K'ang Yu-wei, and outside China there was Sun Yat-sen. As long as these men lived, he indicated, China's situation could not be said to be completely hopeless. When we asked about Mr. Ho's whereabouts, he first said only that he had no contact with him, and then said that he had heard that he was now in Canton. One could see how circumspect he was. That night we spent in a Macao hotel, and the next morning we ate with Mr. Chang and two or three others; that night we boarded the ferry for the city of

Canton. Again it was our purpose to find Mr. Ho. However, feelings aroused by the Sino-Japanese War had not yet left people's minds, and in the Canton area the memory of Sun Yat-sen's abortive rebellion also added to the problem.

People were uneasy, and they were not prepared to talk to total strangers. It was not easy for us to grasp the real situation. But we thought that Mr. Ch'en's letter might provide an opening, and that was why we tried to look up this person named Ho.

Our ship reached Canton the next morning at dawn. We went to Shameen and put up at Queen's Hotel. The next morning, after breakfast, we ordered a sedan chair and went straight to Ho's house on some street. He came out to greet us himself—short, slim, and at first sight, rather nervous. We explained why we had come and surreptitiously handed him Ch'en Shao-pai's letter. Mr. Ho looked to the right and left before reading it furtively, then looked at us, picked up his brush, and wrote a question about where the two of us were staying. He would like to come to see us and learn from us, he wrote; we couldn't have a confidential talk there. He seemed to be extremely afraid of attracting attention. So we told him where we were lodged, and left after agreeing to meet again.

We returned to our lodging. After a bit Mr. Ho came to visit us. He complained about the misgovernment of the Ch'ing and lamented China's weak and isolated position in the world, sounding very much like Mr. Chang. But when we asked about ways in which improvement might be possible, he talked around the subject and didn't say anything. He just talked about the necessity of cooperation between upper and lower jawbones, and praised the chivalrous virtue of the Japanese. We could never get him to come to the point. He protested that he did not know Sun Yat-sen, assured us that he was not a close friend of Ch'en Shao-pai's, and made us think that he was timid. Consequently we were rather disappointed. Then we tried to take it a step further by talking about the present condition of China. We argued that the only way to bring improvement was through revolution, and tried to get him to reveal what was in his mind. It only seemed to make him more fearful and more reluctant. At the same time he seemed to be turning something over in his mind, and out of the depths of his ambiguity he finally provided the name of one party member. "In Hong Kong," he said, "there is a man named Ou Feng-ch'i.[54] He was formerly treasurer of the *Hsing-Chung hui.*" We asked him for an introduction, but he turned us down on the excuse that he was not in communication with him. He cautioned us not to use his name in meeting him, and said we should just go to a certain church. This was like trying to follow a firefly on a dark night. But we had no choice but to try, so we boarded a ship for Hong Kong.

The place he had directed us to was a Christian church. I went there with Hirayama. It was Sunday, and the people had gathered there to listen to a Christian missionary. We mingled with the crowd and listened to him. But our reasons for doing so was not to hear about the Kingdom of Heaven, but to find a Chinese revolutionary and discuss the affairs of all under heaven with him. As people were leaving after the service was over, I suddenly saw that the Mr. Chang whom we had met in Macao was there. We went up to him and asked where Mr. Ou was. He pointed to someone and then went out, pretending that he didn't know him. We got the point and did not ask him for an introduction. We followed the man he had pointed to down the stairs and, as soon as no one was near us, pulled his sleeves to attract his attention and introduced ourselves to him, presenting our namecards. He was pleased, and took us to a room, where we sat across from one another. He asked why we had come.

[54] A Kwangtung Christian, who is credited with a large role in Sun Yat-sen's Christianity, his development of writing style and of thought.

He looked middle-aged, about forty. His skin was dark, his body heavy, neither tall nor short. His eyes were long and narrow, his eyebrows thin. He seemed a pleasant gentleman, quite amicable. Hirayama and I were afraid that if we spoke carelessly he might be suspicious of us, and we wondered how we ought to answer his questions. We were excited and nervous, like hunters in sight of a bird, and whispered to each other as to what we should say. Then I picked up a brush and wrote briefly why we had come: "We are ignorant persons of little ability and quite unable to develop a strategy for saving the world, and yet we couldn't bear to sit quietly either; we have come here to seek the way from men of our neighboring state. Will you not be good enough to educate us in that way?" He answered with the conventional Chinese analogy about upper and lower jaw in stressing the relationship between our countries. Then he lamented the misgovernment of China and expressed his resentment at the corruption of the officials. Nothing he said was more than a little bit stronger than what Mr. Ho and Mr. Chang had said. Finally, we told him of our advocacy of revolution for China and asked whether he agreed or not. At this he came alive, clapped his hands, and said "That's it! If chivalrous Japanese help us we can expect to succeed." Then he talked about the failure of the plot they had formed the previous year and about the latest activities of Sun Yat-sen, their leader. He continued: "If you two plan to help our party's enterprise, you really ought to meet Sun Yat-sen soon. I have information that he left London last month. He should reach your country soon. He is coming to your country precisely because he wants to seek the help of your chivalrous men." This news moved our hearts. We promised to meet again and went back to our inn; talking with Hirayama, we just about made up our minds to return home in order to follow Sun Yat-sen.

The next day Mr. Ou and two other men came to see us. They talked with us for a little while. Before Mr. Ou left, he said, "Tonight we're having a discussion with three or four like-minded men. Won't you come too?" So at the appointed time we went to the church hall. When we got there we found them waiting for us with wine and meat. We sat at a table and drank like cows and ate like horses, discussing animatedly and enthusiastically. The vigor of the controversy was very pleasant. We returned to the inn under a moon at midnight, and once again Hirayama and I toasted each other. It was the first time I had ever had a party like that in a Christian church.

At that time there was another man who had a reputation among the literati in Canton as high as that of Sun Yat-sen. This was K'ang Yu-wei. The two advocated rather similar ideas: that is, they were both for people's rights and a republic. However, Sun Yat-sen drew his views from Western scholarship, but K'ang got his from Chinese. The one was brought up a Christian, the other a Confucian. The one was all substance, the other all theory. Substance emphasized action, theory delighted in debate. Although the two of them saw things very much the same way, they differed in source, background, and character. Sun Yat-sen was in the vanguard of the revolution, K'ang its educator. The vanguard had already risen and failed; consequently Sun had fled across the ocean. People thought it would be hard for him to rise a second time. K'ang, the educator, was in his private academy as before. He advocated the virtues of freedom and republic with much eloquence, and bitterly criticized the evils of the times in trenchant writings. It seemed as though he might rise to any heights. Naturally the minds of men seemed gradually to move toward him. Therefore we secretly wanted to meet him. But since he happened to have headed north it didn't work out. Then we made up our minds to stop everything we were doing and to return to Japan for a while. The reason was that we thought it might be better to get one general than to capture ten thousand privates. But what kind of a man was Sun Yat-sen?

[17]

SUN YAT-SEN, THE LEADER OF THE *HSING-CHUNG HUI*

SUN WEN, ALSO KNOWN AS SUN YAT-SEN, WAS born in Hsiang-shan prefecture in Kwangtung. His ancestors had been farmers for generations. As a child Sun too followed his forebears' calling with plow and hoe. When he was thirteen, he went to be with his eldest brother, who had migrated to Hawaii and was regarded as one of the well-to-do. He went to an American school there[55] and was converted to Christianity. This upset his brother, who forced him to return home, where he worked on the farm once again. He was then seventeen. But the local villagers now realized his ability as a student, and raised money to make it possible for him to go to Canton to study at a medical school.[56]

After a stay of one year there, he moved to Hong Kong just as the English opened Hong Kong Medical College, transferred to it, and studied there for five years. He graduated from the Medical College with a first-rate record, and then immediately moved to Macao, where he began to practice medicine. He became well-known and prosperous with his policy to treat the poor free of charge and charging the rich exorbitant fees. He was so successful there that jealous European physicians did their best to make things difficult for him. During his stay in Macao,

[55] Iolani College.

[56] Canton Hospital Medical School.

there was a movement to establish a China Youth Party. Sun became a member, and freely drew on his profound knowledge of politics to advise the other members. They were so impressed by his insights and aspiration that they elected him leader of the party. This was the origin of the *Hsing-Chung hui* movement.[57] Thereafter Sun disciplined and trained himself and studied hard; he became increasingly concerned with the desperate situation his country was in—so much so that he ended by giving up his career in medicine to prepare for the future as a full-fledged leader. In 1894 and 1895, taking advantage of the Sino-Japanese war, Sun began to purchase weapons and ammunition secretly. But his preparations for a rebellion were delayed, and just as they were finished the truce was made and peace negotiations opened in Shimonoseki. Although he had missed his chance, it was too late for him to stop. Sun himself was in Canton; he organized his rebel troops secretly in Swatow, in the West River Region, and in Hong Kong. In his Canton headquarters he set the time for the uprising and cabled the order to march. But his plot had been uncovered. Government troops raided his headquarters, and he was barely able to escape to Macao. Now he secretly moved to Japan by way of Hong Kong.

In Japan he changed from Chinese clothes into Western dress and cut his queue for the first time. From there he went on to Hawaii, and from the United States to London. It was there that he was apprehended by a Chinese official and held prisoner on the premises of the Chinese Legation. His life hung by a hair. But heaven did not abandon this revolutionary hero; news of his arrest leaked outside the legation. A former teacher and friend spared no effort to get him released, and the protest of the Prime Minister, the Marquis of Salisbury, forced the Chinese Legation to release Sun and narrowly saved his life. Sun expressed his

[57] Founded November 24, 1894, with a handful of members, but in Hawaii, and not, as Tōten has it, in Macao.

gratitude and bade farewell to England by having a publishing company in London publish his own detailed story of his detention,[58] and then, ever more intent upon his lofty purpose, boarded a ship for Japan.

A week after we had left Hong Kong, our ship arrived in Yokohama as the sun was setting behind the western mountain. We landed, went to an inn, bathed, and had dinner. After night fell, I went alone to the residence of Mr. Ch'en Shao-pai. A one-eyed, ruddy-faced maid came to the door. I had met her before. She said that her master had left a few days ago. "Where," I asked, "did he go?" "Probably Taiwan," she answered. "Are you staying here alone in his absence?" I asked again. "No," she answered, "there is a guest in the house." "Is he in?" I asked. "No," she said "he went out for a walk earlier this evening."

I thought this guest must be Sun Yat-sen. So I continued to ask questions. "When did he arrive, and where from?" The maid's guileless voice fell like the music of angels on my ears. "I did not quite understand because I don't speak his language," she answered, "but I think from America. It was hardly a week ago." My heart beat. I was so impatient that I didn't want to waste a minute so I asked her if she wouldn't look for him. I was standing outside the door waiting for her to come back. She did not return until my legs were numbed and a pain had begun in my side. At last, she came back at eleven o'clock and told me that she had done her best to find him, but in vain. All I could do was thank her for her effort; I reluctantly headed back to my inn. There I told Hirayama what I had done that day, drank some sake, and went to sleep.

The next morning I got up early and hurried over to Ch'en Shao-pai's house a second time. The same helpful maid greeted me. When I asked what the situation was, she said the guest was still asleep. She offered to wake him up. I asked her not to do so, but decided to wait in the garden

[58] *Kidnapped in London* (London, 1897).

for him to wake up. I was lost in day-dreaming. Then I heard the creak of a door opening. I looked up quickly, unintentionally, and saw a gentleman still in his bed-clothes stick his head out. When he saw me he nodded his head a little, and asked me, in English, to come in. When I got a good look at him I recognized the Mr. Sun Yat-sen of the photographs. So I greeted him, entered the house, and was ushered into a sitting room and offered a chair. Sun Yat-sen pulled another chair over and sat down across from me. He had not rinsed his mouth or washed his face, and he sat there just the way he'd gotten out of bed. At first I was startled by such casualness, and thought he must be rather unstable. When I presented him with my name card and introduced myself, he said that he had heard about me from Ch'en Shao-pai, and asked me about the situation in the Canton area. I explained that I had had to come back without having the time to investigate the situation there in detail. When I expressed my gratification at being able to meet him this day, he said that he had heard about Yazō and how Ch'en Shao-pai and I had met through the efforts of my late brother. Surely today's meeting, he added, was heaven's will. He spoke as if he trusted me completely. You can imagine how happy I was. On the other hand, though, I was troubled by the fact that the man did not seem to have very much sense of dignity and presence.

Now the maid came, and told him his warm water was ready. He excused himself and went out to wash. While he was gone I reflected in solitude. Would this man be capable of taking control over all China? Could he take power over four hundred million Chinese? Was his the kind of quality that would ultimately justify my committing my full effort to helping him? What it came down to was that I was still going by external appearance.

Now Sun returned again. His hair was combed, his clothes were neat, and as he took his chair his appearance was certainly that of a very proper gentleman. Nevertheless the Sun Yat-sen I had imagined was not like this. I missed something in him; I thought he should have more dignity. Alas, I was still unable to escape the old expectations of oriental physiognomy and bearing to which I was a slave.

I asked the first question. "I know that you are determined to carry out a revolution in China," I said, "but I have only the most general idea of your plans. Would you tell me what the content of your so-called revolution is, and can you explain the steps by which you plan to implement it?" Sun began to talk. "I believe," he began, slowly, "that the highest order of government is one in which people govern themselves. Therefore the political principle I advocate is republicanism. This belief alone would be enough to impel me to take up the responsibility for revolution. But beyond that is the fact that it is already three hundred years since the barbarian Manchus seized power. They made it their first object to keep the populace stupid, and their officials made it their business to wring out the people's sweat and blood. It is because of the perpetuation of this long-standing injustice that the country has come to such a lamentable state today, in which our fertile valleys and lovely mountains are being seized by foreign powers. How can anyone with feeling see this happen and stand aside, without trying to do something? This is why our party, although we realized our limitations, tried to take advantage of the disorder in China to start an insurrection."

His words began gently and quietly and then swelled into a torrent. He became more and more impassioned and enthusiastic, and by the time he finished the gentleman who had begun so carefully was more like a tiger growling deep in the mountains. He continued his argument.

> "Some people argue that republican institutions will not fit a barbarous country like China. But those who take that view are ignorant of the facts. To begin with, republicanism is at the core of our political tradition, and it is a heritage bequeathed to us by our ancient

sages. That is, when you think about our country's ancient times you call to mind the example of the government in the three dynasties. But the government of those days actually contained the essence of republicanism. Do not say that our people have no qualities of idealism, or that they have no spirit of progress because they follow only the past. Actually, when this reverence for the past is properly understood there is evidence of great idealism. Doesn't this bring with it the guarantee of great progress in the future? Look at our people in remote and inhospitable areas that did not fall under the malignant rule of the Manchu barbarians. They govern themselves today; they select elders to judge suits and they follow their directions, they organize militia and prevent banditry, and they make their own determination of all matters that affect the common interest. Who can say that these people are not suited for a republican form of government? Therefore I say that once a hero rises up to overthrow the Manchu barbarians and replaces them with good government, let him promise only the simplest of laws like [Han Kao-tsu's] three codes and the people will reward him jubilantly with respect and gratitude. At that time reconstruction will take place on a basis of patriotism, and the country will spring to life with the spirit of progress.

"This republicanism is the finest natural form of government, and it is essential because it suits the Chinese people; moreover, it will work to our advantage in carrying out the revolution. When we look back to previous periods in China's past, we see that once rebellion breaks out in the land local heroes rise in every region, seize the strategic points, and compete in valor with each other. Often unity is not completely restored for decades. The unfortunate masses do not know how to seek their happiness in such difficult times; moreover, this time no one can be sure there won't be foreign powers trying to take advantage of the situation for their own profit too. The only way to avoid such misfortune will be through a sudden, irresistible revolutionary surge. At the same time, men of prestige in the various regions will have to be placated by having them retain some local political power under the loose control of a central government so they will feel satisfaction with the new structure. Successful control over these local leaders will lead to adequate political unity and avoid a really severe civil war. This is why I hold that republicanism can be advantageous to the revolution."

Sun grew more and more passionate as he described the pathetic state of his country.

"Alas, because our territory is so huge and our people are so numerous, we are like a piece of meat on the butcher block. The ravenous tiger who devours it will grow so strong he will come to dominate the world. But now if someone with moral principles responds to this, he will find himself in harmony with the principles of humanity and renowned throughout the world. I would not have been able to stand aside from such a challenge even if I were an ordinary person anywhere in the world, wanting the way of humanity to be preserved. How much more so when it concerns the country of my birth, the land whose distress I have myself experienced! I know my deficiencies in ability and knowledge, and know that I am not qualified to undertake this great task. But the times do not permit me to stand by waiting for someone else to lead the way. So I am eager to make myself a forerunner of the revolution in response to the times. If my party should be fortunate enough to get help from someone more capable than I, I would be happy to let him take over the leadership and I would work faithfully under him. If there is no one else, I will accept the challenge and

> assume the burden. I firmly believe that heaven will help our cause—for the sake of the Chinese masses, for the sake of the yellow races of Asia, and for the sake of humanity throughout the world. I am buoyed in this conviction by the fact that you have come to me to participate in our work. You are an omen. Now it is up to us to exert ourselves in order not to fall short of your expectations. And you, in turn, must do your best to help us gain our objectives. The way to help the four hundred million of China's masses, the way to wipe out the insults that have been heaped on the yellow peoples of Asia, the way to protect and restore the way of humanity throughout the universe—all this can be done only by helping our country's revolution. When this one cause succeeds, all other problems will find solution quickly."

Sun's words were clear and explicit. He was rational and righteous, fervent and discerning; he burned with inner passion and enthusiasm. He was eloquent but he also spoke with spontaneity. Through all this flow of discourse his true nature sparkled, and it seemed a nature full of the music of the spheres and the rhythm of revolution. No one could have failed to be persuaded by it. Yet as soon as he finished, he relaxed and returned to an almost childlike simplicity, rather like a naive country girl, without a single artifice or concern. At this point I inwardly confessed to my shame; while professing twentieth-century ideas outwardly, I had not emancipated myself from old-fashioned oriental standards of judging people by external considerations. Because of this weakness I often misjudge myself and, even more frequently, others. A person like Sun Yat-sen, however, follows the dictates of his own nature. How noble his thought, how sharp his insight, how great his conception, how burning his fervor! How many persons like that have appeared among our countrymen?

Truly, he is a precious jewel of Asia. At this point I committed myself to him.

Now I told my friend Sun about my friend Hirayama Shū, and went back to my inn half delirious with joy. I took Hirayama to Mr. Sun's place again, and we chatted around his table. We talked about all sorts of things: Japanese political parties and personalities, the politics of Europe and America, the present state of China, religion and philosophy. The more we talked the warmer grew our feelings. As evening fell we promised to meet again. Hirayama and I returned to our inn, and then went on to Tokyo.

When we got back to Tokyo we went to report to Inukai and told him about Mr. Sun. He commented that this was a fine souvenir and asked whether I wouldn't bring him around for a talk. Afterwards I went to the Foreign Ministry and reported to Vice Minister Komura,[59] who asked me to write out a report about my travels in China. When I told him that I had brought him a living document on the present state of the secret societies in China, and asked him whether he would like to talk with him directly, he was startled and said he would pass up the opportunity. But I had made up my mind that officials were officials and I was what I was, and that I would do what I had to do no matter how much it startled the officials. Finally, through the generous assistance of Inukai and Hiraoka Kōtarō[60] we rented a house in Tokyo. There Sun Yat-sen and Ch'en Shao-pai, posing as language teachers, lived with Hirayama.[61]

[59] Komura Jutarō (1855-1911), Meiji diplomat who served as minister to China, the United States, and Russia, becoming foreign minister at the time of the Russo-Japanese war. At this time, vice minister.

[60] Hiraoka Kōtarō (1851-1906), Fukuoka samurai, parliamentarian, and coal-mine operator who stood as sponsor and patron for many Asia-oriented and nationalist causes.

[61] Under the treaty port system Sun Yat-sen required a permit to live outside the foreign zone; this was granted him as servant of Hirayama on October 12, 1897. They first lived in Kioi-chō, and then moved to be farther

At that time my family fortunes were completely exhausted, and my family was almost at the brink of starvation. Therefore I entrusted the details of these matters to Hirayama for a time and returned to Kumamoto. There, thanks to the noble assistance of my "nameless benefactor" Watanabe, I was able to get my wife set up in a coal store. Unfortunately, she found if difficult to get used to this work. The business went poorly, and after a few months she gave it up. As a result I have never been able to repay my benefactor.

Just then I received a telegram from Mr. Matono of Chikuzen, asking me to come to his place right away. I hurried to Fukuoka. He said that he was planning to publish a newspaper and wanted me to stay and help him with it. Mr. Kojima Kazuo[62] was coming from Tokyo to edit it for him. So I became a free-lance reporter, without set duties, and helped him. I worked in all sorts of capacities; translating, interviewing, delivering, reading proof, and even folding newspapers. However, Matono, the publisher, complained that a free-lance like me seemed to be the most costly kind of arrangement possible. Although the salary wasn't fixed, my appetite was very large, and my needs for food and drink were high, as were those of entertainment. After I had been there for several months I had an urgent telegram from Tokyo. My employer provided my travel money and I went back to Tokyo.

When I reflect on the past, I am overcome with gratitude to Inukai for the kindness he showed me. When I went to meet him in Tokyo he pulled several thousand yen out of

---

from the Chinese legation, ending in a residence directly behind that of Inukai near Waseda.

[62] Kojima (1865-1952), a journalist who was influenced by Sugiura Jūgō and Tōyama Mitsuru, edited a Fukuoka paper (*Kyūshū Nippō*), then worked on the Tokyo *Nihon oyobi Nihonjin*, before entering politics with Inukai; he was elected six times to the Diet, named to the House of Peers, and was influential in post World War II politics in association with Yoshida Shigeru.

his pocket and said, "This is the best I've been able to do for you. I imagine you would like to travel for a while. I think it would be well if you set out soon. But this time you will not be on government business, and you can be your own boss." How generous, how kind! That same day, after talking things over, we agreed to wind up the housing arrangements we had made. Sun and Ch'en moved to Yokohama, and Hirayama and I headed for Shanghai.

[18]
AMATEUR DIPLOMAT

AT THAT TIME THE CHINESE EMPEROR ACCEPTED the proposals of K'ang Yu-wei and energetically set about on the reform of the national government. The conservative faction that was in power opposed this, and the political situation in Peking became unstable. Hirayama and I parted company shortly after we reached Shanghai; Hirayama went to North China, and I to South China.

I proceeded to Hong Kong, where I put up at the Tōyōkan. I looked up old friends and made new acquaintances, and met secretly with members of the *Hsing-Chung hui* and *San-ho hui*,[63] to investigate the state of affairs. Then through the help of my friend Usami Okihiko, I was able to meet some men of high purpose, from the Philippines.

Although my aspirations centered on China, I also made friends with men from the Philippines while I was in Hong Kong. When I think about it, it seems fickle of me, but I couldn't help it. Not only did I fail to exercise discipline over myself; I succumbed to this new enthusiasm. The first time I met Mr. Ponce,[64] he pounded the table, as if unable to control his indignation, and said, "There's nothing

[63] One of the principal secret societies of central and south China, often referred to in English as the Triads.

[64] Mariano Ponce (1863-1917), Philippine historian and writer, was educated as a doctor in Madrid and became prominent for his expositions of

worse than to be betrayed by those you have trusted, but that's the state of affairs in my country right now. Did you know that when the war between the United States and Spain broke out, the Americans promised us our independence if we would start an insurrection? We believed what they said, we risked our lives, and we fought because we wanted that independence. Then Spain lost the war, and we all thought that we would now be a free people. How were we to know that we were to become a dependency of the United States? Ah, what are we to do! We who fought the Spanish for the sake of liberty now have to fight the Americans. Yes, there's no alternative to war! Oh, my friend from a chivalrous Asian country, will you not take pity on our spirit?" I was full of sympathy. How could I listen to much of this without trying to help?

We got along well together, and the more we talked the more passionate our talk became. I gathered from Mr. Ponce that General Aguinaldo intended to rely on Japan for help. He indicated that the common people in the Philippines had similar ideas, and indirectly asked me whether I wouldn't look into the possibility of assistance from the Japanese government. It was a serious question. I agreed that Aguinaldo ought to go through with his idea of going to Japan, and said that even if the government wouldn't help him, some private parties would surely do so; he should certainly go. Ponce answered, "Aguinaldo has in fact made up his mind to go to Japan. However, he's gone underground for safety for a while, lest some hothead

---

pre-Spanish civilization and culture. Leaving Spain in 1896, he joined the independence junta in Hong Kong, became secretary to Aguinaldo there, and was sent by him to Japan where he arrived on June 20, 1898, to negotiate for arms and assistance. Colonel Fukushima of the General Staff and Vice Minister Komura were initially encouraging, but the American decision to annex the islands meant that further efforts had to be directed through unofficial, adventurer channels. Ponce later married a Japanese woman, wrote a biography of Sun Yat-sen, and died on his way to visit Sun Yat-sen. Josepha M. Saniel, *Japan and the Philippines 1868-1898* (Quezon City, 1962, Univ. of Phil.).

should start things up too soon, and so he's gone into the interior to give orders. He ought to be here within a week." I waited for Aguinaldo with Ponce, but he didn't come, so I headed for the city of Canton alone, leaving instructions with Usami to cover the period of my absence.

In Canton, the contacts I had made with members of the *Hsing-Chung hui* became firmer day by day. Furthermore, I was able to meet some of the K'ang Yu-wei people through my friend Tano Kitsuji.[65] At that time Mr. K'ang was in Peking. He had become the emperor's right-hand man, and his voice was heard in all corners of the land; consequently the influence of his party also grew very greatly. Unfortunately Sun Yat-sen's followers and other groups distrusted him and regarded him as a turncoat; they bitterly resented and opposed his actions and party. They maintained that he had abandoned republicanism and changed sides to serve the cause of a barbarian king. The two groups were in ever sharper conflict. I took a position between the two and worked hard at being a mediator, thinking to myself that European and American diplomats with starched collars couldn't begin to do as well as I was doing.

One day I was taken to the secret headquarters of the revolutionary party by a Canton member. There was a lot of wine and meat, and as I enjoyed the heated discussions and arguments half the day flew by. In the middle of the banquet, one of the participants said to me, "We have the high determination to stage a revolution, but very few of us know anyting about military affairs. I wish you would familiarize yourself with the government's military garrison within the city. Would you be willing to take this on?" I answered, "Yes, I would. The trouble is that what with the way I look, and because I still don't understand Cantonese,

[65] Tano (1877-1904) educated at Dōshisha and Waseda, had strong Chinese interests which led to contacts with Arao Sei, Inoue Masaji and others; he was an instructor in K'ang Yu-wei's academy in Canton for a time, and later joined with Miyazaki Tamizō in the land-equalization movement.

it's impossible to know whether I will be able to escape observation by the officials and do the job you want done." Seated there was a Mr. ——. He seemed fit and courageous, and he had a very stern look about him. He looked at me and said, "It's true that if you enter the encampment the way you look now, the army officers will probably be suspicious of you. Fortunately, though, your hair is long; what you ought to do is to shave around it and make it into a pigtail, get out of Japanese clothing and put on Chinese clothes. I am registered in the military service, and have a pass; I'll go as your guide. If they should challenge you, what I'm going to do is to say that you are from Shantung. You can be sure of that." I agreed gladly. Immediately they sent for a barber who was a member of the revolutionary party and ordered him to shave the sides of my head and weave my hair into a queue. They all said it looked fine. But what were we to do about my beard? I thought he should shave it off; but some thought that would be a shame; others thought only the beard should be shaved, leaving a mustache, and still others supported taking it all. The argument raged inconclusively. Meanwhile the barber went ahead on his own, shaving the neck but not the upper lip, and leaving a goatee on the chin. Then the argument as to whether this was right or not started up all over again. But now the barber put away his razor and refused to do another thing. He pointed at my head, and shouted, "Good! Good! Don't change a thing." Then he left and didn't come back. Everybody applauded and admired his firmness; we finally decided to leave it his way. Meanwhile one of the party had gone out to buy some Chinese clothes. Everybody set to and helped me put them on. Then they stood around me, saying "Great! Great!" They raised their cups and toasted my change of clothing; I promised Mr. —— to go to the military encampment with him, called a sedan chair, and went back to my inn.

That evening Tano came to see me. As it happened, Mr.

Liang ——— came too and invited us to go to an entertainment boat. I went there in my Chinese outfit. There were about ten sing-song girls. At first they thought I was a special guest from Shantung, and treated me particularly graciously. Before long my sexual desire began to rise and I began to think about spending the night. Then one girl unexpectedly picked up a water pipe and invited me to smoke it; I sucked at this the wrong way and got water in my mouth. When she became suspicious and saw I was a fraud, my hopes were suddenly dashed. We all had a good laugh. After we had exhausted the pleasures of the night, Tano and I returned to my inn.

There were several telegrams from my Hong Kong friend waiting for me there, telling me to return immediately because of urgent business. I wasn't supposed to know the reason why, but it did not seem to be an ordinary matter. Accordingly, I got up early the next morning, wrote to Mr. ——— to postpone our plan to reconnoiter the Canton garrison, and returned to Hong Kong with Tano. There I met my friend right away. When I asked him what was at hand, he replied "We have received a telegram telling us that the reform party in Peking has failed and that the emperor has been poisoned."[66] Just then news came from Hirayama in Peking saying that things were falling into a state of chaos. When we put these together, there clearly seemed to be something going on. Voices of news vendors shouting "Extra! Extra!" were already being heard. As word continued to come in people grew more and more agitated, even though it was impossible to check anything for accuracy; it seemed clear, at any rate, that the situation in Peking was in chaos. Sun Yat-sen's partisans came and argued the case for seizing the opportunity, while K'ang

[66] On September 21, 1898, the Dowager Empress Tz'u-hsi directed a coup, announced that the emperor was incompetent because of illness, and ended the "Hundred Days' Reform" K'ang had inspired.

Yu-wei's supporters argued that the rumors were probably false. More and more people were coming to our inn.

Then a telegram came in saying K'ang Yu-wei had been arrested. Another arrived saying that he had fled. A telegram would start a rumor, and one rumor generated others. People were beside themselves trying to figure out what was true and what was false, but there was no doubt that there had been an overturn in Peking. It also seemed clear that this upheaval had been caused by the reform program. If this was so, then K'ang's life must obviously be in danger. And if K'ang himself was in danger, the effects would be felt immediately by his family and also his academy, the *Wan-mu ts'ao-t'ang*. I discussed some emergency measures with Tano: Tano would take the night boat to Canton, and go to the academy. Once there he would alert only the staff, meanwhile making secret preparations to evacuate the students. I would get the facts, and he would wait for my telegram at the academy. In an emergency I would provide shelter for as many as might need it. This agreed, we had some beer, shook hands, and parted. Tano headed for Canton alone, in high spirits.

Early the next morning four students of the academy came to see me. They were ashen-faced, trembling and their eyes were full of fear. I saw the condition they were in and could guess why, but didn't say anything and just asked them why they had come. They said, "We would like to meet Mr. Tano." When I told them that Tano had gone back to the academy, they seemed so terrified they didn't know what to do. So I took pity on them and invited them into my inn. Only then did they seem to calm down. That night Tano came back, bringing several dozen students with him. He said that K'ang had sent a secret telegram telling them to flee. From then on business really picked up at my inn.

When I was in Japan, I was always poor. However, when I got to travel in China through the help of my superiors, I always had a lot to spend, and I adopted the bearing of a wealthy member of the gentry. When I ran out of money I would just head back for Japan right away. As a result some people laughed at my fakery; others criticized it. But this was my tactic, and it was because of this that within a few days or months I came to be deeply trusted by a group of Chinese patriots. I owe all this to my money. I was able to meet the immediate emergency by using my credit at the inn, but it couldn't go on very long. So Tano and I pooled what we had, and sent a telegram to Inukai asking for his help. I was really a penniless camp follower.

I am essentially small of spirit. When I found myself a penniless camp follower I could hardly stand it. Everyday in our secret dealings several hundred people would write me more or less the same request, and I had no alternative but to write several hundred notes in reply with more or less the same answer. Nor was that all. The revolutionaries would argue that the right time had come for them to seize the initiative; then, seeing me help members of the K'ang faction, they became reproachful, making things worse and worse. I became so distressed I could hardly stand it any longer. If at that time Usa had not come to my inn to help me with my work, and if the Tanakas, who ran the inn, had not sympathized with me, and if it hadn't been for sake, and the presence of a woman called Setsurei, it's possible that I wouldn't have been able to stand the stress and the vexation. Fortunately there was also a private area of pleasure that was a different matter. No outsider could possibly understand that area.

In the meantime another telegram came saying that K'ang Yu-wei had left Shanghai for Hong Kong. Everybody doubted this, and in my heart I could hardly believe it either. However, K'ang's disciples, whose faces had been so pale, seemed to have their confidence restored because of their acceptance of this unconfirmed news. And then, eventually, it turned out to be true. That is to say, the live K'ang Yu-wei arrived in Hong Kong aboard an

English mail ship that was escorted by a British naval vessel.[67] It can be imagined how delighted K'ang's disciples were. The Hong Kong government wanted to protect him, so K'ang was given lodgings above the Hong Kong police headquarters.

The disciples rushed to be first in greeting their teacher. But the police were worried about the safety of their visitor, and did not want to permit this. They let only two of the senior students see K'ang. These two came to me to report how K'ang was, and on his instructions also to thank me for the great thoughtfulness I had shown to his students. Thereafter, for several days the two came to me as messengers from K'ang, sometimes trying to carry on a discussion with me and indirectly trying to get me to reveal my opinions. I thought to myself that K'ang, since he knew of my connections with the Sun Yat-sen group, would not be able to reveal what was in his thought openly and that he was using his students to see what my real intentions were. I thought K'ang was a weak-willed plotter, and I hinted at my intentions with general statements: "You were foolish to think that you could reform China's evils with one imperial edict. China's evils are longstanding, and they have their roots in the people's hearts. Therefore if you had wanted the emperor's reforms to succeed, you would have had to have effective power to dismiss the top officials. What is effective power? It has to be backed by military force. K'ang did not prepare for this; he trusted in the emperor's power, and thought he could carry out this great purpose with a paper edict, but in vain. That is why he failed."

The two disciples then said that there was no use in

[67] K'ang Yu-wei thus received high-level protection from Great Britain, where he was also offered asylum, and Japan, for it would fall to Miyazaki to help K'ang get from Hong Kong to Japan. The Japanese foreign service, operating under the instructions of Itō Hirobumi (who was in Peking) worked through unofficial channels to avoid charges of interference in Chinese internal affairs.

reliving the past: what did I think should be done now? I gave them a lecture on revolution: "If you resolve to carry out a reform and you want to get rid of the traditional mandarins, it's obvious that you need to have force available to you. But it is the officials, and not the talkative idealists, who have the monopoly on force. On the other hand, there are secret societies that are determined to overthrow the Manchus and restore the Chinese. So there's no place where you people can expect to find military help. It seems to me that at present any thought of reform is little more than an empty dream. I am convinced that the difficulty of reform in China is greater than the difficulty of revolution." The two disciples leaned forward: "But, Sir, how could we carry out a revolution?" I answered, "If what your people say is true, your emperor has no equal in the world today. There is not a ruler anywhere in the world who advocates republicanism. So if he is really that remarkable, the only thing he can do is abdicate, become an ordinary citizen, proclaim the republic, order the people to select those of whom they approve, and then wait for the rule of virtue. That way he will see the people realize their hopes. After all, there are secret societies like the *Ko-lao hui, San-ho hui, Hsiung-Chung hui*, and *Pai-lien chiao*.[68] There is bad blood between Manchus and Chinese. Don't the big officials control the troops? This single, great, unprecedented decision, gives you the best method for saving your country before it meets with disaster. Why do your emperor and Mr. K'ang not implement the wisdom of the ancients? Of course it's easy to suggest that he abdicate, and difficult for him to do so. If there's no other way, let Mr. K'ang condescend to stoop to work with idealists among the ordinary people, and raise an army of revolt; as things progress he can have the emperor join him

[68] The first-named, sometimes translated as "Elder Brother Society," was with the *San-ho hui*, a strong secret society, while the *Pai-lien chiao*, "White Lotus" Buddhist messianic teaching, produced one of the most troublesome rebellions of the eighteenth century.

in this effort. To try to put an end to the evils of the past without shedding blood is as impossible as crossing the ocean carrying Mr. Tai. It just can't be done." They made no answer to this, but folded the sheets we had been writing on and left in discouragement.

At that time I still took Mr. K'ang very seriously, and thought there were some real heroes in his following. Therefore, I wanted to take advantage of this occasion to get him to combine with the Sun Yat-sen party, and also link up with the *Ko-lao hui* and *San-ho hui*, with the dream of calling down the lightning for a revolt. I talked to the two disciples in this way in order to acquaint K'ang with my thinking.

On the other hand, it has to be granted that from K'ang Yu-wei's point of view, what I hoped for from him was totally unreasonable. K'ang worked with fledgling literati, and he was moved to tears by his emperor's fate; he had abandoned his previous espousal of republicanism and become a supporter of the Ch'ing throne. For him to change his position a third time now and become a revolutionary was virtually impossible. It was natural for him to sympathize with the emperor, especially in view of his recent involvement. Then again, since the revolutionaries regarded him as a turncoat, he could square himself with them if he asked their forgiveness, but if he expected to take a position of leadership and manipulate them he would have no chance at all. For these reasons he did not take my advice. Furthermore, he was at that time obsessed with his own importance and intoxicated with his recent experience of the imperial favor. He still thought that he could profit from the momentum of the reforms and begin to reverse the present trend, take charge of the government a second time, and carry out his original program. One has to admit that this was not an unreasonable state of mind. But in fact K'ang had no support within the country, and he was in personal danger.

How did he think he was going to reverse this state of affairs?

K'ang himself knew very well that he had no support within the country. But he believed that he would again receive support, this time from abroad. Since he had received the protection of an English warship, his self-confidence became ever greater. Should he rely on England or on Japan? This seems to have been the question uppermost in his mind. Since these were the countries he had to count on, the question seems to have been which of the two he should approach first. In the end he seems to have decided to try Japan. So his disciples came to me and revealed that their teacher was interested in going to Japan. They did not reveal this as their teacher's desire, however, but just as their own guess. Then they indicated that he hoped that the Japanese consul would come to see him. But this too they reported not as their teacher's message, but as their sense of the way he felt. Although this was a very Chinese way of doing things, when I contrasted it with the directness of the Sun Yat-sen group or the jovial drinking parties I had enjoyed with the secret-society members, it seemed rather sticky and shifty. In short, I became a little impatient. In spite of that, I sympathized deeply with them, and I was eager to take K'ang to Japan. Since I had this feeling for him, I was particularly irritated that he treated me the way he did. In order to resolve this puzzle, I went to the Japanese Consulate with Usa and explained things to Consul Ueno.

Consul Ueno was trying very hard to live up to the diplomat's code about keeping a cool head, and he was not prepared to agree to our request. The first time, we returned empty-handed without having gained our point. The next day we made our entreaties a second time, but he still wouldn't give in. Then I tried to get him to let me send a telegram in code, but he would not allow that either. I was at my wit's end and almost in despair, but got hold of myself and went back for a third try. This time the consul was not in. His wife, however, appeared and said that if it was an emergency she hoped I would speak to her. So I told her of K'ang's past, what he had done, and his present situation; I begged her for her sympathy, again told her what it was I needed and entrusted a message to her. The next day a message came from the consul asking me to come to see him right away. When I hurried there wondering what he wanted I found that the cool and correct attitude he had shown on previous visits had suddenly changed. He now showed a warm sympathy, and said that he would go to see K'ang in his personal capacity. It was all due to the influence of his wife.

The next day the consul called on K'ang in his personal capacity. Unfortunately something had come up, and K'ang wasn't there. Consequently the consul was somewhat discouraged. But K'ang was very upset about this and sent his students to ask for a meeting. Several days later K'ang moved out of the police headquarters to a friend's house. The consul got his courage up again, and called on him. After this meeting the consul became a very different person, and developed a warm sympathy for K'ang. One can see from this the power K'ang had to move people. It also seems to me that it was at this point that K'ang decided to go to Japan.

A few days after this K'ang's two students came. They quietly showed me secret telegrams from the emperor in Peking (I still do not know whether it was true or false), and asked me to relay them on behalf of K'ang. One was addressed to Japanese Minister Yano in Peking, and said. . . . The other was addressed to Foreign Minister Ōkuma, and said. . . . I went to Consul Ueno with them and discussed it, and this time he agreed to make the necessary preparations, and sent the telegrams. We waited several days, but no answer came. The disciples came every day, and didn't know what to do. Gradually they became disheartened, and even expressed some discontent. I guessed that what they said reflected K'ang's state of mind. Finally, Minister Yano sent a cable saying that we couldn't do anything without papers, and that we should wait for the instructions that would follow. Sure enough, ten days later instructions came from Minister Yano for the consul. We were becoming a little discouraged but in messages to K'ang we did not reveal this to him. Meanwhile the consul was becoming very irritated, and cabled Foreign Minister Ōkuma a second time. Then an answer came: "If K'ang Yu-wei is. . . ." I had Usa take this to K'ang, and he returned with word that K'ang was delighted and that he had decided to go to Japan. Usa went on: "He's anxious to see you. You should go discuss this with him." Of course I had wanted to see him earlier, but had not done so because I thought that he was an indecisive planner, very self-important as well, and suspected he was rather affected. I considered myself rather indecisive too; now, consequently, the two indecisive plotters would stand face to face.

The next day K'ang's two disciples came to say, "Our teacher has asked us to tell you that he would like to see you, but he doesn't feel it is safe for him to come out. He would be very grateful if you would do him the honor of discussing things with him at his residence." I went with Usa to see K'ang. He was shabbily dressed, and his face was dirty. But his eyes burned so with the intensity of his concern that he would have aroused the sympathy of any chivalrous person. I simply said, "We are all in your debt." He expressed his gratitude for the sympathy of noble-hearted men, but added, "This is no time for ordinary pleasantries; we ought to discuss larger matters right away." His manner had an easy sophistication, and he seemed anything but an irresolute plotter. What was he going to say?

K'ang began to jot down an account of the coup in Peking and described matters up to the time of his defeat. He wrote so rapidly that thousands of characters seemed to flow from his brush. He wrote so well, and his logic was so clear, that it was enough to persuade anybody. His conclusion was that the fault lay with the Dowager Empress Tz'u-hsi. She was the root of all evil in East Asia, and eliminating her was the most urgent thing to do. When I asked how he proposed eliminating her, he began citing the so-called *sōshi* (strong-arm men) in Japan; he took examples from the time of the Meiji Restoration, and then mentioned Tsuda Sanzō,[69] the attack on Li Hung-chang at Shimonoseki,[70] and the murder of Queen Min in Korea. He lauded the bravery and intensity as of our *sōshi* as something quite without parallel. Then, at the end, he revealed that he hoped to get the help of such forces and use them to eliminate the Dowager Empress and asked me whether I thought it could be done. I answered, "There is no problem about that. But to commit this matter to the care of Japanese men of high purpose seems to constitute a confession of your own impotence. You have been engaged in education at your academy for many years. Isn't there a single assassin among the three thousand students you have had? If you really haven't a single candidate, and if it's true that the Dowager Empress Tz'u-hsi is really the main problem, I would be willing to take care of it myself. It only requires one person to eliminate one Tz'u-hsi, and there's no need to use more." I had learned the diplomat's tricks. K'ang, though, looked rather ashamed and changed the subject without pursuing the idea any farther. His brush strokes seemed to lose their force, and his logic was less clear. So I went back home.

Two days later, K'ang's student Mr. X. came to see me. There happened to be a visitor talking in my room with

[69] Tsuda Sanzō, a policeman who was part of the guard for the Russian Crown Prince Nicholas at Ōtsu, turned suddenly to try to kill him on May 11, 1891 (the Ōtsu Incident). Japanese feared a Russian attack and feared for the Meiji emperor's life when he went on board the Russian battleship to bring his regrets and best wishes for recovery.

[70] During the Shimonoseki Peace Conference Li Hung-chang was seriously wounded by Koyama Toyotarō on March 24, 1895.

me. The student hid his face with a handkerchief he held in his left hand and beckoned me into another room with his right. I followed him, curious as to his purpose. His face was flushed and both eyes were tearful. He said, looking at me, "Mr. Y. and I have made up our minds to go north. We do not expect to return. We will never meet again. If you hear of lightning in the northern skies, you will know that my time to die has come. I have just had a tearful farewell with my teacher, Mr. K'ang. He urged me to come to say goodbye to you, and from this I realize how completely he trusts you. I beg of you: please help and protect Mr. K'ang, and thereby save our country's future. I can not restrain myself from kowtowing to you." With that he got up from his chair, knelt, and with tears performed the three bows and nine prostrations before me. How could I control my own emotions? I called for sake and food, and we drank face to face through our tears for a time; then we shook hands and parted.

When it was dusk Mr. Y., who was supposed to go together with Mr. X. came to see me too. He, too, beckoned me into another room, and said, "I think Mr. X. has been to see you already. I don't want to say very much. But I do beg you to protect Mr. K'ang. And I beg you to help my poor country. That is my only prayer." His eyes shone with tears. What could I tell him? I tried to cheer him a little; "It is easy to die, but hard to live. If you carry out your mission successfully, I hope that you will flee to Japan. It is not necessary for a hero's life to end like a piece of jade that has been suddenly shattered." He only wept in reply. Tanaka's wife, Komako, was thoughtful enough to bring us some wine and food. We raised our cups to each other, shook hands, and parted. I then went up to the roof and looked down on the street. I saw him, his face still covered with his handkerchief, walk unsteadily to the pier, where he got on a small boat and headed for a steamer. As I watched this I fell prostrate and could not keep from weeping. After a bit I felt someone tapping my shoulder. Bless her! It was Setsurei. She and Komako took me inside and offered me sake to make me feel better. Then Nagato Takezō came in too. He thought I ought to go to a house of entertainment. Nagato himself was a Christian and a very good person, and he usually warned us against wine and women. But not this night. When I asked him why, he answered, "Heaven will forgive you." And he led me by the hand. Ah, these people little knew the reason for my melancholy, nor did they ask. They just did their best to console me. That is the finest human sentiment. That night I slept by Setsurei's side.

The next day Mr. K'ang sent two disciples over again to ask me to come to see him. When I got there, he wrote that there was a serious matter he had to discuss with me. What could it be? The problem was Li Sheng-to, who was to replace Mr. Huang as Chinese minister to Japan.

K'ang said, "Li Sheng-to is a confidant of Jung-lu, and my enemy. They are now sending him to Japan as minister to replace Huang. The reasoning behind this appointment is that they expect me to go to Japan and want to kill me there. I would like you to report this to Count Ōkuma so that he won't agree to the appointment of Li. Otherwise, I will have to put off my trip to Japan for a time and go to England instead. Just now England is doing all sorts of things to welcome me and clearly wants me to come. They just won't take no for an answer. I have been resisting this, however, and would rather go to your country. The reason is that we are of a common race and our countries are brothers. And your country is rich in chivalrous men of high purpose. In spite of that, Li Sheng-to is slated to be minister to your country. This is not just a misfortune for both China and Japan, but it endangers my life as well. How do you think we ought to deal with this matter?"

K'ang's argumentation was not all unskilled. In fact, however, it was a little too clever, and I felt a slight repugnance for him. I answered, "I can forward your message to Count Ōkuma, but it is going to be difficult for him to refuse to agree to Li's appointment. If you are saying this chiefly for fear of your life, it is unnecessary. Japan has the best-disciplined police force to be found anywhere in the world. But from what you say it seems that you are hesitant to risk offending the good will England has shown for you and afraid that if you ignore it and go to Japan, England might become jealous. As I see it, however, there is a destiny that binds your country to Japan. Whether you decide to go or decide not to go, our efforts to plan for your country are not going to change. All Japanese long for the reform of China. Our sympathy for you will not be affected at all by your decision to come to Japan or not to come. It is not too late for you to decide to go to England in response to their encouragement first and to come to Japan after that. This is not just because the present situation in China is unfavorable for you, but perhaps one way of avoiding betrayal by the English. In fact I would advise you to go to England first."

K'ang looked extremely embarrassed. Then he said, "I have decided to go to Japan. But because of the appointment of Li Sheng-to, my followers have been doing their best to urge me not to go. Fortunately you are here now. Let us convene a small national assembly together in order to settle this matter." K'ang called a number of followers immediately, and the discussions began. Among the followers there was one who thought it particularly dangerous for K'ang to go to Japan. I was very critical of him: "Are K'ang followers such cowards? If your master should fall at an assassin's hand, you people should carry out his work in his stead. Otherwise you are going to spend the rest of your lives here with your master in hiding without doing anything." K'ang clapped his hands and said, "You just made up my mind for me. Don't the rest of you try to stop me." So the matter was settled.

Once the matter was settled, K'ang was impatient to go to Japan together with us. Usa and I agreed. We decided to pick out an early mail boat, more or less settled on the Kawachi Maru, and left. At the inn we found a telegram. Inukai had sent us some money. Heaven blessed us! If the money had not come, I wouldn't have been able to keep my promise to K'ang.

[19]
K'ANG YU-WEI ENTERS JAPAN

K'ANG HAD MADE UP HIS MIND AND THE MONEY had come. I went to see the consul with Usa right away to tell him of K'ang's decision, and he was very pleased. He sent Usa to make convenient arrangements with Mihara, who headed the branch office of the Nippon Yūsen Company. Mihara entered into the spirit of the thing very generously; he said he would see to it that the passenger list was restricted to Japanese and English, and that he would have the steamship leave the harbor on time, and then stop outside the harbor to wait for our party, which would be sent by launch just after dark. He could not have been more careful and meticulous. Everything was ready.

But I was staying at an inn, and it was going to be difficult for me to board secretly carrying my baggage. I thought about it and worked out a procedure. I asked Mr. Tanaka, the inn manager in whose discretion I had developed great confidence, to come to my room, and told him that an urgent matter had come up which made it necessary for me to go to Japan secretly. He was to tell people that I was going to Macao. With that I paid my bill and had my baggage sent. Tanaka is an Edokko, and a Tokyo man's word is as good as his bond; he and his wife Komako did everything that I asked. We went to a restaurant together and toasted my farewell, and then Usa and I went to the house of pleasure and I spent the night at Setsurei's side.

Usa left early the next morning to help Mr. K'ang pack and to take him to the pier that evening. I stayed with Setsurei and waited patiently for the time of departure. Meanwhile Tanaka came in, and before long his wife came too. They knew that I was going to Japan, but Setsurei did not. I sent for wine and food and tried to have a farewell party without saying anything about it. Then Kikuko, Usa's girlfriend, also joined our party. "Is Usa going to Macao with you?" she asked, and then, looking at Setsurei, added "What do you think? Macao is so near that they shouldn't be gone more than two or three days, should they?" The two beamed at each other, seeing how pleased I looked. The Tanakas, on the other hand knew the truth and seemed depressed at the thought of parting.

Ah, what good friends they all were! How could they know the extent of my hopes and plans? Without knowing them, they nevertheless made my pleasures and sorrows their own. When I had met the man of high purpose from the Philippines, I was so moved that I could not help but weep; my friends too had wept to comfort me. They simply assumed that some matter related to the good of the country had gone wrong. In the negotiations between Sun Yat-sen's group and K'ang Yu-wei's group I was often at my wit's end; my friends would share my concern, urge wine on me, ply me with oranges, and sympathize with me. All they knew was that I was working for the good of the country. I often longed for the skies of my old home, and could not keep from thinking of my mother, wife, and sons. My friends would sympathize with me in my distress; they would fan me and massage me to help me sleep. They believed that I was engaged in urgent business for the sake of the country. When I thought about these things and realized that I mattered, I sometimes unconsciously shouted for joy. At such times they would share my joy and dance and sing with me. It was all because they guessed that something good for the country must have taken place. Were they not truly pure of heart? My only fear was that I might fail to deserve their trust. Let no one call Kikuko and Setsurei prostitutes. There are any number of men who consider themselves high-minded idealists who will sell themselves for money. And let no one dismiss the Tanakas as menial servants of an inn. How many of the men of high purpose of our days are really indifferent to thoughts of personal gain and loss? In my opinion it would be hard to find people as truly patriotic as these friends of mine. Truly, I have to say that I had wonderful friends; the only thing that worries me is that I may not have been able to measure up to their expectations.

And so it was that I lifted my wine cup with these close friends and inwardly intimated that it was a farewell. What emotions came flooding in! Before the sake or the emotions were exhausted, however, the clock struck four. When we rushed out and looked toward the harbor, we saw that the ship was belching black smoke and that it had raised anchor and begun to move. Tanaka pulled my sleeve in consternation; he thought I had missed the boat. But I just laughed without saying anything, for my mind was quite at rest. I returned to my place without hurrying, picked up my cup again, and waited for the sun to sink behind the western hills. Then, straightening my clothes, I bade my friends farewell. They all saw me off as I left the entryway, stumbled tipsily down the stone path and headed for the pier. There a small launch took me to the side of the Kawachi Maru, which I boarded. K'ang's party numbered nine, and Usa and I made it eleven. As we greeted each other on deck and gave three banzais the ship left the harbor and began to surge forward; the shore behind us gradually became distant, and we picked up speed. The night became darker; gradually it became impossible to see the Hong Kong mountains. What could have been the emotions of the refugee patriots on this night? I thought about my beloved Setsurei, and could not sleep at all that night.

After three days we could make out the Okinawan mountains. K'ang showed his emotions in some lines he brushed:

> The ocean waters push aside the mountains and lead me to Japan;
> Heaven's winds draw the moon which shines on Liu-chiu;
> Alone, I cross the Southern Seas and move toward the rising Sun [i.e., Japan],
> Like a tortoise, blowing aside the waves as he crosses the ocean.

In the darkness of night of the fifth day the ship dropped anchor outside the Kobe harbor. It was too dark to dock. Our party was still in bed, I myself heavy with sake. Suddenly I was awakened by a member of the ship's company who told me that somebody wanted to see me. When I got up and went out, it turned out to be a certain person from the Foreign Ministry and one from the police who had come to meet our party. They said we should take advantage of the darkness of the night to land unobserved. I passed the word to Mr. K'ang and the others to get up; we transferred to a small police launch and headed for the pier. Once there we were escorted to a room above the police station where we spent the rest of the night in talk. Mr. K'ang was asked to put on western clothes. We waited for the dawn, and then headed by twos and threes to the station, where we boarded a train for Tokyo. When the train reached Shimbashi, Hirayama got on to meet us. He had come from Peking a week earlier escorting Liang Ch'i-ch'ao. Liang was K'ang's most important follower.[71] So both Hirayama and I had returned

[71] Liang (1873-1929) one of twentieth-century China's most important men of letters, was escorted to Japan by Hirayama Shū, also at government direction. In Japan he was to become Sun Yat-sen's principal rival for the resources and support of the Chinese community in Japan.

to Japan as the result of this national crisis in China. Fate still had surprises for us. We were taken to an inn called Sambashi.

The next morning Sun Yat-sen showed up, and asked me whether he could see K'ang Yu-wei. K'ang, however, did not want to see Sun. Sun's desire to see K'ang had nothing to do with ideology or tactics; it had its origin in sympathy for K'ang's present plight. All he wanted to do was to greet him and to share his emotions as a traveler whose fate had also led him to foreign shores; it showed the man's real quality. But it was also natural for K'ang to avoid the meeting. To begin with, from the point of view of the Ch'ing court, Sun Yat-sen was a lawless rebel with a price on his head; Sun, for his part, saw the Ch'ing emperor as an implacable enemy, one he would strike down whenever he had the chance. K'ang had suffered a setback and had to flee abroad, but he still had the idea that once the situation was reversed he would be up there again, serving as the emperor's principal adviser and achieving unprecedented accomplishments. Naturally, then, neither easy-going courtesy nor thoughts about the impact on public opinion created the slightest inclination for K'ang to meet with Sun Yat-sen. On the other hand, we Japanese who were involved found this most unfortunate. However hard we tried to get them to meet, even if only in secret, we couldn't do it. In addition, friction among K'ang's followers gave rise to an unpleasant situation; they started making all sorts of false accusations about Sun to hurt him, and as a result the distance between the two men unfortunately widened steadily.

In actuality, however, K'ang had an additional thought in mind that made him determined to stay away from Sun Yat-sen. What was it? It was a product of his conceit and an idea he secretly expected to see implemented. This is what he thought: my status is so high that I will be able to talk to the foreign minister of Japan; he will surely see things my way, and send out troops to overthrow the conservative clique in Peking. Then I will be able to take power again. Conceit and optimism produced this hope. But it was much exaggerated. The exaggeration produced disappointment, and then resentment. But that is the way human nature is. One has to conclude that the only reason Foreign Minister Ōkuma was able to avoid this embarrassment and maintain his reputation was the timely collapse of his cabinet. His cabinet did fall, and it was succeeded by one under Yamagata.[72] The new cabinet's attitude toward K'ang was very cold, and K'ang and his men put their trust in Ōkuma more and more. Unfortunately Ōkuma was no longer in power and there was no chance of his getting back in. Before very long all the prominent people who had welcomed K'ang and entertained him grew tired of him and started to avoid him. One might lay this at K'ang's door, but on the other hand it also showed something about our countrymen's fickleness in enthusiasm. It was certainly fortunate that during all this time Inukai, at least, remained unchanged in his good will and that Kashiwara[73] did everything he could to help. But still there was nothing that K'ang could do, and it was inevitable that he would decide to go on to Europe and America.[74]

There have always been those who talk about great men and heroes. But all judgments of so-called great men or heroes are relative. If you look for someone completely godlike in his perfection, then all the great men and heroes of the past rank no higher than children or birds and animals. To be sure, even birds and animals amount to more than insects, and children are smarter than birds and animals. That's the way it is with the great men and heroes of this world. Take Li Hung-chang. Everybody praises him and calls him a hero of East Asia. What has been his

[72] On November 8, 1898.

[73] Kashiwara Buntarō (1869-1936), Waseda-educated Sinophile whose career revolved around institutions like the Tōa Dōbun Shoin (see below, 87).

[74] K'ang left Japan on March 22, 1899, with government funds channeled to him through Konoe Atsumaro.

contribution to the state of affairs in the world? Some will answer, "He is great because he finished off the Taiping Rebellion." I disagree. What if Hung Hsiu-ch'üan[75] had succeeded in setting up the Taiping kingdom? The Chinese people might not be in the plight they are today. Others will say, "He hoodwinked Itō in the negotiations for the peace treaty at Shimonoseki and secured the return of the Liaotung Peninsula." True enough, Itō was foolish and was taken in by him. But didn't Li end up an even bigger fool by having the great powers take him in after he had taken Itō in?[76] That is all that Li's supposedly great achievement of extending the life of the Ch'ing dynasty amounts to. You can not get around that fact that it is because of that that China's territory is so threatened today. Well then, what do all Li's contributions to the state of affairs really amount to? All they add up to is insurrection and national peril. And still he's called a great man of China. Surely there has to be somebody greater than that! Li can be described as a great man in only a most relative sense.

As an individual K'ang can clearly not be called particularly great. He was not very magnanimous, he was not farsighted, and he lacked experience. But it is a fact that he won the emperor's favor while he was only a scholar. It is also true that he influenced the emperor and stirred in him the determination to sponsor reform in China. It is also a fact that he assisted the emperor, and worked out the rationale of reforming institutions and strengthening the country. It is a fact that he managed to shake the entire country by this. And it is a fact that he was able to make the Ch'ing court powerless for a time. Although he failed and his plans unfortunately collapsed

[75] Hung (1814-1864) led the Taiping Rebellion; Li gained fame in its suppression.

[76] In the Triple Intervention Germany, France, and Russia joined to force Japan to give up the Liaotung Peninsula which China had reluctantly granted at Shimonoseki, but shortly afterward each of the powers demanded territorial grants; Russia moved into Liaotung.

completely, up to that point facts are facts. And furthermore it is also true that the force of these events was forward-looking and reformist. That is why I consider Li Hung-chang a minor figure and K'ang Yu-wei a major figure. He had the intention of making a contribution to the affairs of the realm, and that is what he should be celebrated for. People who look down on K'ang do not appreciate his true dimensions; they lack a true awareness of China's present state, and they do not realize how relative all judgments are. Truly, China has never had so few men of stature as it does today. At this time men with any familiarity with the state of affairs should put other things behind them and men who aspire to achieve great things should arise. And, just as certainly, it is at this time that valorous men who revere humanity and are mindful of the masses, should move. Do not think for a minute that fellows like Chang Chih-tung and Liu K'un-i[77] are important to Japan. They are nothing more than banners in the sky. They are at the mercy of every shift in the situation, and they think only of their own security. To think that one can clasp hands with men like that to plan for the long future makes about as much sense as to think that one can mount a raccoon as if it were a horse and go for a journey of a thousand leagues. Then what is there to the great officials of the past? In that light, K'ang looks more and more like a hero.

When K'ang first came to Japan he was praised to the skies, and since I had brought him to Japan I shared in some of this praise. But then, partly because of this, I began to coast along, and got used to being entertained, drinking, and partying. It was at this time that I was invited by a certain viscount to the Matsuei house of pleasure. That was when I met the geisha Tomeka. Of course I didn't have a penny of my own in my pocket.

[77] With Li Hung-chang, the greatest viceroys and supporters of the Ch'ing throne.

Despite this the head madam at the Matsuei saw to it that I had the best of everything there was to offer. I became a completely base parasite, a nose-picking beggar playing the gentleman. Despite this, Tomeka didn't seem to mind, and she loved me; I didn't understand why. And though I didn't understand what was going on, I was like a bee intoxicated with the pollen of flowers, and didn't want to leave my lovely Tomeka of the Matsuei. Before I knew it my bills for lodging had run up to several hundred yen and the Matsuei bills were also adding up. And still the head madam carried me. There was nothing I could do about the bill at my inn. By this time K'ang had already moved, and Hirayama too had left on a trip to Hupei and Hunan. The day of reckoning was at hand, but Kiyofuji and I were the only ones left.

Kiyofuji was a very old friend. We had gone different ways because we had different views, but we still had many things in common and felt deeply about them. He had become discouraged with public affairs, and had isolated himself almost completely. Despite this his benefactor, Oyama Yūtarō,[78] was deeply impressed by him, and provided money to tide his family over, and also the resources for him to study and travel. Kiyofuji felt very grateful for such generosity, and had gone up to a mountain temple in Hakone for study to seek happiness and spiritual courage. When he heard that I had brought K'ang Yu-wei to Japan, however, he hurried back to Tokyo and came to my Sambashi Inn. We sat up all night discussing what we should do next. Then, when he saw the financial straits I was in he stayed on instead of rushing back to his mountain temple, so that we could work out some solution. We couldn't find one. The bill collectors became more and more insistent and the situation became more and more precarious. When things were at their

[78] Oyama was a Kumamoto newspaper publisher and entrepreneur who maintained active interests in Japanese and Chinese politics.

blackest, I proposed this step: "I hear that Inukai is ill just now, and recuperating at Ōiso. Why don't we slip out of here and go somewhere to work out our plans?" Kiyofuji agreed. We managed to sell a waistband for three yen without being seen, and then walked nonchalantly out of the inn and headed for Shimbashi. That's how we got away from the inn.

When we got to Sukiyabashi, a two-man rickshaw bore down on us from the right. The passenger waved to us and motioned his rickshaw to a stop. It turned out to be an old friend of mine, Inoue Yoshio. "Where are you headed?" he asked. We told him the truth. He said, "Haven't you got several days till the end of the month? This is the time to exert yourself; when I'm in that kind of trouble, I go on the offensive. Victory is in sight! You two had better come to my place and wait for good news." Spirits matched words. We followed his suggestion, changed direction and ended at Inoue's residence in Mita.

I call it that, but it hardly lived up to the term. It was actually a dirty little house. Inoue, the lord and master, had been born into a family of noble lineage, but he had no use for aristocracy. He was completely cynical about the great and preferred the common people, with whom he affiliated. When he had money he would go out to drink somewhere else, and when he did not he would stay at home and wait for guests to come; everyday he killed time nonchalantly by riding around town. When he had no money his rice supply gave out. As the end of the year drew close, the bill collectors would gather in front of his place as if it were a market. Kiyofuji and I watched from inside as her ladyship skillfully cut her way through this evening host. We were full of admiration and could only hope that his lordship's efforts in the battle outside would be successful.

Then came year's end. His lordship left before dawn and headed for the battlefield. The sun stood in the west and began to fall, and he still hadn't returned. At the tenth stroke of the dragon a telegram came. It said, "Prepare for the siege." He had been defeated. We looked at each other and laughed. Even her ladyship managed a bitter smile. She faced her guests courteously and said, "Forgive us! Please give me your instructions; I'm off to the Sixteenth Bank." With that she loosened her obi and took off her soiled kimono; standing in a simple cotton robe, she brought out a garment; folded it with her own, wrapped it in a *furoshiki*, and went off to the pawn shop with a servant. She came back with sake and rice. At the sight of this, everybody revived. The sake was immediately warmed, and we gathered around the stove slurping it up like cattle. Then her ladyship closed the door and decreed that we should all give vent to song in order to ward off the creditors. So we started off at the top of our lungs. We were particularly lusty in case someone should knock at the door so that we wouldn't be able to hear him. It really is a fine way to avoid bill collectors. Then his lordship, somewhat in his cups, returned too. We ended up by carousing all night. I think that is what a New Year's Eve party should be like.

Now we had used our last coin. There was no point in trying to do anything. There was barley to eat, sake to drink, and a fire to keep us warm. When we got drunk we sang, when we were tired we slept, when we sobered up there was sex, and so we passed the days seizing the pleasures of the moment. When a man comes this far he needs nothing more. However, I felt one element of remorse. I couldn't see my geisha Tomeka. The only way I could deal with that longing was to hoodwink it with sex. My companions, looking at my little black book, would say "My lord, Tomeka is down for only two hours of your time." Including her, they pointed out, the total list came to two hundred eighty-five. It's true; I have to admit that I have had a lot of girlfriends. But while my companions sought relief from boredom for a few hours this way, it seemed to me that there was nothing to be ashamed of in my love affairs; on the contrary, they were to my credit. And so I made much of my love for Tomeka. What of her feelings for me? That was a problem for the future.

Things had been going on in this rather pointless way for more than three weeks, when a friend of mine happened along. We resorted to our established procedures, scraped some clothing together, and headed for the Sixteenth Bank. With some difficulty I was brought back to my original determination and headed for Ōiso.

At Ōiso I spent a little more than a week as a camp follower of Inukai's, just eating and drinking. Since the level of conversation was very good as well, I felt almost as though I were in paradise. It could not be compared to the days that I had just spent in Inoue's besieged house. But our host Inukai was sick, and since we knew that his resources were limited, we did not want to stay too long. When we were able to get travel money together we headed for Hakone, and there entered Kiyofuji's Hōsen Temple. Here things were inexpensive and as I benefited from the trust they had in Kiyofuji it went well. For a while, at any rate, it was a fine way to spend one's life. The two of us would warm unrefined sake and become gloriously drunk after a few bottles. Then, just when we were about done for, a telegram came: "Toki died come immediately." Toki was the head madam at the Matsuei house in Tokyo. I considered this an order; and became so agitated about it that it seemed a matter of my own life and death. If I didn't go, I felt, the blame would be mine. Consequently that night Kiyofuji went to Odawara with me; the next morning we took the first train to Tokyo and headed for the Matsuei, full of uneasiness. There was the head madam; she hadn't died at all. She was all bows as she laughed and said, "Do forgive me. I sent milord that telegram in order to test his spirit. The test is over. Now please feel free to come and waste some time drinking."

If there's a weak point in your heart, even a woman can make fun of you. I knew that emotions connected with the

2. Tōten's brothers: Tamizō (1865-1928) and Yazō (1869-1896), the latter in the Chinese dress he adopted.

3. Tōten with his mother, wife, and infant sons Ryūsuke and Shinsaku, around 1894.

REPUBLIQUE FRANÇAISE

CONSULAT GÉNÉRAL DE FRANCE À BANGKOK.

CERTIFICAT D'INSCRIPTION.

Nationalité Japonais Nous, Ministre Résident de la
Age 24 ans République Française à Bangkok,
Lieu de naiss. Koumamoto certifions que le Sr. Miasaki
Fils de est enregistré au Con-
Petit fils de sulat Général, sous le No 8
Né à comme protégé Français.
Profession agent de l'immigrant japonais A Bangkok, le 26 Octbr. 1895
Domicile actuel
Taille d'un mètre
Signes particuliers

A. Defrance

OBSERVATIONS

4. Tōten's travel permit at time of Siam Immigration Project.

5. Sun Yat-sen with Tōten and other friends during the period described in the narrative. Those mentioned in the text: rear row, from left to right, Kani Chōichi, Oyama Yūtaro, Tōten, Sun Yat-sen, Kiyofuji Kōshichirō; front row from right, Uchida Ryōhei, Suenaga Setsu, Hirayama Shū.

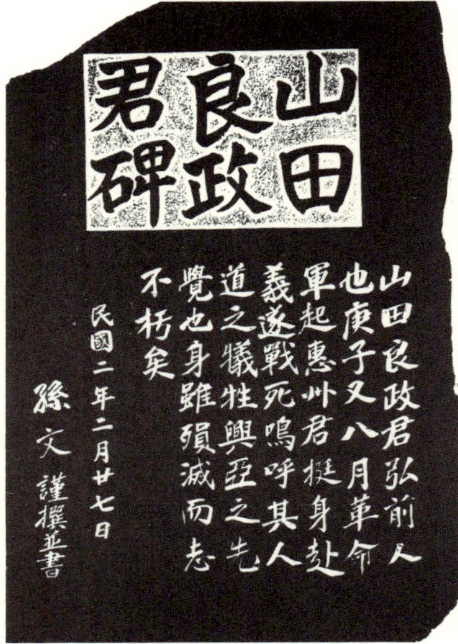

山田良政君碑

山田良政君弘前人也庚子又八月革命軍起惠州君挺身赴義遂戰死嗚呼其人道之犧牲興亞之先覺也身雖殞滅而志不朽矣

民國二年二月廿七日

孫文謹撰並書

6. Inscription Sun Yat-sen wrote in 1913 to honor Yamada Yoshimasa.

Yamada Yoshimasa was a man from Hirosaki. When the revolutionary army rose at Hui-chou in the intercalary eighth month of 1900, he came forward and went to his death in battle for the cause of righteousness. Truly, he sacrificed himself for humanity and became a pioneer of the new Asia. He is no more, but his spirit will endure forever.

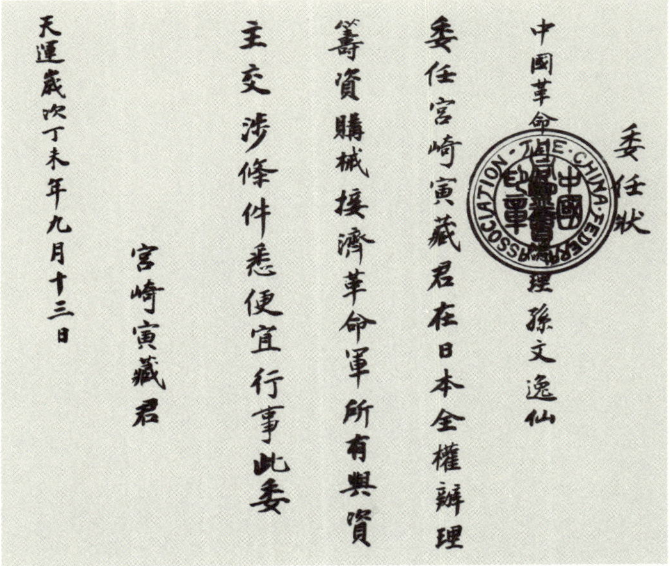

委任狀

中國革命同盟會總理孫文逸仙

委任宮崎寅藏君在日本全權辦理籌資購械接濟革命軍所有與資主交涉條件悉便宜行事此委

宮崎寅藏君

天運歲次丁未年九月十三日

7. 1907 Power of Attorney authorization in which Sun Yat-sen gave Tōten "full authority to raise funds, purchase equipment, and obtain supplies for the revolutionary army in Japan and full discretion to negotiate terms with capitalists."

mystery of death could produce such weak points. But although I knew it, I did nothing to resist. I became more and more entrapped in the jungle the madam had lured me into. But after all I had spent a lot of time drinking at the Matsuei earlier. There were a number of reasons why it had come to this, but the principal attraction was my affection for Tomeka. Later I heard that the head madam had fallen on evil days and gone bankrupt and that she had become an ordinary prostitute to keep herself alive. Alas, I am the one to blame. When the madam got in really desperate straits at the last she hired a strong-arm type to try to force me to pay my bills, but I did not resent that particularly. One bad trick deserves another. My subsequent affairs did not prosper as I had hoped they would, with the result that I was never able to pay my bills. But I think that if she had known the details of my situation she would not have judged me very harshly.

Kiyofuji and I, having been taken in by the fake telegram, saw that the madam was prepared to offer us food and drink, and we were soon well along in our acceptance of that offer. We exchanged cups vigorously before passing out. The next day we sobered up and left for Hakone and Kiyofuji's temple again. We were there for several weeks and almost became mountain ascetics. But our interests were not those of mountain sages. There is no opportunity to take part in affairs of the world if you stay in the mountains in lonely contemplation. So after talking it over with Kiyofuji I headed for Tokyo, took up some of my former connections, and lodged at the Taiyōkan again.

The Taiyōkan was an inn below Atogayama in Shiba. Some ten years earlier, when I had come to Tokyo with my hair grown long, other innkeepers thought I looked suspicious and would not take me in, but the Taiyōkan mistress, seeing that I had been misunderstood, was good to me, let me stay, and treated me kindly. Her husband was a remarkable fellow. He would drink sake every day, and usually erupt into joyful song. I felt very much at home there and the owners were very good to me. We trusted each other fully. I had wandered about a lot before this without a fixed place, but now whenever I came to Tokyo and saw the Taiyōkan I felt at ease. It's not very often that you find a place to which you seem linked by karma. And even when you do, changes in human nature often cancel that linkage. In my present state, however, I hesitated to go there. I yearned for a place considerate of its guests, and I wondered whether it was possible that the old warmth had not cooled or changed. But finally I mustered up my courage to go and ask whether I could lodge and eat there for a while. They welcomed me, and urged me to have at least some rice, and to relax and stay as long as I could. And so I made myself at home. It was February 1898.[79] On the bank opposite the stream floating grass was in flower. It drifted with the wind. Was that not true of me as well? And yet is it not a truly kindly world that ministers to famished spirits?

[79] Tōten's error: it was 1899.

[20]

OUR ACTIVITIES IN THE TROUBLED WORLD OF SOUTHEAST ASIA

THANKS TO THE KINDNESS OF THE OWNER OF the Taiyōkan, I had sake to drink and rice to eat. In comparison with earlier days, I was better off than I had been in body and mind. Still, when I thought of the road that lay before me, I couldn't help but feel that I was not making any progress. Once the Yamagata cabinet was organized, all the help our friend Inukai had been able to provide collapsed overnight. Moreover, I had failed in my attempts to bring about the cooperation between K'ang Yu-wei and Sun Yat-sen that I had dreamed of; K'ang had left the country for different climes, and Sun, although he was still in Japan, was hardly able to lift a finger. At the Ch'ing court the Dowager Empress and Jung-lu had seized all power. Ah, it seemed the winds were howling and dark clouds were gathering in the sky. And all I could do was drink sake and fret in inactivity every day.

Then came news. Aguinaldo and his followers had raised their standard on the battlefield.[80] Already before that, Hirayama had come back after finishing his survey of conditions in Hupeh and Hunan. According to him, he had

[80] The Treaty of Paris, December 10, 1898, which confirmed the United States' intention of annexing the Philippines and ignored the prior declaration of Filipino independence, was followed by declaration of the Republic on January 23, 1899. Hostilities with United States forces broke out on February 4, 1899.

been able to make contact with members of the *Ko-lao hui* through the help of Pi Yung-nien's[81] father. They had pledged themselves, and were only waiting for the right time to rise in revolt. There were many very able men among the society members. If Sun Yat-sen were to raise his banner too, everyone would swarm to join him. So Hirayama said. At that time, many members of Sun's *Hsing-Chung hui* were planning revolt and urging action on him. But Sun, because his preparations were not yet complete, sent word that they were not to do anything rash. Even so, although he was at work on his plans, things were not going the way he wanted them to. In the end it became Sun's plan that some of his followers should go to the Philippines in secrecy, join Aguinaldo's army to speed its victory, and then turn to direct their new power to the Chinese interior, establishing a revolutionary army there.

At that time Sun was living in Yokohama. One day he came to see me in the Taiyōkan. When we were alone he said, "Is there any way you can get guns and ammunition to the Philippines?" When I asked him what he had in mind, he lowered his voice and said, "There is a representative of the independence army in Yokohama. Since I have planned to go to the Philippines with you, I visited this man and revealed my secret support for him. He was overjoyed, and promptly entrusted me with a great matter: the import of guns. It was our very first meeting, and see how he trusted me! I must do everything within my power for this cause. Moreover, this man's spirit is exactly the same as ours. I want to ask you to use all your strength for these valorous Filipinos." My heart was instantly aflame. Sun, Hirayama, and I made secret plans, and I resolved to reveal these to Inukai and to tap his wisdom.

[81] Pi Yung-nien, a revolutionary from Changsha, Hunan. Pi came to Japan after the failure of the Hundred Days Reform, met Sun Yat-sen, and worked effectively for the union of secret societies thereafter.

Inukai was a chivalrous samurai. When he heard our story he was full of sympathy. Then after thinking a bit, he said, "The simplest way to deal with this is to put it in the hands of a merchant. The trouble is, though, merchants are moved by greed and have no knowledge of morality: even if one should take it on, he would betray you. What we have to do is to identify someone with a sense of adventure and integrity who also has some knowledge of business." Then, after a period of silence, he went on, "what about entrusting it to Nakamura Haizan? He has recently come down with diabetes, and he knows that he hasn't got very long to live. Yet he's very anxious to make a name for himself. The other day he talked to me for some time about the Philippines. I think he would like to join the Filipino army, but doesn't seem to have any way of doing it. I think that if you people went to talk to him about it, he would respond with all the desperation of someone who doesn't have very long to live. Wouldn't it work out for him as well as for us? I hear that he can't expect more than three years of life. He doesn't have much chance of making a name for himself in the Diet in that short time. You people can provide the chance for him to make that name. Doesn't that give him a fine opportunity?" We clapped our hands in delight.

When we went to Haizan's residence to explain our secret plot and asked him for his help in purchasing weapons, he agreed immediately. "I have an incurable disease," he said; "I know my life cannot be very long. How fortunate for me, that I can follow you gentlemen and be entrusted with such a noble task! You may be sure that I will do my utmost." His sincerity and fervor seemed to match his words, and we were overjoyed to have found such comradeship. Little did we realize that the seeds of future disaster were being sown.

So Haizan set to work with us at once. The Filipino representative, Ponce, entrusted everything to Sun Yat-sen and didn't interfere himself at all. Hirayama and I were the contacts between Haizan and Sun. Then before very long, our activities were under police investigation again.

At that point the owner of the Taiyōkan took Hirayama and me aside in a separate room and said, "I don't know what you gentlemen are up to, but the police are watching you very closely. I hope you will be very careful." The same night we noticed a plainclothesman standing outside the gate. It was raining hard. Hirayama and I put our heads together, ordered separate rickshaws, and had them take a zigzag route at high speed to the Matsuei house of pleasure. We were pleased with our success, and thought we'd surely lost the plainclothesman. Then we called for Tomeka and another geisha to join us, but for some reason they didn't come. We were told that Tomeka's father had ordered her not to have anything to do with me. Since there was nothing we could do about this, we had to leave the selection of girls to the head madam. She was effusive in her assurances and assured us, "They'll be here any minute now!" But somehow they just didn't seem to show up. Then, when the clock struck twelve she came running up to us and said "Whatever have you gentlemen done! There are four detectives outside the house. Is it any wonder that the geisha turned back on their way to my house? Really, what have you done?" We realized then that we hadn't done as good a job of dodging the detectives as we thought we had, and that they had taken revenge on us. Hirayama and I had to sleep side by side, without company.

The next morning we got up early, called for geisha and for sake. The detectives, unable to stand the rain outside any longer, came in to talk with us. "Why don't you call a halt before you've had too much," they said, "and go back home? We caught cold out in the rain last night!" So we suggested they come upstairs to join us; the four of them sat around our table with us, drinking and singing. After the sake began to take effect, Hirayama called a rickshaw and headed for the licensed quarter. The plainclothesman assigned to him went with him. I went to the kabuki with the head madam and my detective, and then returned to my inn. The next morning Hirayama came back, but without his detective. He explained: "I invited my detective to accompany me to a brothel last night and engaged a girl for him for a night of pleasure, but another policeman found out and he was fired." Later we went to Inukai and told him the story. "That detective is down on his luck," he said with concern; "Let's see if we can't figure out something for him." I still derive pleasure from this.

In the meantime Nakamura was making progress with his work. He said the arms had been contracted for, and that all that remained was to locate a ship. He thought one comrade should go ahead, and recommended Hara Tadashi.[82] We didn't know him at that time. Hara was from Nagano, and he had been an army captain. He resigned his commission and decided to go to the Philippines with five men. Hirayama was to go along as the representative of our group.

Before all this, I had known Uchida Ryōhei[83] in Fukuoka. Uchida had cherished high ideals since his youth. As a member of the Ten'yūkyō he had been in Korea to work with the Tonghaks in the hope of starting a revolution. Later he had gone to Siberia and traveled between Vladivostok and St. Petersburg. We trusted each other immediately. At this time Uchida had come to Tokyo, where he stayed with his uncle Hiraoka Kōtarō. I had visited him and told him of my hopes and ambitions and he had reciprocated with honesty and sincerity, and promised to cooperate in the future. He now helped us quietly.

Then a sudden telegram came to Sun Yat-sen. His

[82] Hara, referred to by Miyazaki as Kondō Gorō, was an army officer with service on the General Staff before immersing himself in revolutionary and independence matters in the Philippines and China.

[83] Uchida (1874–1937), Fukuoka nationalist, was founder of the *Kokuryū-kai* (Amur, "Black Dragon" Society), and a powerful figure in activist circles in Korea and northeast Asia throughout his life.

followers in Kwangtung wanted to rise in revolt. Sun asked me to go there to evaluate the situation for him. So the way it worked out was that Uchida would head for Siberia again, and Kiyofuji was to go to Hunan. The three of us went together as far as Fukuoka, where Uchida said goodbye to me. At parting, he said to me, "When things are ready, just cable me 'Come!' " Now wasn't that a real comrade? Then, with prayers for safe journeys, we parted, I to Nagasaki and Kiyofuji to Kumamoto.

I waited for a ship in Nagasaki for a week. Kiyofuji had come from Kumamoto to see me off, when a servant of the inn informed me that a boat was about to sail for Hong Kong. I immediately said goodbye to Kiyofuji and boarded the ship. A day and a night after we had left port, I saw a peninsula on the starboard side. When I asked a sailor what it might be, I learned it was Cheju Island. I asked what we were doing there and only then discovered that our route was to be via Chefoo, Shanghai, Foochow, Amoy, and Swatow. Then when I asked how long all this would take, I found out that it would take eighteen days to reach Hong Kong. I was astounded and disappointed, but there wasn't anything that could be done about it. We reached Shanghai via Chefoo.

I had acquaintances in Shanghai, and there were many Japanese there. If this had been an ordinary trip a stay in Shanghai would have been very pleasant, but I was on an important mission, and tense, and stayed on board, idly waiting for the ship to sail again. As it happened one of the passengers who boarded for Foochow was an acquaintance of mine, and I was pleased to have his company. The time came for the ship to raise anchor again. Suddenly dark clouds covered the sky and the wind began to howl. When the ship was a few miles off Wusung, it stopped and the anchor was lowered.

There we sat for two days and nights, bobbing about on the ocean. Then the winds began to die down, and although the sea was still rough we headed for Foochow.

None of the other passengers dared eat, and I was the only one to drink my beer and finish my dinner. When I went out on deck, the sun was setting over the clouds and waves and the evening sky was ominous. My spirit rose in exaltation. I could not resist taking up a pencil and jotting down these lines in my pocket notebook. The lines lack balance, but they show what was in my mind and heart.

> The sun has set,
> A bleak wind penetrates my frame
>
> The turbulence of waves
> The passengers descend below
> Above, the call of flying geese,
> Vast sky and ocean; in between, I alone
> The bell! Has midnight come?
> My mother, in our native place
> My anxious wife and children,
> Their bedding thin, their panels tattered;
> What dreams have they?
> Wind, blow gently!
> Grant them quiet sleep.
>
> Clouds have come!
> White waves; will it be rain or snow?
> A moonless night, and no one knows;
> I feel no direction in this blackened night
> Impatient as I am,
> I see what may be mount, or only cloud
> Floating on so turbulent a sea
> When shall I reach port?
>
> Think not of it!
> For thirty years of struggle
> Have I pursued this dream
> A single night or hundred years for me
> Are both a single dream
> The future of this life of mine is like
> The hope to see the moon tonight.

I know nothing of rhyme, of Chinese poems or Japanese verse. This was the first time I had composed one. Was it my premonition or heaven's dispensation? When the ship arrived in Foochow, a sailor told me that a ship called the Nunobiki Maru had sunk off Shanghai the day before. He said it was a Mitsui vessel, but of course I had no way of knowing that it had any connection with our group.

After leaving Foochow we went on to Amoy to Swatow, and then finally reached Hong Kong. It had taken us twenty-two days for the journey. I spent my days on board in talk and drink, and ran up a bill of 23.30 yen for beer alone. My talk was all about Tomeka, my love. I still knew nothing of the disaster that had befallen us.

I arrived in Hong Kong and registered at the Tōyōkan. The first thing I did was drink to my safe arrival, and while I was exchanging toasts with the innkeeper and his staff a friend appeared. He was a Mitsui employee. I said it was a shame that they had lost the Nunobiki Maru, but he seemed quite indifferent. "Oh," he said, "that ship had been sold just twenty days earlier to Nakamura Haizan. So the loss is all his." His answer pierced my heart, for now I realized that this was our project. Nevertheless, I tried to stay calm, and said to him, "That was good luck for you, wasn't it?" But I was in such agony that I could hardly keep my seat. If this was really Nakamura's ship not only was our cargo lost, but two close friends must have gone down to watery graves. I finally found a pretext to excuse myself and rushed off to the home of Ch'en Shao-pai.

I came directly to the point without small talk or apologies for not having kept in touch. The minute I saw Ch'en I told him about my fears. He was quiet for a little while, and then answered sorrowfully "It may be as you fear. Let's go together to see a representative of the Philippine Independence Committee to find out." We called rickshaws, went to Wanchai, and asked to see Mr. A. P. He took us to a place where we could talk in secret. The three of us sat quietly and said nothing for a time. A. P.

was clearly not his usual pleasant self. Finally Ch'en started the talk, and asked him if there had been a cable from Japan. A. P. shook his head, then mumbled for a while, and finally decided to answer. "Yes, a cable did come yesterday, but parts of it don't make sense and I do not understand it. But as far as I can make out it does seem that something unfortunate has happened. Because I'm not sure, though, I have not shown it to my comrades." Then, when we explained our fears and told him that we had come to find whether there was substance to them or not, he quickly asked what the name of the ship in question was. "Nunobiki Maru," I answered. He jumped up, slammed his hand on the table, and shouted "That's it! It has to be!" Suddenly his eyes filled with tears. He said nothing more. We were all silent now; it was quiet as the grave. After a while, A. P. opened his mouth again. "There are still two words I can't make out," he said, "I think they are probably Japanese names." "Could they be Takano and Hayashi?" I asked. He clapped his hands and said, "Yes, that's it. It seems to me the cable says that the two of them were drowned and that the pilot, who was a Filipino, was saved." Now he could no longer control his tears. He covered his face with his handkerchief. "How terrible that Heaven did not favor us!" he sobbed, "It was my responsibility to acquire weapons, and this is the third time I have failed. I have lost a considerable amount of money in this as well. How can I ever face our president and people again? The only way I can make up for this is to commit suicide to apologize for my crimes." His appearance and his words were equally agonized. Yet the rest of his group didn't know the story yet.

It was impossible to look on this scene without tears. Least of all for us who were involved in the matter, and especially for me, who had now learned of the tragic death of two comrades. After a while Ch'en raised his head and tried to console A. P. "Revolutionaries have always had to overcome many difficulties," he said, "now and in the past.

Are you going to let this incident break you? It is easy enough for you to put yourself to death. It might even be a good choice from your own point of view. But what about the tens of thousands of your comrades who are fighting on the battlefields? What you do affects the destiny of the Philippines—ruin or rise. Do not be too hasty in making up your mind." I too tried to take heart myself, and then tried to encourage him. Gradually he recovered his spirit a little and said he would not decide before giving it twenty-four hours' consideration. I advised him against telling the story to his comrades in the Philippines, and then Ch'en and I left.

Two days later we visited him again. A. P. looked a little less distraught than he had. "I called a meeting of my comrades in Hong Kong. I asked them what I should do and how we ought to plan the future, and I told them the advice you two had given me. Everybody there wanted us to make another attempt to get weapons. I beg you, and the comrades in your countries, to help for the sake of our group." We were very much encouraged to hear him talk like this. We continued working with them. But what was the sequel? Alas, how was it all to end?

The Nunobiki Maru had sunk. Takano and Hayashi had been killed at their post of duty. What about Hara, Hirayama, and the others?

A Western-language newspaper in the Philippines reported that six Japanese military men had landed in Manila and made their way inland. There was a rumor that two of them had been captured and that the others were missing. Japanese merchants in the Philippines, it went on, had begun to leave, one after another. Because they were suspected of hiding Japanese army men, they were being arrested by the American military frequently; a number were in prison, and no Japanese merchants were able to do much business. Rumors like this went the rounds, everyone whispering, "This is secret, it's a secret story," until they reached me. But no rumor could be trusted, and I wore my spirits out trying to verify them. Neither Setsurei nor Komako was in Hong Kong. The only sources of comfort I had were sake, and Masako. And Tanaka, Komako's husband, understood my problem and did everything he could to bring me rumors and leads.

One day he came hurrying into my room and said, "A man who traveled together with Hirayama has just disembarked and registered. His name is Kiuchi. He says he has heard of you, but that he hasn't made your acquaintance yet. He asked me not to tell you about his arrival; please think about this." The man in question was one of Hara's companions, a man I hadn't met. I took out a name card of mine, and asked Tanaka to take it to Kiuchi requesting a meeting. Kiuchi agreed. I went up to his room on the fourth floor and entered. When I asked him about the situation in Manila, his reply was very ambiguous. Since he could see I had some connection with the movement, it was hard for him not to respond with something to my question, but to say too much might endanger the trust of his comrades. I too pretended not to know very much about the matter, and asked him if he knew anything about Hirayama and Hara. He looked very embarrassed, and finally answered, "No, I really don't." I went back to my room. After a bit Tanaka came to my room and asked how things had gone. Instead of telling him, I asked him to bring in sake and food, and then had him bring Kiuchi in, explaining that I wanted to show my hospitality in a toast to him for the long trip he had completed. Kiuchi declined, explaining that he did not drink. When I pressed him a second and a third time he finally gave in. After we had exchanged cups and drank to each other several times, he began to get tipsy. I kept drinking and singing, meanwhile passing him one large sake cup after another. His spirits rose as he drank, until he was beginning to feel quite happy. Then I got the others to leave and talked with him directly. "I respect the way you keep faith with your comrades," I said, "Your conduct makes you a shining example of Japanese army men; this is in fact a new experience for me. I suspect you already realize that I am somehow involved in this matter. I don't know how long it has been that rumors and stories have been worrying my spirit. Won't you take pity on me and tell me about the fate of my comrades?" Now he finally relaxed and began to talk. He described for me how they had gone from Manila into the interior to President Aguinaldo's headquarters, and told it so graphically it was almost like seeing it all. "Hara and Hirayama," he said, "were the only two to meet with the president. The rest of us were not let in on all the details. I have been ordered back home to relay the word of an urgent need for weapons. Three of us were ordered back for this. I don't fully understand this, but decided I had to obey the orders of my section commander. When I started on the homeward path, Hirayama gave me letters to carry back to Inukai and Sun Yat-sen. On the way, though, I burned the letters because I was afraid of being captured and getting into serious trouble on that account. On the way out I became separated from the other two. If they haven't been captured, they've been unusually fortunate." This story relieved my anxiety for Hirayama a little.

Nevertheless, I was worried by the way he talked. He seemed to have some resentment toward Hara and Hirayama. He seemed to be asking himself, "I know I have to obey my section commander's orders. But why would he have dispatched three comrades to carry the message about an urgent need for weapons? Hasn't he kept me at arm's length while pretending to flatter me with an important mission?" Although I tried to reassure him and reason with him on the matter, nothing seemed to relieve his anxiety.

Only later did I find out why I hadn't been able to reassure him. He had read the letters he was carrying and found that they contained the recommendation that the three men be demoted, and consequently he had burned them. I had no idea of this, and I trusted him with a letter to Nakamura Haizan in which I warned Haizan about my doubts about him; explaining that he seemed to harbor some kind of resentment and might well give our plans away to some outsider, and that he should be treated carefully if we expected to be able to call on him again. Since Kiuchi had already read the letters from Hirayama and Hara (before burning them), he undoubtedly read mine too. I must say that was stupid of me. Still, we have reason to be grateful to him, for he controlled himself and kept from getting back at us by revealing the details of our plans to other people.

[21] A DRAMATIC CHANGE

SHORTLY BEFORE THIS A LETTER FROM OUR comrade in Hunan, Pi Yung-nien, arrived with the news that the top leader of the *Ko-lao hui* would be in Hong Kong soon accompanied by several of his men. Ch'en Shao-pai suggested that I wait for them in Hong Kong rather than proceed to inland China for the observation Sun Yat-sen had asked me to undertake. Then one day Ch'en came to me and said, "The *Ko-lao hui* group has arrived, but Pi is not with them." He showed me a letter from Pi that introduced the group to Ch'en and to me. The letter added short accounts of each member of the group, and made them sound like heroes in the *Three Kingdoms* and the *Water Margin*. Before long we met Mr. N. and Mrs. M., two leaders of the group. They behaved in strangely old-fashioned ways that were completely different from those of modern scholars. One of them said, "These days the world is opening up rapidly, and national sentiment is very different from what it used to be. How can our society expect to retain its old ways? That is why we have come here to learn from you." They hinted at a plan to have the three secret societies—*San-ho hui*, *Ko-lao hui*, and *Hsing-Chung hui*, unite into a single party with Sun Yat-sen as its leader. "We do not know a great deal about things abroad," the man went on. "And if we were to raise the banner of revolt without sufficient deliberation we might invite some unexpected disaster that would take a century to overcome. It is because we do not have among our members anyone familiar with the outside world that we are relying on Sun Yat-sen. We want to talk this over as soon as Pi arrives." Wonderful! This was exactly what we had been hoping for, the dream of all these years! And here it came, not from us, but from him. How perfect! Of course it was not entirely accidental either. Hirayama's trip to Hunan the year before had started it all and Pi Yung-nien's work since then had set it into motion.

Unfortunately Pi Yung-nien, who was central to this, was now stuck in Shanghai without boat fare. After consulting with Ch'en I sent him what he needed, and urged him to join us.

Pi arrived. Before the meeting to discuss unification of the secret societies opened, Shih ______ and Liu ______ both of them *Ko-lao hui* chiefs, also arrived from Shanghai. The others were all suspicious of Shih, however, because they thought he was a collaborator with K'ang Yu-wei's group, and they wanted him excluded. I was afraid that if we left him out he might give our plans away, and persuaded them to treat him cordially in order to secure his good will. One day when Ch'en and I went to the place where the secret society leaders were staying we found Shih not there; he had gone to Canton. When he came back his face was flushed with excitement. "An urgent message just reached Canton," he said, "our comrades in the Yangtze Valley have risen. We leaders are all here. If we do not rush back to take charge and control our people, they could get into real trouble. Those of you who want to stay here can do so, but I for one am worried by this news, and do not feel that I can stay any longer." And with that he started collecting his things in a great hurry. The others became restless. Some said, "We've got to go back!" while others argued, "Let's wait for more details!" Still others said, "It's probably just a rumor." The argument went on and on without coming to any conclusion. Ch'en looked at me, and asked me how to solve this problem. I got up and spoke to them as follows: "I feel sure that this story has no basis in fact, and that it was made up by someone on purpose. It can't be true. If there were anything to it, I would have had word from my comrades there, and the Japanese consulate would certainly have had word of it. But my comrades have sent no word. Nor has the consulate had any word. That's why I conclude that it is false. But if you gentlemen are genuinely uneasy about it, let me cable my comrades there, so that you can make up your minds whether to go or stay on the basis of the answer I get. After all, haven't you gentlemen come a great distance to meet here for the purpose of working out a grand design of high purpose for the long future? Are you going to set it aside incomplete on the basis of this one rumor? That does not seem what one would expect from great men. I beg of you to be calm and to reconsider. If anyone is unable to do this, let him go. But if not, I beg you to wait for the reply to my inquiry." Shih looked crestfallen and said nothing. The others clapped their hands and backed my suggestion and decided to wait for the answer to my telegram. There upon I left and went back to my inn.

Shih's tactics in this had been like those of conspirators in the era of the Warring States. Having worked with the K'ang partisans, his real purpose was to divide them from Sun Yat-sen's group. Knowing this, I decided I would have to do a little conspiring of my own. Of course I did nothing about sending a telegram. Instead, I scribbled a whole series of meaningless numbers on a piece of paper the next day, pretended to have received a coded cable, and put their minds at ease. They were taken in. They denounced Shih and urged that he be excluded prior to the opening of serious discussions on unification. But I still thought it would be unwise to antagonize Shih. After talking it over with Ch'en, I provided travel money for him to return to the mainland on the pretext of controlling his followers. Before he left he came to see me and said, "It seems that some people do not trust me. But actually I make no distinction between K'ang's group and Sun's group in my heart. The only thing I hope for is their full cooperation in order to speed the day of revolution. I hope that you understand my feelings." I organized a farewell party for him, and provided a little money from my own small budget as a farewell gift so that he would feel better about things. After this he headed for Shanghai, where he joined T'ang Ts'ai-ch'ang[84] in his planning for a rebellion. He was later captured and executed. Truly, it is hard to know what lies in wait in the affairs of men.

With Shih gone, everybody relaxed. Immediately they began the talks for unification of the secret societies. The total number of participants in the conference was twelve. They included: from the *Ko-lao hui*: Li Yun-piao, Chief, T'englungshan Branch; Yang Hung-chün, Chief, ______ shan Branch; Ku Hung-en, Chief, ______ shan Branch; Ku Jen-chien, Chief, ______ shan Branch; Li Ho-sheng, ______'s right-hand man; Shih Hsiang, ______'s right-hand man; Chang Jao, ______'s subordinate. From the *San-ho hui* there were Tseng Chieh-fu, head, and Tseng Yi-hsiang. From the *Hsing-Chung hui* there were Ch'en Pai (Ch'en Shao-pai), Cheng Shih-liang, and Yang Chü-yun.[85] The time was ripe, and it did not take very long to reach agreement. Sun Yat-sen was to be the leader, the organization was to be named the Rise, Chinese Party [*Hsing-Han hui*]. They agreed on three articles of incorporation, swore to this in sips of pigeon blood, designed a seal, and sent it to Sun. I had never taken part in anything quite so wonderful before. I have not begun to describe it here. It may well affect the lives of men far into the future.

[84] T'ang (1867-1900), Hunan revolutionary who was central to plans for union with the secret societies. He was killed in a 1900 revolutionary *putsch* in the Yangtze Valley.

[85] Tōten, writing at a time the Ch'ing empire still existed, protected the conspirators by leaving names and places incomplete.

The deliberations for unification of the revolutionary movement concluded, I invited everybody to a Japanese restaurant for a feast. The guests totaled sixteen with four outsiders in addition to the original twelve. I had ordered the restaurant to provide each guest with a raw carp. All the guests were queasy about this. One asked whether it was meant for decoration or for eating. In answer I picked it up with my chopsticks, pulled back some skin, and ate a piece of the meat. I asked them to do the same, but they just looked at me and didn't make a move to use their chopsticks. I explained to them: "In Japan this is a customary courtesy tendered to samurai who are about to go off to battle. Your three societies are now one, united in an organization that is going to spark a revolution to oust the Manchu barbarians. So this is really a party for you who depart for the battle, is it not? Won't you follow my example and eat?" My guests finally began to use their chopsticks and began to nibble. The raw fish was very fresh, and sometimes pieces moved and even popped off the plates. There was soon a pleasant chatter of astonishment. We toasted each other, and ended by becoming quite drunk. One of my guests asked me, "How do Japanese drink sake?" "We show close friendship by exchanging sake cups and drinking to each other," I explained. Next he wanted to do this with me. I agreed. He passed me a large bowl of almost a pint capacity and I ceremoniously drained it. The others thought this quite wonderful and each drank in turn and passed it back to me. I downed it again, a second and third time. I was so full of sake that it was almost running out of the corners of my mouth. I retired to another room, bent over, and out came the sake with the force of a waterfall. After wiping my face, I returned to my place at the banquet table. They wanted to toast me again, and so the process went on. Each time I would go to the other room to vomit. In the course of four such trips, I managed to exchange bowls with all sixteen of my guests. They did not realize that I was unloading in the next room, and by now they held me in respect as a more formidable drinker than Li Po. Later in the evening I invited those who were game for more to accompany me to a Japanese brothel. It had a rule against serving Chinese, but the madam relaxed the regulations for this occasion and extended her hospitality. Bless her! She is a good friend. In fact, I still have a considerable bill there that I never paid, and I feel guilty about it.

Shortly afterward the group departed. They divided into three parties: one went to Kwangtung and Kwangsi, another to Fukien and Chekiang, and the third to Shanghai. They were all on their way to report the results of the conference to their comrades. But I did not go on to Canton and inland China, but decided to return to Japan with Ch'en Shao-pai. I wanted to tell Sun about our progress, and I wanted to present him with his new seal as head of the organization.

The day before I was scheduled to leave Hong Kong, a young man came to see me. He was under twenty, and so slender and attractive that he resembled a heavenly maiden. He bowed with great courtesy without even verifying my name and presented his card with a smile. I accepted it, and saw that his name was Shih Chien-yu.[86] I had never heard it. "Sir," he said, "my elder brother will probably come to call on you today. If he does, I would appreciate it if you would tell him that you plan to take me to Japan with you. Mr. Ch'en Shao-pai can explain it to you." I agreed, without knowing what it was all about. A little later Ch'en Shao-pai came with the explanation. "This is a very high-spirited young man," he said. "He decided he wanted to go to Shanghai and then on to Hunan and Hupeh in the company of the *Ko-lao hui* comrades, but his elderly mother and his elder brother would not permit him to do so. But the family head had heard of you and greatly

[86] Shih Chien-ju (1879-1900), Kwangtung revolutionary who was to die in the Huichou rebellion, was widely praised as a person of charm and sincerity.

admired the gallantry with which you had helped K'ang Yu-wei. So the young man took advantage of this and used your trip as an excuse by telling them he wanted to go to Japan as a student. This they permitted, and his brother is going to come to express the family's thanks to you. They were afraid that if you were not tipped off to this in advance the whole scheme would come apart. So I hope you will be tolerant and cooperate." I was impressed by Shih's shrewdness, and asked him about his motivation in all this. "Sir," he replied, "I believe the world is a single family and that all men are equal. Consequently I have always been an admirer of Dr. Sun Yat-sen's noble character, and I have been eager to work under his direction to implement his goals. Yet I have not yet had the privilege of meeting him personally. Recently I had the good fortune to meet Mr. Ch'en; I discovered that his goals were no different from mine, and I resolved to devote myself to his cause. Then I happened to learn of the unification of the three secret societies. Unable to contain my enthusiasm, I was burning with eagerness to go to Hunan and Hupeh to investigate their activities there and involve myself with them in preparation for my future contribution to the cause. Unfortunately my elder brother lacks the courage of his convictions; we agree in principle, but he is too cautious to take any risk. If I were to tell him the truth he would be so terrified that he would never allow me to leave. That's why I used your name as a way of getting his permission. I know I must seem unfilial and unfraternal in deceiving my family in this way, but I really believe it is filial and fraternal of me to do it this way in order to keep them from worrying about me. I do hope I will have your understanding in this."

What was the secret of this youth's confident idealism? He told me himself: "I am a Christian, therefore I believe in a single Heavenly Father who loves all human beings as His children. And that is why I deplore the present state of the world with its survival of the fittest, and yearn for the fulfillment of the great principles of liberty and equality." When young Shih talked about his country's troubles he stressed the necessity of revolution. His rhetoric was remarkably confident and his logic was irrefutable. He was particularly striking in his analysis of contemporary China. "Someone who kills another deserves a sentence of death. Is it not just as serious a crime to kill the people's spirit and stunt their intelligence? That is exactly what the present dynasty is doing." And again, "The highest circles in our government are doing this. People who aspire to high office now want only to keep ordinary people stupid and bleed them. The path to office is through the examination system. But in China today those who follow this path do so in order to practice evil and selfish exploitation, and not to rule the country and order society by regulating themselves. No river can run pure if its upper streams are polluted. Such a country must inevitably decline, however some may seek to save it." And again, "There are people who talk about reform. But they can never be moved from talk to action. For those who really seek to bring about reconstruction, it will be necessary to cleanse the people's spirit with blood. Without that, it will all remain idle talk." He was not even twenty! And yet he had such maturity, and such a firm and integrated view. I was astonished by the clarity of his understanding and the practicality of his grasp. He was fully determined to travel to Hunan and Hupeh. I was equally impressed by his inflexible will. Consequently we became fast friends and pledged to work together in the future.

That same evening I was drinking with my friends at the Nomura Restaurant. As the sake took effect, I began to sing. Suddenly someone shouted my name and opened the door to the room we were in. I looked at the man without recognizing him. I studied him, and still couldn't bring him into focus. He, meanwhile, took off his shoes and came into our room. He grasped my hand and said, "You mean to say you don't recognize me?" Then suddenly I knew: it was Hirayama. He had had his hair cut very short (before, it had been long), his beard shaved off: his white clothes were dirty, and he looked like a nondescript sailor. We were both speechless. Then, since others were present, we felt it best to wait with talk until later, and drank instead. Much later the two of us staggered off to a brothel and fell into a drunken sleep.

The next morning we woke up early. Hirayama told me about the Philippine adventure, how he had managed to extricate himself from great danger, and come back. I told him what had happened since we had parted, and why I was now going back to Japan. I also suggested that, now that I had to return, he might go inland to Kwangtung province to carry out Sun's mission in my place. We discussed the work that lay ahead for us, and then headed back for the inn.

Shih and Ch'en were there waiting for me. Before long Shih's elder brother came. I saw immediately that he was a warm and trustworthy person. He expressed his gratitude to me for my kindness to his younger brother, and asked me to look out for him; indeed he seemed to trust me completely. How could I keep from feeling somewhat pained by this? But I had already sworn a life-and-death oath with the younger brother. Was I to let personal emotions interfere with high purpose? So I encouraged myself, and helped Shih to deceive his brother.

As soon as the ship raised anchor and sailed for Shanghai, Shih lost his appetite; he had never been at sea before. But his spirits never fell. He took up a brush, sketched a picture on the back of my *haori*, and said it was my souvenir from him. Alas, how was I to know that this would indeed become my memory of him? When the ship docked at Shanghai I went ashore with Shih, visited with *Ko-lao hui* comrades to tell them about Shih, and asked them to take care of this fine young fellow. I also went to the Tōa Dōbunkai[87] and met Kiyofuji there. I persuaded him to come to a Japanese restaurant with me, and we drank the night away before I returned to the ship.

After a few more days the ship arrived in Yokohama. There we went to Sun Yat-sen's house and told him everything, from the sad fate of the Nunobiki Maru to the plans for a new insurrection in China. Sun said, "Our plans for the insurrection are complete, but the Japanese government is watching us so carefully that we are unable to get our supplies out of the country." What Sun said pleased us, and he in turn was bouyed up by the news that Ch'en said I brought for him. So, far from being dispirited, we were happy and flushed with the hope of new successes. We returned to Tokyo, where we once again registered at the Taiyōkan.

I had not seen Suenaga Setsu since our adventures in Siam. One day he came to see me at the Taiyōkan. He was now using a different name from the one he had used at that time. When he saw me he smiled with pleasure, and said, "You're still at it, aren't you! But that Nunobiki Maru thing was too bad. I came close to sailing on that myself. I had heard about the matter from Uchida Ryōhei, and I was all set to go when I was delayed by a fever. That was good luck!" He was entirely relaxed, completely his old self, and he put me quite at ease. "Well," he went on, "what are you planning to try next?" Again, he was detached and impersonal about it. I answered, "Oh, we're just going to try to implement J. S. Mill's *On Liberty* in China." He burst out laughing. "However are you going to do that? That's going to take a lot of capital." "Well," I answered, "if we were going to do a thorough job there's no limit to what we'd need. But actually a thousand rifles is

[87] Founded in 1898 by Prince Konoe Atsumaro for the promotion of cultural and commercial relations between Japan and China, with the establishment of stations and offices in regional centers and a major educational institution (Dōbun Shoin) in Shanghai.

a lot, and even that isn't easy to come by. If we have to, we'll just have to resort to banditry to steal money." And with that I told him about the unification of the three secret societies. Suenaga clapped his hands and said, "Are you that far along! I'd like to work with you on this! But you can always resort to banditry if you have to. It would be better to try to attract some capital legally first." He then proposed a plan, and introduced me to Nakano Tokujirō. Nakano provided five thousand yen, and that became the starting point for the Huichou [Waichow] Rebellion. From this time Suenaga too moved into the Taiyōkan Inn, and it became the conspiratorial lair for revolutionaries.

Sun Yat-sen had now decided to start an insurrection. One day he came to the Taiyōkan, fretting impatiently, and said, "The preparations for another try in the Philippines are now ready. But we are under observation by the government because of the last incident, and there is no telling when we will be able to ship any guns out again. In view of that the Philippine revolutionary committee has agreed to let us use the guns instead. There is neither first nor last in a single cause of great virtue. If our party seizes the opportunity to launch a revolutionary army, it can realize longstanding goals. And if we succeed it should also lead to independence for the Philippines." With Nakano's pledge of help in hand, Sun's optimism grew by leaps and bounds. "It's time to get rough," he said. From this time on every day was filled with rushing about and planning. Suenaga said to me, "There is a compatriot of mine from Fukuoka named Fukumoto Nichinan.[88] He's over forty, and although he works as a writer I don't believe he is satisfied with that. How would it be if we tried to recruit him for this, so that he could still make a name for himself through great deeds? This would give him that

[88] Fukumoto (1857-1921) was a prolific writer and journalist who traveled widely in Asia before settling down as publisher of the *Kyūshū Nippō*. Somewhat older than the others, and perhaps wealthier, he clearly assumed a commanding stature among the adventurers.

opportunity." I took this up with Sun Yat-sen, who also liked the idea. Thereupon Suenaga and I went to visit Fukumoto at his house, revealed our secret plans to him, and asked for his participation. He promptly gave his approval, saying "That would be a fine way to die." We were deeply impressed. Then, after consulting the others, I sent a cable to Uchida Ryōhei in Vladivostok asking him to join us as he had promised to do.

It was unfortunate that at this time none of us had any money. But for the nobility of the Taiyōkan manager we would not even have had food and drink. Is there anything as expensive as not having enough money? If I had had some coins in my pocket I would have been able to hail a rickshaw on the street. He could have waited for me, and I could have eaten simply. But because I didn't have such coins I had to lease one on contract for my affairs. Anybody seeing me would have thought I was a person of influence. So many sessions had to be held at good restaurants that our debts piled up, and I became a burden to the good-hearted manager of the Taiyōkan. In all the world there is probably nothing so inconvenient as bills. If I weren't careful about leaving they would think I was trying to get away and try to catch me, or they'd send somebody to speak to me. To keep going meant drinking, and drinking made the bills worse. That was why I did so much of my drinking at the Matsuei. The reader will see that I had several concerns at this time. On the one hand there was my love, the geisha Tomeka, on the other the management of the Chinese revolution. Each enabled me to relax from the cares of the other, and to marshal my courage and work diligently. And as a matter of fact all sorts of preparations were coming along in the meantime.

Uchida Ryōhei also arrived. He settled in at his uncle Hiraoka's house and sent word to meet him there. I hurried over in my rickshaw. When I started to fill him in on all the details to get his approval he interrupted me with "I don't want to hear any more about it. Everything that's been done is fine. But what is it that you still need? What do you want me to do?" I must say one word like that is worth a fortune. Right away I asked him if he would not organize and lead a group of adventurers to help Sun Yat-sen. "Fine," he said. One word, but what weight it carried! I had no way to thank him. With this we went along to the Taiyōkan and put our heads together to discuss managing the affair. Uchida started lining up his group, quietly making preparations for what lay ahead.

Meanwhile Kiyofuji returned from Hankow, intent upon the same business. Efforts to collect funds for military equipment had struck a snag and were behind schedule. After talking it over we went to Kyushu to try to make up the difference; Fukumoto, Uchida, Suenaga, Kiyofuji and I headed for Fukuoka. We were there the better part of a month, with Shimada Keiichi[89] and Uchida doing wonderful work for us. When we had collected several thousand yen we returned to Tokyo. By then Hirayama was back from Hong Kong, and Captain Hara from the Philippines. The Taiyōkan became more of a conspirators' lair than ever.

The Taiyōkan also became busier and more prosperous than before. But as the proverb has it, "if there are so many people the very mountains eat"; how much more with one little inn! And again, how much more so when applied to a few thousand yen worth of military funds! If one is fortunate enough to put a few thousand yen together, and then people eat it up, there will be nothing left for military expenditures. It follows, then, as day follows night, that more money has to be raised. It can be seen what kind of pressure we were under. Consequently Sun Yat-sen came up with the suggestion, "We're wasting our time this way. The situation is getting worse, and we're not doing any good. Let's get things started." We agreed, and it was decided.

[89] Shimada (1866-1927), a Fukuoka-Hakata nationalist close to Hiraoka Kōtarō with a record of educational and commercial efforts on the continent.

[22]

OUR EXPEDITION TO THE SOUTH

SUN YAT-SEN ASKED HIRAYAMA TO GO ON TO Hong Kong and wait for our group there. There were six in our party: Sun Yat-sen, Cheng,[90] Ch'en, Kiyofuji, Uchida, and I. Fukumoto and Hara were to take the next ship, and Shimada and Suenaga decided to remain in Fukuoka and bring their men to join us when Sun Yat-sen's preparations were complete.

Once our departure date was set and we were about to leave, the thing that was most on my mind was my Tomeka. She had been living with me and taking care of me for several months. I was able to give her almost nothing in the way of support, and couldn't even provide pin money. Although it pained me to see how little she had, it was impossible for me as a man to give a woman anything from our war chest. It was also impossible for me to disclose our secret plans to her. The conflicting claims of duty and love are agonizing indeed. So I deceived her by saying I was going to Kyushu. We parted: I went to Yokohama and there boarded the Nihon Maru for Hong Kong. I could not take my mind off her, even in my dreams. After we left Nagasaki I wrote her a letter to say

[90] Cheng Shih-liang (?-1901), Kwangtung native, acquainted with Sun Yat-sen for many years, began as a member of *San-ho hui* and was involved in the 1895 Canton revolt. After the Huichou failure he went to Hong Kong, where he was killed, either in a traffic accident or by poison.

that I was bound for Hong Kong, and mailed it in Shanghai; this eased my mind a little. I had a wife I had married during our struggling days ten years earlier, three beloved children by her, and an elderly mother almost eighty years of age, but now my thoughts were all of Tomeka. What was one to make of this?

I did not expect to return from this trip. Therefore I thought more than once about returning first to my home to bid farewell to my mother and my wife and children. Although it may seem that I was heartlessly nonchalant about this, the reverse was actually the case: I could not trust myself to do it. Having resolved on death, I did not have the courage to look my aged mother in the face. My family had fallen into extreme poverty; my wife and the children had had to move in with her family, and I simply lacked the courage to see and experience those conditions in person. The actions of a coward often resemble those of someone with courage. That was the case with me. When my spirits flagged I called for sake, and when my heart was pained I relied on Tomeka. How can this behavior be confused with the way of a hero? Yes, sake was my stimulant, and Tomeka my solace.

I put Tomeka's picture up in my cabin in the ship. The French cabin boy saw it, and asked who that might be. My mistress, I explained. Thereafter every morning when I went up on deck while he cleaned the cabin I would come back to find that he had put the picture upside down to tease me. I don't know what he meant by this, but I do know that my emotions were at cross purposes.

However, I know that my love did not bring happiness. I could not help having doubts about the lasting nature of love and therefore I could not be enslaved by it. In view of this I had to rely on impersonal thoughts about higher virtue. I was at ease with the affirmation of higher principles. That is the reason I was setting forth on this pursuit. I was supposed to be exhilarated by this course, but then why did dark clouds remain in my heart, and why was I unable to repress feelings of agony and pain at times? I had three children, a wife who was not well, and an aged mother. I was concealing ordinary emotions of family loyalty and love. Neither love nor sake could suffice to overcome those emotions. It was only when we had secret meetings on board, planning our future steps, that I was able to forget those concerns and relish the blue sky and broad ocean. You could say that my spirit hadn't died completely yet.

Yes. Shipboard was a splendid place for secret meetings. There were no policemen to watch and no detectives to follow us. There was a policeman from Tokyo Metropolitan Headquarters on board, but he was a strange sort of fellow; he loved to play cards with Kiyofuji and me, and there was no need to worry about him. Sun Yat-sen laid down the general policy that was to be followed in the future. "I cannot land at Hong Kong because I have been expelled under provisions of the Public Security Law there, so I will go straight to Saigon and wait until Fukumoto arrives there, at which time we can proceed to Singapore together. Uchida, Kiyofuji, and Miyazaki should land at Hong Kong and take care of things there. After you're through come straight to Singapore; when you get there we will review the entire situation, and then make plans for further action. If we see the likelihood of being able to collect funds for a war chest we will spend some time there doing that; if not, we will turn back right away to enter Kwangtung." That was his plan. I proposed one plan myself: "We ought to try to make friends with K'ang Yu-wei and work together with him on this." I knew that K'ang was in Singapore. Sun Yat-sen approved my idea, and the others agreed that we should try to form a common front.

Before this, when we were still in the Taiyōkan, Suenaga had said to me one day, "What should we do when this insurrection breaks out?" I said that Fukumoto should be in overall charge with Uchida acting as his chief of staff. "Do you really mean that?" Yes, I said, I did. He clapped his hands, and said that if that were really our plan then we were sure to succeed. Sun Yat-sen also spoke with me on shipboard: "I want you to be in overall charge of the Japanese section." I told him about my conversation with Suenaga about Fukumoto, but Sun wouldn't listen to me. I said to him, "The ideals we fight for are enough for me, but we should make provision for others who seek to die for glory rather than for ideals. Don't you think we should put Fukumoto, who is oldest among us and the most mature, in general change, and Uchida, who is young and full of spirit, in a position to achieve fame?" Sun agreed. My argument seems rather disrespectful to Fukumoto and Uchida. But that really is the way I felt at that time.

The ship reached Hong Kong. One Chinese gun boat came out to meet Sun Yat-sen. We wondered why it was meeting Sun. He refused to come forward, however, and instead sent Uchida, Kiyofuji, and me as his representatives. Why didn't Sun come forward himself, and what was it we were to do on his behalf?

Uchida, Kiyofuji and I boarded the Chinese gunboat. The person who met us was Mr. ______ , who had been an officer in the Peiyang fleet at the time of the Sino-Japanese War. There was also Mr. ______ , son of ______ . The only conversation we could manage was in my broken English. However, the three of us could give each other looks and laugh, and even talk about the future, and gradually we spoke quite freely to each other. Meanwhile, we were examining the lay of the land as we neared Canton; we entered some great mandarin's imposing estate about ten o'clock at night.

The host, Mr. Liu Hsüeh-hsün, came out to welcome us. I made the most eloquent speech of my life in my broken English, and when that didn't get through I took up a brush and wrote it down; by doing so, I was barely able to get an occasional nod from my host. What did I say? While I was in the full flow of my eloquence and sometimes filling a sheet with Chinese characters, Kiyofuji was choking with suppressed laughter, and Uchida took up a fan to hide his face. How could they behave like that! After a bit the banquet began. While we drank, while we ate, and while we talked, the gunboat was prepared for the return trip to our ship. Taking advantage of the darkness of the night, we returned to Hong Kong. It was now three A.M. As the gunboat entered Hong Kong harbor we saw that Sun's ship was raising anchor and about to sail for Saigon. We waved our hats and shouted, but to no avail. There was nothing we could do but turn our faces to the pier, go ashore, and head for the Tōyōkan. This whole affair was a little like a novel. But I am sorry I cannot explain it here, for it would affect the safety of other people.[91]

In Hong Kong we found Hirayama and also Ch'en Shao-pai in addition to my old friend Tamamizu Tsunekichi who was staying at the Tōyōkan on his way to Siam. He looked at me and said, "I'm completely out of travel money and can't move one way or another. Have you got anything interesting planned?" He had participated in Ōi Kentarō's plan for an insurrection in Korea in 1885, and so his history of participation in rebellions was a good deal longer than mine. Furthermore he said importantly, "I'm rather good at making bombs." So I answered him, "We may have something interesting. Why don't you go into the Chinese interior with me instead of going to Siam or returning to Japan? If you're interested, wait in Hong Kong until I come back from Singapore." He was delighted and answered, "You don't need to say another thing! I'll wait for you." This is how he joined our party. We remained in Hong Kong three days. Then, in line with Sun's orders, Uchida, Kiyofuji, and I headed for Singapore. It was at this time that the Boxer Rebellion was raging in North China and the treaty powers were taking steps to send their troops.

[91] In fact, however, Miyazaki does say more about it below, pp. 238-40.

We were all watching it closely and agreeing that things were becoming interesting.[92]

We arrived in Singapore, registered at the Matsuo Inn, and waited for Sun, Fukumoto, and their party. I knew no local people or Japanese in Singapore, but I did know K'ang Yu-wei, who was now living there in seclusion. And since it was one of the hopes of our trip to make contact with K'ang and his group, I wanted to see K'ang first of all so that I could introduce our group to him. Consequently I visited a man whose name was Ch'iu, who I had heard was K'ang's right-hand man, and asked him to help me get in touch with K'ang. He agreed right away, saying, "I'll take care of it myself and let you know what day would be convenient." I thanked him for his kindness, said goodbye, and went to my inn to wait for word. One day a Japanese named Kitamura, whom I had known earlier at Hong Kong, came to see me at my inn. He said he had come to Singapore recently, and was writing for K'ang's newspaper. Then, lowering his voice, he went on, "They say that assassins who are out to get K'ang have come from Japan. A number of K'ang's people think that your party is on such a mission. Isn't it terrible how suspicious these Chinese are?" Since he knew the story of my relationship with K'ang in detail, it never occurred to me that he could put any stock in these rumors. I just smiled and said, "That's impossible. You must be wrong." He didn't show any further suspicion; the conversation gradually changed to other topics, and after we drank for a while he left.

The next day a disciple of K'ang's named T'ang came to see me. He showed me a letter and said, "This is Mr. K'ang's present position. If you have any important business, please be in touch with me, and I will transmit it to Mr. K'ang immediately." When I looked at the letter he

[92] In 1900 the foreign powers strengthened their legation guards at Peking (May 28); an additional international force was attacked by a Boxer force on June 10: within a week the legations were under a siege broken by the foreign expeditionary force on August 14.

had shown me it turned out to be from K'ang to Ch'iu, with reference to my request for a meeting. The letter went as follows:

> "Miyazaki Tōten is my benefactor. Now that I know he is in Singapore, I would like to see him very much. I will make application to the government to request this immediately, but, as you know, the government's protection of me is so close that I almost feel as if I were in prison. Consequently I am not sure whether I will be able to see him or not. If it should prove that I am unfortunately unable to see him, would you please give him a hundred dollars for me as a farewell gift? As for the things Tōten wants to take up with me, please have my disciple T'ang learn those from him so that he can transmit them to me. As I have the fullest confidence in T'ang, Tōten can feel free to tell him even the most secret matters."

It seemed to me that however strict the English government's protection of K'ang might be, there was no reason for them to forbid his meeting with me if K'ang really wanted to. Yet here he was beginning by making provision for a farewell gift through Ch'iu. Did this mean he didn't want to see me, or was he taking the assassination threat Kitamura had talked about seriously, and feeling suspicious that I might in fact want to kill him? Hate begins with doubt, and hate goes on to paranoia. I answered with some agitation, "I wish you would tell this to Mr. K'ang for me. 'Are you doubting me on the basis of an idle rumor you heard on the street? If so, I'm the one who doesn't care about a meeting. How could I accept a hundred dollars from you? I am free, but you are in exile. The last thing I had in mind in coming to see you was getting some money. Quite the contrary: I wanted to provide support for you to show sympathy with your difficulties and to discuss things we might do in the future.' " T'ang saw that I was angry. He tried to explain on K'ang's behalf. But I wouldn't listen to him and he left rather depressed.

The next day Kitamura came to see me again. "The assassination story I told you about the other day seems to have become an obsession with K'ang's group," he said, "and it is clear that they suspect your group. I know a man named Ōshima who is close to K'ang's people. He told me that he happened to visit at Ch'iu's last night. He found a number of K'ang's followers sitting around discussing the assassination rumor and arguing the pros and cons of having K'ang meet with you. What bothered them was the fact that the relationship between you and K'ang is rather widely known, and they wondered whether K'ang's reputation might not suffer if he refused to meet you because he would be thought ungrateful. On the other hand, it might be dangerous for him to meet you. Ōshima became angry and argued that they were being very unfair to Japanese."

Listening to him I became angry too, and ended up writing this letter to K'ang:

> My Dear Friend K'ang Yu-wei:
>
> Word has come to me to the effect that your friends have warned you by cable of the departure of Japanese assassins from Yokohama for Singapore. Now it seems that you and your associates suspect Uchida, Kiyofuji, and me of being the assassins mentioned in that cable, and that you consequently refuse to meet with me quietly. On hearing this I was first amused, and then incredulous. I thought to myself, aren't we on very friendly terms together? That's why I laughed when I first heard of this rumor. But now I gather from what Mr. T'ang says that you may actually harbor some suspicion of me. That does create misgivings in my mind.
>
> In Japan we had one mad patriot who tried to slay the Russian emperor with his sword, and another

assaulted Li Hung-chang. It would be hard to count the number that have assassinated their own countrymen. Our country has had an abundance of such madmen; everybody knows this. But is it not also the case that men of high purpose of many lands have come and entrusted their lives to this country of mad patriots? And is it not also true that not one such has ever been assaulted by such a madman? I think that although our *bushidō* may have declined, some chivalry[93] remains. Chivalry! That is a quality that my countrymen revere, and it is also something that our group has set as a standard for itself. Surely, Sir, I do not need to detail the bonds that held us together at a time of national crisis. I have come a great distance in order to see you and to discuss in profound concern a grand design for the present situation. What could have prepared me for the fact that I should no longer regard yesterday's friend as a friend today? Or that I should be thought capable of such infamy? Such shifts of circumstances and pendulum swings of human emotion are like a dream and an illusion. They are truly devastating. My friend Fukumoto, who is also anxious to see Your Excellency, has already left Hong Kong and is on board a ship bound for Singapore. When he hears this upon his arrival, how will he feel? Alas, what am I to do? With whom am I to discuss the rise of Asia? To you, who were moved to tears by your emperor's favor but who cannot understand the loyalty of a friend, I respectfully bid farewell with this letter. May it go well with you."

I was not the only one to be angered by this suspicion of us; Uchida and Kiyofuji were angry too. We also were quite disappointed. Since K'ang was so narrow-minded we could not ask his cooperation in our great undertaking; thereafter we quietly watched his activities from a distance.

[93] *Kyō* (otokodate), has a "knightly" unselfishness in its classical usage.

Before all this, Uchida had abruptly announced that he was going home alone the day after we arrived in Singapore. When I asked him why, he had no particular reason and said only that he wanted to get back. Once he had made his decision there was no use in arguing with him. However, since we had sworn to give our lives together if necessary, and since Sun Yat-sen and Fukumoto had not even arrived yet to complete our plans, it seemed a little too much to have him leave without any reason at all. We didn't try to argue with him, but I just begged him not to do it. "Won't you at least wait until Sun and Fukumoto arrive?" I asked. He agreed, and postponed his return. But then, when a ship was scheduled to sail for Japan, although it was still three days before Sun and Fukumoto were due to arrive, Uchida suddenly changed his mind again and said he was going to go. He was so insistent about this that no one could stop him, so we bade him farewell with very little effort to dissuade him. At his departure he said, "Last night I had a strange dream." He went on to explain: "All of us were going off together. I got in a horse-drawn carriage first. The horse was frightened and bolted, and I was the only one who got to our destination. The rest of you were all left behind in difficulty in the road, and you came later after undergoing much hardship." With that Uchida got in the carriage together with his favorite geisha, Otaka, and headed for the pier. Who would have thought that his dream was a portent of what was to come?

[23]

ARRESTED IN SINGAPORE

KIYOFUJI AND I HAD GONE TO THE ENTRANCE OF our inn to see Uchida off. We came back to our room and, amazingly enough, put some of our papers and belongings in some kind of order, and then picked up a broom to clean things up a little ourselves. We said to each other "That's that!" and then Kiyofuji ordered the girl to cool some beer in preparation for the night's drinking. Then he called in the houseboy, who was named Yoshimura, and began to play *go* with him. I had no difficulty in keeping up with Kiyofuji when it came to drinking, but I had no comprehension of *go* at all. So I sat down in a nearby chair and started strumming on my *biwa* to pass the time. Then a Chinese coolie came shuffling in. Standing beside me, he said, "Is your name Miyazaki, sir?" I nodded. He bent his head and left. Then I heard someone wearing shoes coming. But the inn didn't allow shoes upstairs: I'd never heard them in the hall. Thinking this strange, I looked down the hall, and saw an enormous Westerner stooping to keep from bumping his head, coming toward me. On closer examination it was a policeman. He came closer and closer to the entrance of our room. As he stood there he straightened up, pointed a pistol in his right hand at me, and shouted "Quiet!" at the top of his lungs. I had no time to wonder what was happening to me, but I got up and shouted at him. He put his pistol away and seized my hand; another fellow came along and grabbed the other hand, and the two of them dragged me down the hall. They searched me for dangerous weapons. All I had on was a thin short gown. I didn't even have a loincloth on; where on earth would I have carried a weapon? They grunted "All right, all right," and let me go back into the room. By now five or six policemen had come in, one after another; two of them sat facing me on chairs. Then I realized this had to do with the story about Japanese assassins.

The first thing I said was, "Aren't you mistaking me for somebody else?" In answer one of them pulled out a warrant, showed it to me, and said, "Is this your name?" Yes, I agreed it was. But Kiyofuji was still playing *go*. One of the officers pointed to him and asked me who he was. I told him his name. He promptly compared that with another warrant and announced, "That's him!" They promptly seized Kiyofuji, searched him, said "Good! Good!" had him sit down again, and resumed their seats. Then, turning to me, they pulled out more warrants and asked where Uchida and Hirayama were. Uchida had left that morning for Japan, I told them, and Hirayama was still in Hong Kong. They seemed a little disappointed, looked at each other and said "That's funny."

After a while one of them took pencil and paper and began to interrogate me, writing down my answers to his questions. They went as follows: First: Why did you fellows come to Singapore? Second: What's your connection with K'ang Yu-wei? Third: Have you tried to meet K'ang since you came to Singapore?

I certainly didn't have the courage to tell him why we had come to Singapore.[94] They weren't going to get that out of me if it cost me my life. So I told him we were just on a pleasure trip, with no other purposes than sightseeing and visiting friends. But in response to the second and third

[94] That is, to start a revolution in China.

questions I explained how I had met K'ang in Hong Kong, and I told him in great detail about events since our arrival in Singapore. I went on to explain that I had heard a rumor that K'ang seemed to fear that we were out to assassinate him, and consequently had refused to see us, and I showed him the draft of the farewell letter I had written to K'ang. The interrogation took almost two hours, during which there didn't seem to be any points that aroused suspicion. They looked disappointed, and muttered "That's funny" to each other.

The interrogation over, they started to examine our baggage. When they found two Japanese swords, their attitude suddenly changed. "Why are you carrying dangerous weapons?" they demanded. I immediately became an advocate of national character. "A Japanese sword is the very life of a Japanese," I said; "it is like a Christian with his cross." But they did not pursue the point further. They went on to inspect every single item, one by one, and opened my wallet. At the time we had about thirty thousand yen with us. This astonished them. "Incredible!" they muttered. Then, after counting it carefully and putting it in their bag, they resumed their seat opposite me again. "You two are under arrest by the orders of the government. If you want something to eat or drink before we go you may do so." So the two of us cleaned up, called for the beer that Kiyofuji had asked to have chilled, poured ourselves some, offered them a little too, decided against dinner, changed, and waited for their instructions. They carried out our baggage first, meanwhile keeping a close eye on us. I seized the opportunity to say to the boy, Yoshimura, "A man called Fukumoto Nichinan is coming the day after tomorrow on a French ship. I want you to get word of what has happened to him before he disembarks, warning him to go on to some other place." When we went down the stairs and out to the entrance, there were two horse-drawn carriages there. One was for Kiyofuji and one for me. A policeman climbed aboard and indicated that I should follow him. I did so, and after me came another policeman. Then there was a woman's voice; "Where are you going, Sir? Can't I come with you?" It was the maid, Omura. I answered, "I'm off to jail." She started. "Really?" and then saw that it was true." "My goodness! No! Whatever did you do?" She called out in a frightened voice that remained with me as the horses' hooves clattered down the street.

I had known that Omura since the days of my adventure in Siam. When I had contracted cholera there she, a woman, had been kind enough to come to see me at a time when even the settlers who had sworn eternal cooperation had fled from me and refused to come. Now we had met again by chance in Singapore after an interval of several years, and my arrest had come before we had had an adequate chance to see each other. Apparently her affection had not lessened. What could her emotion be on this new separation? I wondered also what the inn manager, his wife, and their little girl Kikuchan must be thinking. I was paying scarcely any attention to where we were going when the carriage pulled to a stop in front of the police station.

Several policemen led us down a dark corridor, opened an iron door, and took us into a long, wide room. Kiyofuji and I seated ourselves on the wooden floor and looked around; it would be hard to describe our emotions. Soon the manager of our inn and his wife came with one of their helpers to bring bedding, lemonade, bread, and so forth. Kiyofuji and I were resting on the soft bedding they had been good enough to bring, but he soon became sleepy and before long he was snoring loudly. I could not get to sleep as I was thinking of one thing after another. Finally my thoughts and spirit settled on the person of my Tomeka and I gently slipped into a lonely dream. The next morning we were suddenly awakened by an ear-splitting voice; when we raised our heads we found that we were to be conducted to a prison. After we had straightened our clothing we were taken outside, put in the horse-drawn carriages a second time, and taken to the jail.

The jail was encircled by a double wall. The carriage stopped outside the entrance and they had us get down. One policeman went through a side gate first and had the guard open the main gate. We followed him inside; there were two soldiers standing with bayonets at attention on each side of the gate inside. Two policemen took the lead, and two soldiers came behind me. Then, after a proper interval, Kiyofuji received the same ritual. It was a method more appropriate to preventing murderers from getting away. When we had passed through another gate and reached the entrance to the prison we came to the warden's waiting-room. We waited there. The warden first examined the documents the police had brought and made notes in his register; then he examined us personally, even going so far as to remove the sash of my *haori* (coat). He explained that was because they were afraid we might hang ourselves. Yet curiously he did not take our *obis*.

When this was over, we were taken to still another room. A large black man sat on a chair with a pen and record, and another measured and weighed us while he recorded everything. Then they examined us carefully right down to bumps and moles and recorded all that too.

When that was over they took us to what was to be our cell. Its size was about twelve mats.[95] The floor was brick and there was a bunk on each wall. On each bunk there was a grass mat and a single blanket, and next to each was a wooden coal-box. This was to put clothing in and it could also serve as a seat. Also, in the corner there was a bucket to serve as urinal and toilet. Another corner had a small bucket of water, which was to be used for drinking and washing. The door was made of heavy wood covered with metal, with a rather large hole in the middle. The guards would occasionally come to look through this.

[95] Thus 216 square feet.

When it was opened and closed it made a very frightening noise.

The prison was a brick building, so the three outside walls of our cell were brick. The ceiling was about five feet up. There was an iron-framed, two-foot-square window in a corner of the ceiling for ventilation and light. When I lay on the bunk and looked up, it was like looking up from the bottom of a well. It is impossible for me to describe how unpleasant I found this. I looked over at Kiyofuji with a grin in spite of myself. "Compared to a Japanese jail," he said, "this is like a guest room." He went on to tell me that in Fukuoka he had been arrested for drunkenness once and jailed for two days. I realized then that he was my senior in experiences of this sort.

I had never been a firm believer in justice under law. Furthermore, since I myself might have to break the law, I had rather expected that I might myself some day be on the receiving end of hardship behind bars and perhaps even execution. Nevertheless, I had never expected to undergo calamity at this point. That it did come now seemed to me particularly unpleasant, the more so because nothing remotely like this had ever happened to me before. Still, as I calmed down and thought about the series of events that had led to this, I began to see how it had all come about. As a result I couldn't be too hard on K'ang, or too critical of the British authorities for what they had done. What I could not help regretting, however, was K'ang's excessive intolerance and my own lightheartedness.

Be that as it may, it is inevitable to be uneasy about such a situation even if you understand how it came about. From the minute I was put in jail I couldn't wait to get out. Kiyofuji warned me: "If you're not patient the boredom will be terrible. Just remember we're lucky to be put in here together." No sooner had he said this than the door opened with a shattering screech and a dignified policeman appeared. He stared at us for a few minutes, and then called the warden in a loud, cold voice, and said to him in a sadistic tone, "They are not supposed to be together. Put them in separate cells." At that we were taken out separately and put into cells so far from each other that we couldn't hear each other cough. So the arrangement we had regarded as fortunate disappeared in a flash and I became an isolated convict behind bars.

My detention proved to be for six days. It was not terribly long, but to me it seemed hundreds of thousands of days long. The first day was a Sunday, and there was no interrogation. We were taken out for exercise on order at noon. There were about forty of us, all awaiting sentence: Malays, Chinese, Indians, and one Japanese—myself. They were even keeping Kiyofuji and me apart at exercise time. There is a proverb that even enemies will help each other if they find themselves in the same boat, and there was indeed something special about the sympathy we prisoners had for each other. It was a collection of what the world would consider evil fellows: murderers, incendiaries, robbers, thieves, ruffians, and gamblers. And yet there were neither murderers nor incendiaries within those walls. Evil fellows they might be, but among themselves no one was evil. We were members of a society outside society, and siblings of a family outside the family system. They talked honestly and openly, and tried to conceal nothing. Murder, arson, rape, robberies: they held back nothing. It should have been frightful, and yet there was also something attractive in this directness. Truly, just as it is hard to find a real sage in this world, it is rare to see a totally evil person. I was an enigma to them. Some thought I must be a murderer; they had a certain amount of respect for the murderers in their number. Others thought I must be a rebel; this judgment too was not without its overtones of admiration. As a result my fellow prisoners rather looked up to me, the more so when I was able to do something for them.

That day about two o'clock they brought me a package. I went back to my ward and opened it as I was ordered to, and found that it contained rice balls, cooked fish, meat, and the like, which I proceeded to eat. Before long the warden came in with things like cigars, cigarettes, confections, and lemonade. "The other prisoners are not allowed to have things like this sent in," he said, "but I hear that you gentlemen are very important people in Japan, and I have decided to ignore the rules." Then he winked at me and raised his index finger and thumb in the shape of a coin, and said, "They say you have a lot of money," and hurried out. This fellow, who had been like an ogre, had changed in the twinkling of an eye into an amiable saint. Why? In the distance I thought I could hear the landlady of my inn in conversation with the warden. Then I understood: it was all her work! Soon the warden came back. "After you've had yours, we'll take the rest to the other prisoner," he said. He meant Kiyofuji. I thanked him for his kindness. "You are very kind; I will see that you are rewarded after I am released." He showed his pleasure, and assured me: "Please tell me if there's anything you would like. I will send word to the landlady of your inn. So I ordered books, pencils, paper, and so on. I became a lord among prisoners.

When I went back to the exercise ground with a cigar in my mouth, the other prisoners pressed around me begging for cigarettes by holding their palms together. So I first of all gave the guard a cigar and then presented each of my prisoner friends with a cigarette. I became king of the prison! Or, perhaps better, honorary president.

At four o'clock we were ordered to return to the ward. By five o'clock it was dark in my cell, and impossible to read. I finished eating the things that had been sent in the package as my dinner, smoked, sat down on my bunk, and tried to meditate. Then, after reflecting somberly on the recent past for a while, my spirit tired and I fell asleep. At six o'clock the next morning the guard came to wake me up and take me outside for exercise again; then back to the ward at ten, back out again at twelve, and in again at four:

in short, I was given eight hours' exercise outside each day and the other sixteen hours I was confined in my cell. While in my cell I could lie down, sleep, or read, but after five o'clock the darkness made reading impossible. It was impossible for anybody used to late hours to sleep so long a night. I tried to drill myself in sitting in contemplation, Zen-style, but idle thoughts and vain regrets came crowding into my mind one after another. In the end I would find consolation in thoughts of Tomeka. Her virtue alone sufficed.

That second day there was no interrogation. When night fell the prisoners sang songs, and their thin voices reminded me of the cry of cicadas. When the guard shouted at them they stopped for a few minutes, and then started up again. How relaxed they seemed! Although some of them were prepared for sentences of execution or life imprisonment, it did not seem to trouble them. Were they so courageous? Or simply lethargic? I could not help envying such nonchalance. I myself was full of concern because Sun Yat-sen and Fukumoto were scheduled to arrive that day.

The third day came. At six o'clock in the morning the chief warden opened the door to my cell and came in. Lowering his voice, he said quietly, "Follow me to the lavatory room and wash there. I'll let you see your friend there." When I did as he said I found Kiyofuji, naked, at the well. We greeted each other with smiles: "How are you doing? How are you doing?" I followed suit and stood next to him at the well, and we planned our strategy for answering questions that would be addressed to us in court. We would not have needed to do so if we had any thought of telling the truth, but the truth had to be kept secret. How could we reveal our plans just to clear ourselves of charges of planning to assassinate K'ang? We simply had to prepare false statements for our depositions and it was the magic power of the money we had that provided us with this opportunity to prepare our answers. Money can do everything, can it not? Now the chief warden, who had become so wonderfully thoughtful, came to get us. He said, "If you talk too long it will attract attention." And he went on, "Your interrogation will be held today." Ah, the hearing! It is the prisoner's hope. Kiyofuji and I dressed again, parted with smiles, and headed for the exercise ground. My fellow prisoner friends were waiting for me in the hope of getting more cigarettes. I distributed one to each again. They said to me, "Today is your hearing, Sir." It seemed as though they were congratulating me on an enviable early end to my imprisonment. It is really true that a fierce tiger can be trained and tamed and that a vicious criminal can be transformed through friendship to behave like a child. How compassionate they were! If one compares them with so-called gentlemen who are wolves in sheeps' clothing, they will surely rank higher in the heavenly court.

Ten o'clock: the bell to summon us had rung, but I had not been called out yet. I lay on my bunk and tried to read a book, but couldn't concentrate on it. My mind had already taken flight to the hearing room, and I was imagining the interrogation. I certainly could not be called courageous at this time. At twelve o'clock the bell, and orders once again summoned us to the exercise area. I ate more of the food that had been sent in for me and went on out to the exercise area. As I did so, the head warden called for me to tell me that I was to go to the court for my hearing. My fellow prisoners advised me to dress carefully for the occasion. Was that not kind of them? I put on a light summer kimono with black silk *haori*, white *tabi*, and went to the warden's waiting-room.

The court building was near the prison gate. The warden went in the lead, and two soldiers followed with their bayonets at the ready to guard me. When we went up the stairs, we found the Japanese vice consul and three other Japanese gentlemen. One was a Honganji priest and the other two were interpreters. I stood there waiting for a time, and then I was taken into an adjoining room. This proved to be the courtroom.

In the center of the room there was a large table about twelve feet square. Behind it, and facing me directly, was the judge; next to him was the colonial governor.[96] I was ordered to stand facing them. Policemen stood at my left and right, and behind us stood two soldiers with their bayonets. On the left side of the table sat an associate judge, and next to him was the Japanese vice consul. At their right sat the two interpreters, facing me across the corner of the table. Across from them, on the right, sat the police commissioner and police chief. Those were the two that had come to our inn to arrest us. Ah! They no longer seemed to be as haughty as they had the other day! They seemed to be trying to be as polite as possible now. Probably a good sign, I thought. I had become so petty as to study other people's faces for their possible significance.

The interrogation began. Their questions and my answers were pretty much what they had been a few days before at my inn. Nor did they seem too suspicious of me. But the amount of money we had in our possession did seem to draw their attention, and this was also one of the points on which we had to dissemble. He asked, "Why were you carrying such a large sum of money?" I answered, "It is not unusual for travelers like ourselves who go from one country to another to have an amount of this sort with them. Do people in your country consider it too much?" "Do you come from a wealthy family?" he asked. "No," I answered, "they were very poor." "Then how did you come by so large a sum?" he asked. "Although I myself am poor," I said, "I have a good number of wealthy friends." "And they supply you with money?" he persisted. "Yes Sir," I answered. He seemed to have some difficulty in understanding this, and cocking his

[96] The Governor's Open Dispatch to London of July 26, 1900, with reference to Sun Yat-sen makes note of the arrest of two Japanese on July 6.

head he went on: "What kind of return do you offer people who put up so much money?" It seemed a reasonable question. I replied as follows: "Mutual profit is the sort of thing merchants think about. But not men of high purpose of our country. We have everything in common and help each other when in need. This has been the custom in our country from antiquity, and the standard pattern among our high-minded idealists. Is there nothing like this in your country?" The judge looked more and more puzzled. He turned to the Japanese vice consul and said, "Do you really have a tradition like that in your country?" The vice consul nodded and said that we did. But the judge still didn't understand. The next question he raised had to do with the swords we had with us at the time of our arrest. "Why did you have a sword with you?" I explained to him about Japanese spirit and swords. He seemed increasingly distressed, and once again turned to our vice consul to ask him if what I had said was true. The vice consul assured him that it was, and volunteered the information that he too had a sword. When he turned to the interpreters and asked them, they assured him that they had swords too. For the first time the judge began to look as though he might believe what I had said.

The examination went on for three hours. Except for the points about money and swords, things seemed to go well enough for me, and I was a little more at ease. The rest of the evidence seemed to contradict the charges against me. I was sent back to the chief warden's room with the same ceremonial procedure, and there I found Kiyofuji sitting on a chair, wearing a black silk *haori*; he seemed very relaxed. It was his turn to be examined. But my interrogation had taken so long that it was already growing dark, with the result that instead of taking Kiyofuji on to the court they took him back to his cell. The warden assured me triumphantly that the next day I would be found innocent and released. Of course I believed this too, and I was overjoyed to hear him say so. That evening the warden was exceptionally kind and made it possible for me to see the landlady of my inn and her servant. But what motivated his exceptional kindness was his intention to fix the amount of the bribe due him in front of my landlady. Let us not make too much of the fact that this Western policeman was corrupt. For a mere twenty-five dollars he provided for my comfort in prison and made it possible for me to be in touch with my considerate landlady and her faithful servant. That meant more than a thousand dollars to me.

Moreover, the landlady and her servant brought me very important news. Sun Yat-sen and Fukumoto Nichinan had landed; they had registered at a hotel, and three followers who came with them were at the inn. I was tremendously relieved to hear this. The news that they were safe had the value of a relief army of one million men for me. My spirits revived, I went back to my cell and fell into a deep sleep.

Day dawned once more. My friendly warden again conducted me to the wash-tub. Before stepping in I went to the lavatory at the wall and found Kiyofuji crouched down relieving himself with his clothes wound above his buttocks. I stood next to him at the urinal telling him about my interrogation in court, but I couldn't tell whether his grunts signified his comprehension of my story or not. When I asked him if he understood, he finally smiled and answered that he had in a loud voice. The smell was so bad that I hurried out, went to the well, took off my clothes, and washed myself. I felt much refreshed. I went back to my cell, finished my breakfast, dressed, and went out to the exercise ground. My fellow prisoners gathered round and congratulated me on the release that seemed likely to come soon. I gave each of them a cigarette again.

After a bit the warden summoned me again. I expected this to be the end of it, and was delighted. Instead, when I responded to his call, I found to my disappointment that it was for a return to the court for further hearings. I dressed immediately and returned to the courtroom with the same ritual of my first visit there. This time the colonial governor himself took the central seat and asked the questions. He began with questions about Sun Yat-sen.

"Do you know Sun Yat-sen?" "Yes, I do." "How did you come to meet him?" I explained that I had known him since we met in Yokohama some four or five years earlier. He went on: "Do you know an Englishman named Morgan?" He was a member of Sun's group. "Yes," I said, "I know him." He asked how I had come to know him. I explained that Sun had introduced him to me. Again: "Do you know a man named Fukumoto?" "Yes, I know him." "And do you know a man named Ozaki?" When I asked his first name, he provided it: "Yukimasa." I was somewhat surprised at this, becaused I did not realize that he had come together with Sun Yat-sen. But since Ozaki was a friend of mine, I said as much.[97] Next he asked me about Nakanishi Jūtarō. I was more and more surprised. But he was an old friend so I identified him as such.[98] At this time the prosecutor got up and showed me a short sword. "Do you recognize this sword?" I wondered if Fukumoto and his party had been arrested too. So I answered that I did not recognize it. The governor asked again: "Have you not been requested by the Chinese conservative party to assassinate the leader of the reform party?" I raised my voice: "I work for the enlightenment of the world. No matter how deeply I might sympathize with Sun and K'ang, it would be impossible for me to assassinate the conservatives. It is even more inconceivable for me to assassinate Sun and K'ang at the request of the conservatives. I would have to be completely out of my

[97] Ozaki (1874-1934), youngest brother of the well-known *Kaishintō* politician Ozaki Yukio, who was a close associate of Inukai's.

[98] Nakanishi (1875-1934) was a member of the first class at Arao Sei's Trade Research Institute, served as interpreter during the Sino-Japanese War, thereafter attended Waseda, guarded K'ang Yu-wei on his departure from Japan, and later served as educator.

mind to do that." He asked, "Why are you so intent upon working with Chinese?" "Because I share their anguish over the weakness of China and want to help to reform that country." He smiled. "Why should you commit yourself, body and soul, to a foreign country?" I answered, "The answer to that question goes to the heart of my being and belief. It does not bear on today's business, and I shall not respond to it here. If you would like to discuss it with me, let us do it as friends after I have been released." He smiled and did not press me. His questioning moved on to other matters.

The governor's attitude now became conversational as he went on to ask me about the Tōa Dōbunkai. He also asked about the policy of the Tōhō Kyōkai and the Ajiya Kyōkai.[99] He seemed to want to know about the attitudes of the Japanese people toward China. I responded in a rather non-committal manner. That day's hearing ended up taking three hours too. Then Kiyofuji was questioned after me for an additional two hours. The chief warden assured me, with pleasure in his face, "It's over now. I'm sure you'll be released tomorrow!" He was not just pretending to be pleased, although his interest in the matter was a little different from ours. His interest? He was to receive his twenty-five dollars at the time of our release. Ah, interest! Does its secret lie in the manipulation of lesser, selfish types for the development of truly large groups and purposes? Isn't that the basic point that our politicians have to get through their heads today? If so, the landlady of my inn may be said to have mastered such politicians' tactics very well. That evening the guard brought a special mattress into my cell. Apparently this was special consideration on the governor's part. I was able to sleep soundly without feeling the hardness of those boards in the bunk.

The fifth day. At about eight o'clock in the morning

[99] The principal Meiji associations for personal, scholarly, and cultural communication with and about China.

Kiyofuji and I were ordered to go to the administrative office. I dressed and went to the chief warden's office, where two or three policemen were waiting. They handcuffed the two of us and took us outside the gate. Two horse-drawn carriages were waiting for us there. Kiyofuji and I each climbed aboard and two policemen accompanied each of us. After the horses trotted about a mile we arrived at the government office, where we were taken to a room on the upper floor and kept waiting for over an hour. Then the Police Commissioner came in and took us to another room, where I found a dozen gentlemen sitting around a table. The governor was facing me, and the others were councillors. The man next to the governor seemed to be a clerk.

We stood at attention facing the governor. The councillors were around the table, and Japanese interpreters were standing on the left of us. The governor opened the proceedings with a smile: "At this time we propose to determine an appropriate sentence for your guilt in plotting to assassinate a member of the Chinese Reform Party. Have you any objection to that?" He addressed the question to me first. I answered "The charge is false. I cannot accept it." He asked Kiyofuji's opinion with the same smile. Kiyofuji raised his voice, heatedly denied his guilt, and began to argue the point when the governor cut him off. "No," he said, "we have not determined the matter yet, but we are about to do so. I will let you leave while we deliberate." And with that the policemen took us to another room.

We had waited for a little more than a half-hour when we were summoned back into the council chamber. The governor proceeded to read the text of the sentence: "The sentence for the two accused is as follows: The government of Singapore considers that you are a danger to public security. Consequently it directs that you be expelled from the territory under its jurisdiction for a period of five years." He asked if we had anything we wished to say. I spoke: "The word 'considers' you used reveals an arbitrary decision. In my view it leaves no doubt about the nature of your procedures. So be it. Man is created by heaven, but he retains freedom to question its ways. How am I to interfere with your freedom to be arbitrary? I can only conform respectfully with your decree. But I consider the world the garden of mankind, and you are depriving us of a part of it. I shall long remember this." The governor grinned and said, "You shall regain that freedom after five years." Then he looked at Kiyofuji and asked him if he wished to make an statement. Kiyofuji replied angrily that he was absolutely unwilling to accept such an illegal decision. "But," he said, "you have political power. I have no desire to continue a hopeless dispute in this tropical heat, and I see no alternative to a reluctant acceptance of your decision." They were all watching his face tensely. The governor, though, grinned again and said, "Then that settles the matter." Then he began to tease us.

First he asked us our plans for departure and our destination. I said I wanted to board the first ship headed for Japan. The governor went on, "If you will travel third class, the government will provide each of you with a ticket, but if you want second or first class the expense will be your own." "We travel first class," I said. We decided to board an N.Y.K. ship that was due to leave the next day. The governor once again asked with a smile, "Is there anything you would like to have Nakanishi know?" "Is he here?" I asked. He shook his head and said, "At any rate, if you have a message for him, we will forward it." That was the first I knew that Nakanishi was in Singapore. "I believe Nakanishi must be on his way to Europe with K'ang Yu-wei," I said; "please extend my regards to him and ask him to pass along my best wishes to K'ang for a pleasant journey." He said, "And do you have any message for Sun Yat-sen?" And so I knew that Sun was in Singapore too. I said, "Please tell him that I shall leave for Japan tomorrow." The governor nodded and agreed. Then he became more serious. "Sun Yat-sen claims that the money you had on you at the time of your arrest was his and that he had entrusted you with it. Is that true?" This was a little embarrassing, since I had insisted from the first that the money was my own. But it would have been even more embarrassing to tell the truth now. So I suppressed my amusement and said, "No, it's my money. But he and I share almost everything, and if he feels that he needs it you may let him have it. I would appreciate your excellency's sending that word to Sun." With that the governor burst into laughter and said, "As it happens Sun Yat-sen, Nakanishi, Ozaki, Fukumoto, and Morgan will all board the same ship tomorrow and travel to Japan with you." I couldn't help smiling myself.

After all this was over, we requested permission to return to our inn, but this was not allowed. They said we were to be taken to the ship directly from the prison the following morning. So there was nothing for it but to climb aboard the buggies again and return to the jail. But we, who had been handcuffed three hours earlier, now rode back unfettered; we were allowed to stay together that night. That night the landlady of our inn came to see us. We were allowed to see her and able to confirm the fact that Sun and Fukumoto were to board the same ship the following day. She also carried out the terms of her agreement with the chief warden. After she left Kiyofuji and I lay down on our bunks. The five days we had been separated gave us so many thing to talk about that the time shot by. By midnight we were tired enough to fall asleep for a while, and then the happy day of our release dawned.

We got up and bathed, and then the warden came to order us to go to be photographed. A policeman took us to a room where a white photographer took two pictures of each of us. One picture was full face, with both hands flat on my chest, and the other was a profile view of the upper half of my body. The photographer was a young and good-looking lad; he did not seem very coarse, and yet he wore prisoner's clothes. When I asked him what he was in for, he answered shamefacedly, "I forged a half-million dollars' worth of notes in Germany, and when I came here I was sentenced to eight years of hard labor." We were astonished by the discrepancy between his appearance and his actions.

This done, we went back to our ward for breakfast. We gave our fellow prisoners what remained of the food our landlady had sent in to us, and tried the prison fare for the first time. There was a choice between Malay and Chinese food. As I was used to Chinese food I tried the other, and found it was just like European rice curry. But it turned out to have a lot of hot pepper in it, and it was very hot for me. Still, it did not seem inferior to what even middle-class people might eat in Japan.

Then came the time for our release. We distributed the things we had no further use for to our fellow prisoners, and shook hands with them to say farewell. They seemed sad at the separation, and we too were moved to sympathy with them. Is not that the way of human emotion? If I harbor no evil intentions toward others, they in turn will be good to me. When the innocent meet with misfortune the fault is usually with society, not with them. They have been influenced by the circumstances in which they found themselves. There must be almost no one who is not influenced by his circumstances. Therefore I conclude that people should be enlightened and not punished, that the basis for that enlightenment must be that of equal rights, and that the recovery of those equal rights must be sought through a revolution of our social structure.

The chief warden, however, was still not satisfied and wanted more. As we shook hands in farewell he pulled at my sleeve and whispered, "You are an important person in Japan. When you return home won't you send some kimonos for my wife and children?" A villainous-looking Indian clerk made the same request. We said we would, but we never did. That was not very noble of us.[100]

[100] Literally, "we did not behave like *chün tzu*."

When a policeman took us to the gate the chief inspector and the police commissioner were there and the things they had confiscated at the time of our arrest were on the horse-drawn carriage. They all rode to the pier with us. It was a fine day and our spirits soared. We got out of the carriage, boarded ship, and finally saw Fukumoto and Sun Yat-sen. We embraced each other and rejoiced that we were safe. Then we went below and found the other members of our party. A number of Japanese had come to see us off. It was truly as if I had encountered a long lost sweetheart. Nakanishi was also there. He had apparently come to see us off, having found himself in Singapore with the purpose of accompanying K'ang to Europe. I talked to him in that vein. He pointed to the Police Commissioner who was standing by and said, "That fellow had me arrested and detained for two days. I gave up trying to counter his stupid arguments and I've decided to go home." Then he glared at the Commissioner, and shouted, "Give me my sword back!" He resembled a tiger about to jump an elephant. The Commissioner returned the sword to him. It was the one they had shown me in court the previous day.

The landlady of our inn and her husband were there; she wept when she saw us. Little Kikuchan's eyes filled with tears, and she bowed without saying anything. How were we to restrain our emotion? The maid Omura gave me a rosary of fragrant wood, and Otaka some canned coconut. Much later we heard that Otaka, as soon as we had been arrested, had cabled Uchida warning him not to disembark at Hong Kong. Was she not a chivalrous one? Now we entered the dining room together and toasted our departure in champagne. It was indescribably crowded. As the bell rang and departure time neared we shook hands all around to bid farewell. The ship began to move, but our friends did not leave the pier and continued to wave their handkerchiefs and hats. But the ship moved on without thought for our sentiments, and within a half-hour we could no longer see our friends. We drank together for a while. Gradually I became tipsy, and then drowsy, and fell asleep. When I woke up and went on deck, the sun had set and the air was cool with evening. All I could make out was the dim outline of the Malay Peninsula. I was deeply moved. I finally raised my arms and shouted, "Farewell! For five years!"

[24]

GENERAL HEADQUARTERS ON BOARD THE SADO MARU

WHEN WE WOKE UP THE NEXT MORNING WE began to swap stories and complaints about the events of the previous week. Fukumoto began with his account of the situation when he arrived:

> "When the ship docked somebody showed up asking for me. When I asked him what he wanted, he looked around him as if he was afraid somebody would see him. I thought there was something wrong with him. Then he put his mouth to my ear and started whispering what had happened to you. Was I surprised! He gave me your message that we should not get off the ship; but when I asked him why we shouldn't he didn't seem to know. I couldn't figure it out and took it up with Sun; he was incredulous too. Sun said "Look, if we all get arrested, we're done for, so let's see if we can't get away instead of going ashore." But of course we didn't have any idea where, since this had come up all of a sudden. We checked to see what the next ship we could get on might be, and learned that something was leaving for Colombo within the hour. But there's no reason for us to want to go to Colombo, is there? If we didn't go there we'd have had to wait two or three days for something else, and if we took it we would have had to board immediately. Sun and I didn't know what to do. Then

a man from the Japanese consulate fortunately showed up. He too warned us that it would be a good idea not to go ashore. When we asked him why, he told us that we were suspected of setting up a plot to assassinate K'ang Yu-wei. Now we began to understand, and we felt a little better. I went to Sun's cabin and found him stuffing things into his bag in a great rush. I told him what I'd learned and suggested that he wait for a little while while I went to the Japanese consulate to get the details; if I didn't come back, it would mean I'd been arrested too and that he'd stay on board. With that I went ashore and headed for the consulate, and got the general details. But when I came back to the ship I couldn't find Sun anymore; he'd gone ashore quickly. He made just the right decision, like the revolutionary leader he is. So then I headed for the hotel where I'd been told Sun had gone, and he said that he wanted to talk things over with us and figure out a way to help you. According to what they'd told me at the consulate, the only thing they had on you was the money and your inability to explain where it came from; aside from that things looked all right. When I told Sun that, I said he ought to tell them the money was his and that that might solve it. Sun agreed, and went right to the governor to tell him that was the way it was. That's why the governor was kidding with you after he decided on the sentence. We were afraid that if things went wrong we might be detained too, but fortunately all they did was interrogate us and it didn't go that far. That's the only good luck we had in all of this. But it's really too bad about poor Nakanishi. He had actually been invited by K'ang, but then ran into bad luck just because he happened to be on the same ship with us. He was at K'ang's, and then he was held for two days by the police. If K'ang had not distrusted us a little bit, he would have been able to take our part and these stupid things wouldn't have happened. That K'ang is just too nervous, isn't he? I went to see him, too, and he had all sorts of excuses. For half a day he just scribbled excuses at me; it was amazing. I tried to say it was enough now and change the subject, but he just kept at it. He thought it was terrible that he'd been responsible for having the man who'd helped him thrown into jail, and he couldn't talk about anything else. But it's all over now. What do we do next?"

It was true. All our plans for Singapore had gone glimmering into the void. So what were we to do now? This was the problem we had to take up in our shipboard meetings. We decided that we would have to decide on the basis of the situation in Hong Kong and that we just would have to make up our minds when we got there. If we had to, we could try to go inland from there. That was the decision.

We were confused about our next move, and like people groping their way through a heavy fog. But in fact the ocean was calm, and the ship made good progress. The Sado Maru was scheduled to dock at noon, but it arrived four hours ahead of schedule and berthed at Kowloon, across from the island of Hong Kong. Kiyofuji and I disembarked immediately in order to acquaint ourselves with the state of affairs. The first thing we did was to go to see Hirayama and Hara. We were delighted to see each other again, and immediately ordered sake and caught up on each other. After we had drunk and talked for a little while, a letter came which proved to be from the Japanese consulate. "We have something to talk with you about," it read, "please come right away." I called for transportation and headed for the consulate. The consul said to me, "The Hong Kong government is watching you very closely. It's not out of the question that you might be arrested and detained again. If it came to that we would do our best to explain things and argue that you should be released, but in the meanwhile you would be obliged to put up with the hardship of imprisonment, and it might be bad for your health. An epidemic is spreading here day by day. If you're on very important business that you can't put off then it can't be helped, but we think you ought to head for home at the earliest possible opportunity." He was extremely considerate. After thanking him for his kindness, I deceived him by saying that I had already decided to return home and that I had my ticket, thereby easing his mind. Then I left. I had learned this from heroes who had to resort to strategies of deceit in the past.

When I returned to my friends' place I found them still drinking and talking. They looked at me and said, "The English police chief was just here looking for you and Kiyofuji. We told them you had left, and they headed back for your ship to look for you there. He asked us to tell you that he was looking for you. There's someting going on here. We told him Kiyofuji had just gone out too, so he didn't see him. We've been waiting for you to come back." Now I knew that the situation was very serious. When I told my friends what the consul had said, they were impressed by the danger we were in. But after we had downed a good deal more sake we stopped wagging our heads about that danger. Kiyofuji and I headed for the pier, hired a small launch and headed for Kowloon and the ship. We boarded and headed for Sun Yat-sen's cabin.

When Sun Yat-sen saw us he closed the book he was reading and said, "A policeman was just here looking for you two. The situation seems to be very tight. Shouldn't you talk to him to see what he wants?" We then went with Sun to talk to the policeman, identified ourselves, and asked what it was he wanted. The officer slowly produced a document and announced "This is an order of the government. By the provisions of the Security Law you are expelled for a period of five years." We knew it would do no good to protest. But we did joke with him, "There is no K'ang Yu-wei in Hong Kong. Even if we were thinking about assassinating somebody we would have no target. Why are you persecuting us with this expulsion order?" He was a rather gentle policeman. "I am just following government orders in this matter," he said; "I have no explanation. But my own conjecture would be, that it has no connection with K'ang Yu-wei, but rather bears on some other important matter. I have no way of knowing all your secrets." Then, having said this, he looked at us, laughed loudly and said, "Do you still want me to explain it to you?" He had us there. We too laughed in turn, thanked him for his good will, and went back. So now we once again were prisoners of our ship.

It should not be thought that Hong Kong is just a small island. For me it had been a very big island. Here I had rested on my way to and back from Siam, and this island had been my base for the last seven years. Here I had made contacts with the members of the *Hsing-Chung hui*, and those contacts had made my meeting with Sun Yat-sen possible. Here I had met the leaders of the *San-ho hui*. Here too I had met the heads of the *Ko-lao hui*. Here the ceremonies marking the union of the three secret societies had taken place. I had made contact with the representatives of the Philippine Independence movement here. So too with K'ang Yu-wei and members of his group. It was so too with Kiyozō and Okoma, with Setsurei and Masako. Consequently most of the memories of half of my life were centered here. This is why I love Hong Kong and do not consider it a small place. And now suddenly this place was stolen from me in one morning. How painful this was! The more so in that we were about to launch a great event here. The expulsion of Kiyofuji and me from Hong Kong was not just a personal misfortune for us, but really a direct attack on our entire party. Consequently we had to take counsel immediately to decide our next steps. But the policeman hadn't left; he was still on board. All we could do was make signs to each other and head for our cabin.

We all agreed that however stormy the way ahead, we should persevere in our journey. But how were we to reach our goal? What road should we take? That was our problem. Kiyofuji and I had now been barred from Hong Kong. Sun Yat-sen, our leader also, although he had gained the tacit approval of the Hong Kong Governor General to enter the Kwangtung Province interior, now found himself unable to implement these plans because of the events in Singapore. Try as we would, we couldn't seem to work out a satisfactory plan. Time after time our shipboard councils got nowhere and broke up at dusk without having come to a decision.

After dinner, the evening breeze would bring cooler air and as the deck became quieter our secret deliberations would resume. Our leader Sun Yat-sen made the following proposal: "Let us have Fukumoto take charge of all preparations in Hong Kong; Hirayama and Hara will assist him. After those preparations are made we'll have Cheng take over and raise the flag of revolution. Hara can be his chief of staff, and the other Japanese comrades can help by occupying ———; after that the rest of our force can march in the direction of Amoy." Sun himself was to make a secret crossing from Taiwan to establish contact with the insurrection, and Kiyofuji and I were to accompany him. No one commented on this, one way or the other. Then Fukumoto made this proposition: "Things have begun to move. It is clear that the Japanese government is watching us carefully. If Sun returns to Japan, we have to realize that he will not be able to move freely. And as for Kiyofuji and Miyazaki, we have to realize that they may be arrested again too. Consequently if they go back to Japan it is likely that the morale of the comrades in Hong Kong will be severely weakened. What we need is a quick strike. I think we ought to go ashore tonight under cover of darkness at Kowloon, go inland with our comrades and attack Canton, with a sudden strike, an insurrection like that of the

Shinpūren."[101] Everybody applauded this, none more so than the two of us. It seemed a very bad idea to me to return to Japan, and we were afraid that it would produce setbacks we could not foresee. We asked Sun's opinion of the strike on Canton. Sun shook his head and said, "It's a terrible idea. Like throwing meat in front of a starving tiger." When I argued the disadvantages of my going to Japan and the dangers that would bring, Sun stubbornly refused to agree, shook his head and said loudly, "My life is not so worthless that I am going to throw it away in a desperate move. Even if this whole plan should come to nothing, I am not ready to take such a suicidal step." I answered that if the three of us went back to Japan morale in Hong Kong would be so damaged that the larger plan would end in failure. "If you rule out Fukumoto's plan," I said, "then perhaps we ought to give the whole thing up and wait for another opportunity." Tempers rose, words became vehement, and violent arguments broke out.

I became agitated, lost my temper, and became insulting. "A revolution isn't something you can work out on an abacus. You can't wait until you're sure you have the answers. If you do you'll spend a lifetime waiting and achieve nothing. They say a smart man spends years planning a revolt and gets nowhere. Is that your idea? If so, I'm through working with you." Sun became angry too. "Are you crazy? If so, why don't you just jump overboard and commit suicide? You'll never make it by trying to go ashore at Kowloon at night to go into the interior!" Fukumoto left first to go to his room. Sun tapped me on the knee and said, "When did you become so stupid?" I answered, "When did you become such a coward?" It was like a children's quarrel. When Sun heard my answer he put his hand on my knee, pressed it, raised his voice, and said, "Surely you know I'm not a coward. And you certainly ought to know that I'm not afraid of giving up

[101] See n. 4, p. 11.

my life. Yet now you are reproaching me so. Why is that?" And, pressing my knee convulsively, he burst into tears. We were both silent for a time. Kiyofuji too left for his cabin and finally Sun went off to his. I was left alone. I wiped my eyes and raised my head; everything was quiet; all I could see was the stars and the rays of the street lights. I could no longer think clearly, and went off to my cabin too.

When I stretched out on my bed a thousand thoughts came flooding in. The walls were hot from the midday heat and I was unable to sleep. I got up, poured myself a whiskey, and after drinking it lay down a second time. I heard footsteps in front of my door. The door opened, and I heard Fukumoto: "Are you asleep?" "I can't sleep." I answered, and we went up on deck together. "There's something funny. When I tried to sleep a stranger looked in. He may be a thief," said Fukumoto. We walked the deck together. We saw two English policemen standing there. Then we also saw Chinese policemen standing in two corners. Fukumoto said, "Aha! That's it. Those Chinese cops were the ones." We exchanged bitter smiles. "We can't get away from these fellows very easily." We walked around the deck side by side. Fukumoto stood still. He pointed toward the policemen; "This is hopeless." I looked down and saw a small police launch, and immediately realized that our plans for going ashore would not work. Fukumoto said, "We'd better apologize to Sun." I went to Sun's cabin and knocked. He apparently had not been able to sleep yet either. "Yes." He came to the door and said, "What's the matter?" I told him what we had seen and that he was right, and apologized. He accepted my apologies and then we went up on deck together so that he could see for himself. He started when he saw what I meant; he laughed bitterly and agreed that he had shown foresight. We bowed and apologized, and I said "You were right. From now on we will defer to you." We each went back to our cabins.

Truly, the human spirit is vulnerable. When you are distressed, sleep is impossible. Although it was past two o'clock I could not sleep. I took several drinks and was close to sleep when someone came knocking at my door. I got up rubbing my eyes, opened the door, and found it was my beloved Masako. At the very first glimpse of her I forgot the pains of agony. I took her by the hands, led her in, and asked "Why did you come?" She answered, "Tonight I heard someone outside my door calling my name. When I went out, it was a Westerner I'd never seen before. He told me that you were on this ship and advised me to come. I didn't believe him, and thought it was a bad joke. But he insisted it was true. He came in, took me by the hands, led me to the pier, hired a launch, and had it bring me here. I half believed and half doubted, but came anyway." I knew it was Morgan, because that morning he had asked me repeatedly what my sweetheart's name was and finally had me write her name on a fan. Wasn't he a gallant Lafayette? So I was finally able to have pleasant dreams.

The ship served as our president's quarters, and also as general headquarters and as a social club. Consequently the coming and going of our comrades was like the shuttle in a loom, and other people who watched were open-mouthed in astonishment. But headquarters still hadn't settled on its policy. The party members were impatient for decisions and they made difficulties for the members of general headquarters. That is why I was in need of sake and of Masako. Therefore I was grateful to Morgan. How much is required for someone as insignificant as I am to try to play the role of hero!

The next morning Sun Yat-sen came to wake me up and took me to another room. "A problem I would like your opinion on has come up." He lowered his voice. "On one occasion my friend had a secret conversation with the governor of Hong Kong. He had the idea of getting Li Hung-chang to declare the independence of the provinces of Kwangtung and Kwangsi and have me organize a new administration, while he himself would covertly stand as protector to prevent interference. My friend then discussed this with Li, who agreed to raise that banner as the last act of his career. But then the Boxer Rebellion became more violent, and the court suddenly ordered Li to come to Peking. Consequently Li had no choice but to give up the plan and schedule his departure for the north. The governor, however, wants to keep him from going, and has proposed a secret meeting with Li at eleven o'clock today. Last night he sent someone in the middle of the night to tell me that if Li agrees to stay in Canton I might be released from my expulsion order and go ashore to join in a secret meeting. He asked whether I would be prepared to do that. What do you think?"

Sun went on: "Li really can't be trusted, and he doesn't have a very good understanding of what's going on. Still, he's old now and no longer very ambitious for glory. He's probably not going to let the governor's suggestion stop him from going to Peking. Consequently this is only a long shot. But in any case I'd like your opinion." I answered, "If the secret meeting actually takes place, then you ought to go. You, with your wisdom and talent, must decide the future of the matter." Sun said "Good," and waited for word rather indifferently. In the evening word came: Li had decided to go to Peking. This too became a dream.[102]

At this time the foreign powers were practicing dual diplomacy in China, pursuing one policy in the open and quite another behind the scenes. That is, while they acted like supporters of the Manchu dynasty in Peking on the one hand, they were working with secret societies on the

[102] Li had first been called to Peking by the court on June 18, and was summoned again on July 3 and 6, and in all about a dozen times, but he delayed his departure for Shanghai until July 21, and he remained there at the advice of the British until the siege of the legations was broken. He arrived in Tientsin September 18.

other. For instance, if a certain foreign power worked with the Boxers, another power would work with the regional authorities to prepare for any eventualities; and if one power cooperated with the Ch'ing court another power would line up with the secret societies in order to counter its rival. While they practiced the art of diplomacy in Peking, elsewhere they protected themselves against change by working with secret societies. This can be seen very clearly. For instance, when, at the beginning of the Boxer Rebellion, the governor of Hong Kong wanted Li Hung-chang to declare his provinces independent and wanted Sun Yat-sen to head the administration, he was developing a crafty plan for new circumstances. He calculated that if the two provinces were declared independent they would end under British influence, south China would not become a problem, and French initiatives there would be contained. The only way to achieve all this was to back Li Hung-chang. If Li cooperated with this, however, the secret societies might resist. Consequently it was necessary to bring Sun Yat-sen into the picture, and it was necessary to have Li and Sun cooperate. If they did, and the two provinces became independent without the use of any force, then England would have achieved hegemony. That was his real goal. He was close to his goal, but his plan collapsed just short of it. Collapse it did, but the basis for it was still there. It was still possible for someone to utilize that basis. It was obvious to everyone that the power of the Ch'ing court was no longer sufficient to control China. It was also obvious that it was impossible for the powers to divide China. Then how was China to be helped to build a state? Certainly not by simply discussing it with its professedly virtuous neighbor. Ah, that neighboring country of virtue![103] Does it still dream of preserving or dividing China by itself?[104] Open your eyes and see what the powers are doing in secret!

[103] Lit. "country of sages" (*kunshi koku*).

[104] *Shina hozen ron* (preserving China) had been a slogan of the political groups aroung Ōkuma Shigenobu since 1898.

That day so many visitors came that the time was full. When things quieted down at night we discussed our plans. Fukumoto, Kiyofuji, Hara, Hirayama, and I were the participants in the meeting. All of us agreed with Sun's proposal, to wit: Fukumoto would stay in Hong Kong and make preparations. If preparations did not go smoothly, we would go forward with what we already had. When it came to leading our forces, Cheng Shih-liang would be in charge, Hara and Yang Fei-hung would serve as his staff. Fukumoto would act as the head of the military government, with Hirayama as his assistant. There was some debate and disagreement, but in the end we followed Sun's proposals. Consequently Sun had Commander Cheng work out the military plans. The other Japanese comrades were all to go inland to assist Commander Cheng. They were: Tamamizu, Noda, Itō. They all were to wait for things to start in Hong Kong. With this settled, the Sado Maru raised anchor.

[25]
THE FAILURE OF OUR PLANS

IT IS THE LANDSCAPE OF JAPAN THAT ALWAYS warms my heart. Lake Biwa and Mt. Fuji, to which I had bade farewell so recently, seemed to smile at me on my return. The white clouds that touched Fuji's peak mirrored the tranquility of my mind.

When my train reached Yokohama I parted from Sun and went on to Tokyo, where Kiyofuji and I lived quietly in Shibaura near the shore. From Uchida and Suenaga Junichirō I learned what had happened since our departure and that Suenaga Setsu and Tajima were in Shanghai organizing comrades there. As old friends gradually located our residence it once again became a conspirators' lair. Consequently, before a week had passed my funds were running out. Tomeka appeared quite by chance. After my departure she had moved to a house in Ueno near Shinobazu Pond, and she had gone back to work as a geisha. She said that she and her mother were living alone, and asked whether I would like to avoid observation by moving in with them, for the first time. I did so, and became a geisha parasite. Kiyofuji meanwhile moved in with his elder sister.

I seemed to be living a leisurely life, but such was not the case. This was the time to develop our plans further. Our Tokyo comrades gathered secretly every day at the— Club, and Uchida organized about forty men with the intention of leading them to join Cheng's army; some of them had already left Tokyo for Kyushu. Hara returned suddenly from Hong Kong, and a few days later Fukumoto came too. Sun was extremely discouraged by that. He thought that because Japanese leaders were coming back like this the spirit of cooperation among the members of the league of secret societies would decline, and that because of that the enthusiasm of the Chinese comrades would decline as well. He seemed to be giving up the plans he had had for action in the south, and instead began to think about starting something in central China. He had Uchida and Suenaga give up plans for taking men to south China and instead made up his mind to go to Shanghai with Uchida and two or three other comrades.

Then came the rebellion of T'ang Ts'ai-ch'ang and his group.[105] Manchu officials cracked down on the Reform Party just as Sun and his companions reached Shanghai. Because of this Sun could not carry out his plans, and he returned to Japan empty-handed. Then hope began to dawn again. Sun planned to go to Taiwan with Uchida. Uchida had his mind on Korea by that time, however, so Sun went to Taiwan together with Kiyofuji instead.

Then a telegram came from Taiwan. It said that a revolutionary army had risen at Huichou [Waichow] on the sixth. I went to Yokohama with Hara, ordered Chinese clothing, and with my preparations made waited for further word. Then another cable came: "Prepare to send arms." The reference was to the arms we had bought for the Philippines. At that time we had not been able to send them because of government surveillance, and we were told they were stored with the Ōkura company. Since the Philippine effort had failed, as will be recalled, the weapons were of no further use there. Sun had received the permission of the Philippine comrades to borrow them for

[105] An effort mounted in cooperation with secret societies in September 1900; twenty persons, including T'ang, were executed. See also n. 84, p. 189.

his own use. He entrusted the negotiations to secure them first to Hara, and later I took part in them too. From this time on Nakamura's crime became apparent, his forgery of private documents became known, and the matter became a problem for our group and the basis for Nakamura's expulsion from our ranks. While we were wasting time with these complex matters the Huichou insurrection came to an end, and Sun Yat-sen returned to Japan. The matter went on to become a court case; Kōmuchi Tomotsune[106] became the arbitrator and finally resolved the issue after a great deal of wrangling. But even then Sun did not despair. He ordered me to go to Shanghai. This was our last-ditch plan.

Until I arrived in Shanghai I retained a certain amount of optimism. But after two days there I saw that it was hopeless, and returned home to report this to Sun. Sun, who had already seen that things were not promising, did not blame me for my incompetence but instead reluctantly resigned himself to the necessity of putting a stop to everything for a while. And so all our hopes came to nothing.

Even before then, Sun had said gently to me, "While you were in Shanghai some of the comrades spoke ill of you." He showed me a letter, then went on, "I hope you will be big-hearted about it, and not be angry with them. Everybody competes to take credit for success, but failure is often blamed on an individual. It has always been that way. Most people, knowing that ordinary people resent those who blame things on them, would conceal it from you, but I'm going to show this to you. I know you can take this like a hero; take it as a challenge." After I had finished reading it he burned it, and said with a laugh, "If you have anger in your heart, burn it like this." His attitude matched his words. My spirit was relieved because

[106] Kōmuchi Tomotsune (1848-1905), Diet member from 1890 to 1905, and Director General of the Cabinet Legislative Bureau, 1896-1898.

of this, but I was unable to suppress all unpleasantness from my thoughts.

I left Sun's place for Tokyo, spent the night with Tomeka, and headed for Inukai's residence the next morning. Inukai smiled when he saw me: "You're not a ghost are you? A lot of talk has been going around to the effect that you'd never come back. I am not impressed by the way you fellows talk about each other. There must be some misunderstanding. Why don't you all get together and talk it out over sake? Can you do it tomorrow? I'll provide the place, the sake, and the food." I thanked him for his kindness and made the round of my comrades to tell them about this invitation. When I got to the Taiyōkan the owner and his wife greeted me warmly: "Welcome back! While you were away there was one story after another about you until we flushed with anger. Those idiots talked about your taking ten thousand yen and their taking your head in revenge. Did you see Mr. Kani? He went to your place, didn't he? If he took your head, you must be a ghost!" They went on and on about this. Alas, I am an ordinary person. Outwardly I had a smile on my face, but inwardly I was in a rage. I tried to take it in my stride, but inside my anger flared. Yet on the one hand there was Sun's warning and on the other hand Inukai's friendship to help me. I consoled myself with the knowledge that they were real friends. The next day Takeda Shishū came. We went to Inukai's together. The others had preceded us there. The seats were arranged. Our host, Inukai, began: "It is easy for misunderstandings to arise when we don't talk together. The purpose of this meeting is to patch up old friendships. I hope that friendship will be restored and harmony will mature in the course of drinking and talking." One round of sake. Uchida addressed a question to me: "How did you finish off the Nakamura matter? Give us the full details of the story." I answered, "I have to be faithful to my promise to keep it secret. Without permission from Kōmuchi I can't reveal the matter." He was supposed to be there, but he had not arrived as yet. Uchida would not give up. I refused to talk. With that his questions became insulting. "Nakamura made a fool out of you," he said, "Why don't you have the guts to kill him?" and so on; he spat out insults at me. I am not very good at fighting, but I also lack the capacity to endure insult indefinitely. The thing that kept me from hitting Uchida was that I had some concept of courtesy, but I could not endure much more. My voice betrayed my anger. With respect to Uchida's charge that Nakamura had made a fool of me, I said it was his privilege to be suspicious if he chose; in response to his demands that I kill the man, I said that when I was convinced somebody ought to be killed I would do it, and not until then. As I look back on it, it must have seemed a childish fight. When our deepest emotions are at stake we all seem to become like little children. Finally Uchida shouted that he was going to beat me up, and I invited him to try it. How stupid we were! Suddenly he hit me in the forehead with a bowl. I immediately forgot all about courtesy and the challenge of remaining calm, forgetting what I was supposed to remember. Without realizing what I was doing I was on my feet and wrestling with him. When we got to the passageway others pulled us apart and I gradually got hold of myself again; then I saw the hot blood. I went to another room, where I was well taken care of. They sent for a doctor, who put on a bandage. It healed completely within ten days or so, but even now the scar looks like a new moon. It is a fitting reminder of my disgrace.

[26]

MY LETTER TO SUN YAT-SEN

I WANTED TO BE GENEROUS OF HEART. IN THE daytime, when there were other people about, the matter did not seem so important to me, but at night when everything was quiet and the wound hurt I would shed bitter tears of indignation. I thought of how little one could depend on people, and what a terrible thing the human heart was. And I myself became suspicious of people. I began to suspect that our Japanese comrades distrusted me. And what about Sun himself? Wasn't he somewhat suspicious of me too? Since human nature is weak, it wasn't at all impossible. I would have to explain the details of the Nakamura matter to him myself in order to resolve his doubts in case he had them. So in the end I wrote a letter from my bed of pain and sent it to Sun. It was the sort of thing a woman might have done. The letter went as follows:

> My Dear Friend Sun Yat-sen:
>
> Four years have passed since I had the honor of making your acquaintance. One can call it a short time, or one can call it a long time. During this period our friendship has been mature and principled; our focus has been not on selfish desires but on making plans and developing strategies. Several times our great undertaking has failed at the very point of success. But while the Way is limitless, it can be brought about

only by man. Our friendship must continue in an unchanging manner. Like the Way, our plans must not be abandoned but they must endure like the world. Truly, I believe, with you, the bond of our friendship will be of this nature. This is why I retain my hope in this world despite the failure and withdrawal, even though the path we took may have been mistaken. That is why I followed your instructions to disband our group of comrades temporarily, for I hope that we will plan and rise with you again. Of course I expected to become the target of abuse. I was not surprised that slander and calumny were directed toward me today. You have insight into my state of mind. I do not need to describe it at length. We have not yet reached the promised land. We are still far from the state of enlightenment and bliss. Nor can we be sure that we can avoid separation from each other in the trials through which we are passing. Therefore I follow the path of ordinary men and take up my brush to tell you the details of the Nakamura matter and explain my own state of mind. If there are doubts in your mind I pray that this letter will resolve them. If there are no such doubts, then please laugh at me and discard this. I do this foolish thing because I am concerned with justice and with human nature. I beg you not to scorn me; do not scorn me.

When you cabled us from Taiwan to ship the military supplies some time ago, I got together with Inukai and Hara to see how we could do it. Everybody thought it would be very difficult. We did not go to Nakamura with this immediately because we were a little suspicious of him because of the previous disaster.[107] At that time Nakamura had handled all the negotiations himself from the first, and he had not allowed anybody else to get involved as middleman.

[107] The Nunobiki Maru disaster.

Consequently, we had no chance to check on him. I myself had regretted that. But this time, by good fortune there was a story that Nakamura was going to go on a trip in the provinces, and we thought that this would give us a good opportunity. So Hara went to him first and said, "Sun has just sent us a telegram ordering us to get ready to send the guns and ammunition. We have no way of knowing when his order to send them right away will come, but once it does come we will not want to lose any time in delay. It would be good if you would delay your trip and take care of this yourself. But if you can't, you must delegate somebody who can take care of it in your place." "I've already promised Ōhigashi," Nakamura answered, "and I can't delay my trip. I would appreciate it if you would wait for my return to Tokyo." Hara explained the situation and said that was impossible. Nakamura finally was not able to resist any longer, and gave Hara papers authorizing him to act as his representative. This gave Hara the opportunity to check on Ōkura.

When Hara first went to Ōkura and asked to have some of the ammunition, they told him the timing was very inconvenient, and that they couldn't let him have any just then. Hara charged them with being very highhanded. He argued that the goods were fully paid for, and consequently his property. They answered, "The goods are yours, but we retain the right to set the time of shipment. This is all provided for in our contract with Nakamura." When he heard this Hara was incredulous and started to have his doubts, and demanded to have a look at the material. To this they said, "These goods are still in the warehouse. Not even we can get access to them very easily." Then they went on, "Anyway, how could you examine 2,500,000 bullets one by one?" Hara retorted, "I'm a professional army man and I know something about these things. Even without examining them all, I can base my conclusions on a spot check." At this they said to Hara, "Well, the material is defective to begin with. Only a few bullets out of a hundred would go off if anybody tried to use them. The thing to do would be to ship it all overseas when the chance comes up and make a big profit. That would be best for both Nakamura and you, wouldn't it?" Those Ōkura people probably thought that Hara was as crooked as Nakamura, and so they told him the truth. Hara tore off to tell Inukai, and he also telephoned me. I rushed over to hear Hara's story, and learned about all this for the first time.

The goods had already been bought and the money had been handed over. And still we couldn't move the materiel, we couldn't examine it, and then we were told it was all defective anyway and that we ought to try to make a profit on it. Was there ever anything so outrageous? We were stunned and had no idea what we should do. All we could do was to rail against Nakamura's dishonesty and lament our own unwisdom, all in vain. That was why we sent you the cable saying that it would be difficult to send the equipment. You cabled back an order to send equipment rather than money. At that point Inukai was good enough to visit Ōkura to demand that they buy back the ammunition. The Ōkura people said, "We'll buy it back for 12,500 yen." Inukai said, "twelve thousand five hundred yen in return for the original 65,000 yen? How can you be that unfair?" They interrupted him: "No. All we got was 50,000 yen. We don't know anything about the rest. But most of the profit went to Nakamura, and we ourselves made very little on it. We heard that there were a lot of people involved along with Nakamura." So then we knew that Nakamura had made an enormous amount of money. But we still didn't know about his rascality in preparing the fake documents. Inukai then pressed Ōkura by explaining something about you, and urged them to pay at least 30,000 yen. Ōkura chose not to make a blunt refusal, and asked for time to consider; two days later they sent an inside man to Inukai and raised the offer by 2,500 yen. It was the best they could do, he said. He was willing to buy the ammunition back for a total of 15,000 yen. Now we had no idea at all as to what we should do.

Then Inukai proposed a plan. "It's clear that Nakamura cheated you;" he said. "I think he pocketed a lot of this money. But although his action was abominable, it won't help things any to sit around blaming him now. Moreover, once people learn what he has done he will be ruined permanently; maybe we should even feel sorry for him. Wouldn't it be better to make a deal with him for restitution, and put that money together with the Ōkura 15,000 yen to respond to Sun Yat-sen's emergency needs? Nakamura, however, camouflages his ill-gotten gains by living very modestly. Even if you confront him directly with the facts and demand the money back, it's certain he will not agree. It's going to be hard to do. Therefore the best thing to do would be to arrange with Ōkura to have it look as if there is still no settlement, and wait for Nakamura to come back to Tokyo. Then, when he does, get him to take over the negotiations with Ōkura; Ōkura can warn him that the facts are going to come out, and then he can still cover himself by making restitution in Ōkura's name. That's the way to have Nakamura pay back the money without being disgraced. You may not get enough money back to meet Sun Yat-sen's needs, but this is the only way to get a quick settlement." Hara and I thought this was a fine suggestion, and agreed to follow it.

When you cabled that you had begun a rebellion at Huichou Hara and I came to Yokohama and got ready to travel, and planned to settle this quickly. However, since things had gone this far, we decided we had to wait for Nakamura to get back to Tokyo in line with our plan. When word came that your forces were winning, our spirits soared and we longed to be there. Then Nakamura came back to Tokyo. I first went to see him and said, "Ōkura says that this is a bad time for him to send the ammunition, and there doesn't seem to be anything we can do about it. When I cabled this news to Sun, he cabled back ordering me to send money right away instead. Inukai, Hara, and I took this up with Ōkura, but he won't agree to give us more than 15,000 yen. There's nothing further we can do. But with things the way they are in Huichou, and Sun Yat-sen in this position I wish you would talk with Ōkura yourself, and see if you cannot get him to raise his figure to 30,000 yen." Nakamura showed some reluctance, and so I pressed him: "This is a critical matter for East Asia. It is no time for you to hesitate. Moreover, I'm afraid that if this matter of the ammunition isn't settled, it could give you trouble for a long time to come." Nakamura suddenly seemed to understand. He agreed, stood up, and telephoned immediately for an appointment with Ōkura. It was arranged, and I left. Everything seemed to be going according to plan.

The next day I visited Nakamura again. He said, "Yesterday, I had an appointment to see Ōkura, but something came up and we didn't meet. I was just on the point of going now." We went out his door together right then; Nakamura headed for Ōkura, and I went home. That afternoon Inukai telephoned to ask me to come over. When I got there Hara was already there discussing things with Inukai. Hara didn't seem to have his normal composure. I wondered what was wrong, and sat down. As the story came out with all its details I understood things for the first time.

Hara repeated his story for me: "I have just seen Nakamura. He said, 'I just got back from seeing Ōkura.' I could see from his face that he was very upset, and in fact he was. He looked at me angrily and said, 'That Inukai is unfair and heartless. Despite the years of our acquaintance, I've never really known what he was like. Today, for the first time, I appreciate him for what he is. What's the idea of going to Ōkura and slandering me? Who is this Ōkura? Isn't he just a merchant? Compare that with the relationship between Inukai and me! Don't we work together as political allies in matters of national importance? Despite this, Inukai has the gall to forget all this and slander me to a merchant. What kind of man would have the heart to do that? He's really a contemptible scoundrel.' Nakamura was almost beside himself. Of course he was just compensating for his fraud, and trying to get out of it by attacking Inukai. It was really intolerable, and I could hardly control myself. I almost wanted to take revenge on the spot. But I managed to hold on and left without saying anything, because I was worried about future plans. We can't give in to frustration. That's why I came here to talk about it."

I think that what happened is that when Nakamura went to Ōkura to advise him to return the money, Ōkura countered by advising Nakamura to do so. Their talk then came to Nakamura's fraud, and as they went on they got to the business (the discrepancy between 50,000 yen and 65,000 yen) that Inukai had talked about. When that came up Nakamura realized for the first time that his friends knew he had been dishonest and in his consternation he wanted to evade that. And so he put on that crazy performance for Hara. Who knows? He was probably covering up for even more serious crimes than the things we already knew about: forgery and fraud.

The next day I went to see Nakamura. Hara was

already there, but I pretended not to know about the things he had told me the day before. Instead, I asked Nakamura what sort of an answer he had received from Ōkura. He answered me with a loud voice and his face flushed. He said, "I don't want to have anything further to do with the ammunition. I don't want anything more to do with you people either." "Why on earth?" I asked. With that he began reviling Inukai in about the same way Hara had described the day before. I listened quietly for a while, waiting for him to finish. Then I said, "This is not Inukai's project, but it's Sun Yat-sen's. No, it's not even Sun Yat-sen's; it is the moral imperative of the entire world. From what you say, you are prepared to abandon this higher duty because of Inukai. Does that make sense? You ought to put your argument with Inukai off to some future date. I beg you to settle this matter immediately so that we can respond to Sun's emergency." I urged him on; "Do not abandon this great cause because of your personal resentment." But he wouldn't listen to me; his mind was closed, and he wouldn't give in. He kept raising irrational arguments and denouncing Inukai. I managed to control myself and argued for a while, but it didn't do any good. Finally my irritation got the better of me. After a few hot words, I left with Hara. But even so we still did not denounce Nakamura as a crook, for we were worried about what we could do after that.

And so our first plan for a solution failed. Still, we couldn't risk losing the sum that Ōkura had agreed to repay. Since we had lost the document that had been drawn up between Ōkura and a German company for the exchange of goods, we had to make up another nominal contract. That we couldn't do without Nakamura; there was no way around it. We finally had Fukumoto take it up with Nakamura, and he got him to draw up the contracts for a German firm so we could finally finish off with Ōkura. Fukumoto was a big help with this.

Nakamura now put up a final defense with the courage of desperation. There was nothing we could do publicly. But of course he knew that he was wrong, and his conscience must have been very uneasy indeed. Finally he invented a mean strategy. He agitated among a number of members of the Progressive Party, trying to stir them up with a twisted story that "Inukai's real purpose in slandering me is to break the influence of our old reform faction." At this time Inukai was still keeping Nakamura's deceit quiet. Nakamura had made a hasty judgment because of what Ōkura had said; because he was nervous about that, he tried to counterattack by distorting the story. As a result people in the political world gradually began to sense the hostility between him and Inukai; some came to Inukai to ask him what the facts were, and others wrote letters to inquire. Gradually it became a problem within the party. But Inukai still didn't make it public, and just gave the facts in confidence to a few party leaders he had to inform. It was at this time that you came back from Taiwan and that we saw from the documents you showed me that Nakamura was guilty of fraud and forgery as well.

At this time Kojima Kazuo came to see me. He was quite fully informed on the entire matter. He said to me, "Yesterday Nakamura Haizan asked to see me. I haven't seen him for a long time, but there is this business now—I believe you're involved in it. Should I see him, or not?" Inukai was out of town that day in Sendai. I encouraged Kojima to see Nakamura on my own, and he did so. When he came back, he said, "Well, that's the way it is. He takes a hard line in public, but privately he's very uneasy. What he wanted was to have me mediate on his behalf." When Inukai came back I told him this, and he was very pleased; he wanted to resolve the problem peacefully.

Soon Nakamura asked Kojima to arrange a meeting for him with Inukai. Of course he was still uneasy about matters, but unless Kojima had worked quietly to explain the pros and cons of such a step to him he never would have come to it. Inukai said, "A meeting is fine with me. But tell Nakamura this: We can't have it in a tea house or restaurant. And I want one or two friends with me. Pick them from Kōmuchi, Yamada, or Hiraoka,[108] and have the meeting at one of their houses." Kojima took this to Nakamura, and then returned to Inukai to say a certain day at Yamada's house would be fine. The other two were to come too. The day came. Inukai had me make a copy of the document Nakamura had forged and took it with him to the meeting. Inukai came back and said to me, "Nakamura's speech took almost two hours. It was a skillful camouflage of what he did. I didn't say much, because I didn't think argument was called for, but when I took out the copies of the forged documents I had with me I said, 'What you say sounds good. But what about these two documents?' He said nothing, bowed his head, and admitted his guilt."

This was a secret meeting, and of course it wasn't supposed to be made public. Everybody there maintained secrecy in order to protect Nakamura. He too, having admitted his blame, wanted to make up for it. So there was now some hope. Then by bad luck a newspaper[109] published the story of Nakamura's misdeeds and attacked him. Although the article didn't talk about his forgery as yet, he was now in danger of losing his reputation and having his political career

[108] Yamada Kinosuke (1859-1913), who was selected, was a leading figure in Meiji law. After Tokyo University, he was associated with the Ministry of Justice, the *Kaishintō*, the High Court, and the Diet.

[109] The *Yorozu Chōhō* broke the story.

brought to an end. It can be imagined how great his consternation was. The next thing that happened was that Uchida asked to see Nakamura. Since Uchida had a reputation for being aggressive and tough, the guilty man was naturally afraid. We ourselves of course know nothing about this meeting; Kojima tipped me off to it. Kojima said, "Nakamura thinks that Inukai put Uchida up to this, and he resents it very much. This sort of thing can only hurt matters. It's probable that others will not understand Inukai's real purpose and consider him a bully. You people ought to think about this." We had heard that Uchida was responsible for the article in the paper, and so we went to Uchida and asked him to call off the press and postpone his meeting with Nakamura. After thinking about it, he agreed. But the newspaper didn't stop its attacks. Before long it revealed the details of the forgery and exposed Nakamura's deceit. Wasn't this the death sentence for Nakamura? Now he was cornered, and he would fight to the end. Once again our compromise settlement had been destroyed.

That's the way it went with Nakamura. But for Inukai a new problem now came up: the problem of how Nakamura was to be punished within the political party. Once the paper reported the story of the documents Nakamura had forged, Inukai found himself under great pressure from many quarters to punish him. When that happened Inukai knew that he would not be able to protect Nakamura any longer, and he quietly advised him to resign from the party. Nakamura refused. As a result Inukai, as a member of the party's General Affairs Committee, had no choice but to expel Nakamura from the party.

The basis for a peaceful solution to the problem was now destroyed. Things moved inexorably to the final step: a court battle. Nakamura had promised Inukai that he would make some sort of restitution and now we needed a firm commitment from him. So I went to see him and showed him your letter. Of course this was a formality; Nakamura responded to your letter with the same excuse he had used previously. You were angry and proposed that we sue, and we all agreed. Furthermore Kojima, who had been trying to act as mediator, realized that mediation was no longer possible, and he did not resist our decision. The suit now became inevitable. We decided to entrust the legal aspects of the matter to Mr. Miyoshi Taizō.[110] In the middle of all this the matter involving Mr. Gotō came up, without being solved; you were angry on that account and we were too. All this made our determination to go to court even stronger. The force of circumstances drove matters forward.

One day I happened to meet Uchida at Inukai's house. When he asked how the matter was coming I explained its course in general terms, and stated that it was our intention to sue Nakamura. He was emphatic in his approval, and said, "You've made your decision. Now you must fight Nakamura head on." He went on, "I have a friend called Sakurai.[111] What he has heard about this matter has infuriated him. He wants to represent Sun without charging any fee. I think you ought to meet with him and discuss the matter." I agreed with this, and so did Inukai. As a result we decided to have Miyoshi act as our attorney, and have Sakurai assist him.

The next day a relative of mine named Ichiki sent word that he would like to see me. When I went to his house a man named Fukui was there. "I am a friend of

[110] Miyoshi (1845-1908) began as an official of the Justice Ministry and resigned to take up a distinguished private career in law: he was named to the House of Peers shortly before these events took place.

[111] Sakurai Kumatarō (1861-1908), a Meiji jurist who resigned from government shortly before this and devoted the rest of his career to public causes.

Nakamura's," he said. Ichiki first asked me, "Are you at peace with your decision to destroy Nakamura forever?" "No," I said, "I'm not." "How about Inukai?" he asked. "Inukai feels the way I do," I answered. He shook his head: "Inukai's persecution of Nakamura is becoming too cruel. The newspaper stories; expulsion: these two things have already made people see Inukai as pitiless and heartless. But now I hear he wants to take Nakamura to court. His aim may be to cut Nakamura up, but isn't he himself going to end up hurt? Shouldn't you try to have Inukai look at the pros and cons of this?" I explained the progress of the matter and stressed the hatred that had been aroused. He answered, "Inukai has more to think of then his own gain or loss, doesn't he? Since there is also his duty towards Sun Yat-sen, and since he is the one responsible he should do what's right and not take time worrying about his own interests." Then he flushed and suddenly changed his tone: "This is the way it is. If it really comes to this, aren't you the one to issue the warning and wave your arms to stop it? You've been obligated to Inukai for many years now. This is the time for you to repay that obligation." I asked him what he meant. He straightened himself up and said, "You know that I've been much more sympathetic to Inukai than most people. But even from watching this matter from the sidelines I'm beginning to see Inukai as heartless. Although I've fortunately been able to have your explanation and I can understand things now, ordinary people are going to be much more doubtful about Inukai, and they will have no way of getting to understand it. Isn't this too bad for Inukai? Although one shouldn't deny the wrong that Nakamura did, aren't you the people who entrusted important matters to him? If he did something wrong, don't you share in the blame for lack of foresight? What you have to do is show generosity and meet Nakamura half way and save Inukai from the distrust that this action will generate." His thinking seemed very clear, and I was almost persuaded by him. Nevertheless Nakamura was a person of great cunning, someone who always suited his tactics to the enemy's weak points. I was quite sure that he could not change his nature and deserve forgiveness. I declined to accept the suggestion, but thanked him for his advice. He told me that Nakamura was coming in the morning to ask me to mediate the matter.

That day Inukai sent me a telegram asking me to come. When I got there he said, "Today Kōmuchi came and argued that it was a mistake to prosecute Nakamura. I argued with him, but I didn't seem to be able to persuade him. When he left he asked me to tell you that he wanted to see you. He's going to be at the Kōyōkan this evening. I think you ought to go once to see him." That day I had arranged to meet you at Kojima's house so we could go to the lawyer Miyoshi together. I hurried to Kojima's in a rickshaw to meet you and go on to Miyoshi's. As it happened, Miyoshi was not there. So I left immediately and went to the Kōyōkan. Kōmuchi took me to a separate room and said, "I wanted to see you in connection with the Nakamura matter. I want you people to let up a little bit." I explained the general process of the matter and why we had become compelled to sue Nakamura. Kōmuchi said, "I understand that pretty well. However, I'm a close friend of Inukai. I think you are too. And you are also Sun Yat-sen's closest friend. I am full of admiration for the idealism with which you and Inukai work for the cause of a refugee from another country. But you must know that Nakamura and Inukai are also political allies of many years' standing. But now you propose to destroy Nakamura for Sun's sake. How can you consider this humane?

Inukai says that he has no pity for anybody who is low enough to suck the blood of high-minded refugees. That makes sense, and it's all very well; but sometimes compassion is more important than sense; it respects the weak more than it does the mighty. If you people persevere in this then the sympathy of the public will end with Nakamura, and Inukai will seem pitiless and cruel. On the other hand if you give Nakamura a reprieve Inukai will be out of this and his good name will be preserved. What you must do is spare Nakamura; that way you will advance Sun's work and at the same time you will save Inukai's good name." I told him that we had decided on this step because we had no alternative. He shook his head: "No, that's not so. If you agree I will approach Nakamura myself. Don't set a fixed sum, but I will take it upon myself to get as much money as Nakamura can manage, to placate Sun Yat-sen." His sincerity was moving. I agreed to that.

Kōmuchi went on: "If you agree with that, then stop this suit." I said this was impossible; "We have an appointment with Miyoshi the day after tomorrow. We still have two days to go. I think that any discussions you have with Nakamura should take place at once and be concluded right away." He agreed. Then he went on, "I'm ignorant of money affairs, and need an advisor." I suggested Kojima, and he agreed.

Two days later you and I went to Kojima's house, and the two of us went on to Miyoshi's office from there. Miyoshi made the following comment: "There is a law that applies to Nakamura's deceit. But this affair came up in connection with a plot, and those who were involved will have to be interrogated time after time. Even worse, there are people of four nationalities involved, and if it blows up into a major scandal it would require several years before a decision is reached." Because of this your determination was shaken. But if Nakamura realized the truth of what Miyoshi said, it was probable that his attitude would harden as a result. That is why I didn't reveal this to even my close friends, and also acted toward Kōmuchi as if the suit were surely going forward, in order to be able to put pressure for a settlement on Nakamura behind the scenes. Ah! At last I became a plotter who deceived Kōmuchi. Kōmuchi consequently hurried his negotiations with Nakamura because he was afraid the day of the court case was coming close. In the end Kōmuchi persuaded Nakamura to give up his house, which was valued at 13,000 yen. We were surprised the sum was so small, and so was Inukai. However, I had promised Kōmuchi that I would insist on a fixed amount. If we had not been prepared to accept this, the only alternative was for me to retire from the negotiations and entrust them to somebody else. So then we asked the opinion of you and your associates. Everybody said, "If the negotiations break down over a specific sum the matter will have to go back to the courts. But there the problems are as Miyoshi stated them. We had better settle for what we have." Kojima went to Kōmuchi and relayed your decision, and the agreement was made. Kōmuchi said angrily, "Nakamura will cheat all the way to the grave." He knew his assets were well concealed. He was so angry that he wanted to supplement Nakamura's payment with a thousand yen of his own. But you were too honorable to accept that. Consequently Kōmuchi went back to Nakamura and had him issue promissory notes of 2,000 yen, and since you were reluctant to accept the house in payment, that payment was changed to 13,000 yen in cash. The matter was concluded at a final meeting at the Yaokan. All this you know.

The facts are really as I have reported them here. Shall I sum it up? At first it was Inukai's hope that we could maintain our honor with you and keep from destroying Nakamura. In the end Inukai was fully resolved to keep honor with you even if it meant being criticized as heartless and cruel because he had destroyed Nakamura. It was Kōmuchi who proposed that we give Nakamura a reprieve and spare Inukai those charges. I was unlucky enough to be in the middle and to be fully aware of the sentiments of both Inukai and Kōmuchi. But I was also deeply conscious of your position, and I had to endure the distress of making the right decision. It was only because I was aware of your full confidence in me that I presumed to go forward unflinchingly.

I am almost through. When I look back at this letter I am astonished that it is so long, and also that I can be so foolish. But what is it that brings me to this point? Knowing it to be foolish, why have I nevertheless done this? It is because I fear the desolation the loss of our friendship would bring. I fear that, because I hope our affection will endure forever. If you do not laugh at me it will be my great good fortune.

[27]

THE HUICHOU INCIDENT

ALAS, WHAT AGONY MY DREAM HAS BROUGHT! During the period that it possessed me, the dream of Philippine independence failed, and so too the Huichou (Waichow) revolutionary rising. The Philippine story is now widely known; the Huichou story is not. Let me tell of that dream, even though only the foolish talk of dreams.

In June of 1900, when we left Yokohama for Hong Kong with Sun Yat-sen, he sent orders to his lieutenants in Kwangtung province to assemble six hundred volunteers at a mountain stronghold in Sanchout'ien [Samchautin]. (Sanchout'ien is near Tap'eng Bay [Mirs Bay] in Kwangtung, and about a day by ship from Hong Kong.) When our ship arrived in Hong Kong he issued orders to construct facilities and make other preparations. From there Sun went on to Saigon and Singapore; we went on to Singapore after finishing our business in Hong Kong. We were to meet in Singapore to work out our detailed plans, then return to Hong Kong, and from there we were to go secretly to Sanchout'ien to join the insurrection. That was the general plan, but of course our imprisonment in Singapore came between. Kiyofuji and I found ourselves banned for five years; Sun and the others no longer had any reason to try to keep their presence secret, and we all sailed to Hong Kong together.

At this time the mountainous area in Sanchout'ien had

Huichou Revolt

been prepared, but although there were six hundred volunteers there were only three hundred rifles, and only thirty rounds of ammunition per person. However, some of our party were in secret communication with a certain commander in the city of Canton. He agreed to sell guns and ammunition at a high price. Sun provided the money and ordered that this be done, and he also directed the purchase of a small steamer. By that means he planned to be in direct contact with the forces at Sanchout'ien. At that time the Hong Kong government banned Kiyofuji and me. Although we made adventurous plans for going inland despite that, the surveillance of the police made it impossible to carry them out. Sun Yat-sen therefore had no choice but to order that the base at Sanchout'ien should be held and that the partisans should wait for further instructions. Meanwhile he returned to Japan together with us on the Sado Maru.

After Sun returned to Japan he rushed around desperately for several months trying to work out a plan, but not one succeeded. Consequently the food supplies of the volunteers at Sanchout'ien diminished day by day and they dispersed to seek maintenance from the homes of sympathizers in the area, with the result that only eighty men remained to hold the base. However, for several months the volunteers at the base had detained villagers who wandered into their area by mistake, and did not allow them to leave. They did this to keep information about the base from leaking out. However, the villagers in the area, when they saw that people that went up there never came back, gradually became suspicious, and before long all sorts of rumors started up. "There are people planning a rebellion at Sanchout'ien," they said. The story grew with the telling: one became ten, ten became one hundred and then one thousand, until there were said to be tens of thousands of men and horses in the mountain base. Because of this the Governor General of Kwangtung and Kwangsi ordered the fleet commander Ho Ch'ang-ch'ing to take four thousand men from the Boca Tigris base to Shench'ou [Shumchun] and also ordered the military commander Teng Wan-lin to lead the forces at Huichou to Tanshui [Tamshui] and Chenlung [Chanlung] in order to blockade Sanchout'ien. But, the Ch'ing forces, having heard that we had a large army, were timid. As they were torn by doubts they didn't know what to do. Our forces were great in reputation, but they were very weak in fact. If the enemy had advanced with eight thousand men they could have finished us off in one morning. Therefore the comrades outside the base were extremely worried, and they cabled Sun Yat-sen to advance immediately. In response to this Sun sent word that since they had been discovered they should disperse for a time in order to avoid the enemy's attack. The volunteers on Sanchout'ien, since they knew the enemy's strength, did not want to advance against him; but since they also thought they had the cover of their mountainous terrain, they didn't feel like giving up their base either. They sent word to Sun a second time, saying that if he could send them ammunition to a point in Kwangtung, and let them know where it was, they would sally out of their fastness to get it and then turn to fight the enemy. At that time Sun was in Taiwan. He sent word again that if they could really extricate themselves they should immediately dash for Amoy and that he would be able to do something for them when they got there. It was at this time that Sun sent us the orders to ship the ammunition from Japan, and it was at this time that Nakamura's trickery became apparent.

Before Sun's directive reached the partisans the naval commander Ho had moved his spearhead party of two hundred men to Shawan, and he was about to scout the base of Sanchout'ien by advancing to Hengkang [Wongkong]. Our forces soon knew of this, and, realizing the dangers of waiting for the enemy, thought it better to raise their morale and anticipate the enemy by attacking him. Commander Huang Fu[112] therefore led eighty partisans in a night attack on Shawan in which forty enemy soldiers were killed. The rest of the enemy troops fled. So he had added forty rifles and several cases of ammunition to his supplies. Our people were greatly encouraged by this. At dawn they mounted a pursuit of the enemy with the goal of seizing the town of Hsinan [Shinan]. Meanwhile Commander-in-Chief Cheng Shih-liang arrived from Hong Kong with Sun's cable. Therefore the orders were changed, and the army headed northeast in the direction of Amoy. At that time our forces were already halfway to Hsinan. Having followed Sun's order, the force reached Hengkang, where they were joined by the rest of the six hundred volunteers who had been in the mountain base. Furthermore some five or six thousand sympathizers from Taku were gathered in the area between Hsinan and Boca Tigris. Their original idea had been to join forces with the six hundred volunteers from the base and take the town of Hsin-an. But when the order to reverse directions came, the main force turned to the northeast and the town was not taken, and they lost their chance to join up. This lost opportunity was due to rigid compliance with directives sent from a great distance.

By this time Cheng had replaced Huang as our commander. After the encounter at Shawan the enemy troops had fled, but the main force had not yet been defeated. It consisted of three thousand troops encamped at Tanshui. Chenlung also had one thousand troops. On the other hand our forces numbered only six hundred, of whom only three hundred had weapons. They were able to recruit another one thousand men from P'ingshan and Lungkang [Lungkong]. Consequently the men who lacked guns were given spears and that raised morale; they immediately marched toward Chenlung. Meanwhile the

112 Huang Fu, Kwangtung revolutionary and leader of the *San-ho hui* who was active in Southeast Asia.

enemy forces reached Futzuchieh and waited for our army in a mountainous position. Our men advanced on them; the spear bearers were in the front showing their high morale, men with rifles were on the right and left sides of the line; they crawled up the mountain and attacked the enemy from both sides. This surprise attack terrified the enemy, and our men pursued their soldiers as they fled. Enemy casualties were heavy. In this attack our troops captured several dozen prisoners, and enemy commander Tu Feng-wu was among them. More than seven hundred rifles were captured along with twelve horses, banners, and all sorts of insignia of rank and merit decorations. More than fifty thousand bullets also fell into our hands. That night our army camped at Chenlung.

At that time a comrade came from Huichou. He reported that the comrades in Polo [Pokloh] were unable to rise. (This group had been expected to seize the city of Huichou). There were already more than five or six thousand Ch'ing troops on hand there. Moreover Admirals Liu Pang-sheng, Ma Wei-chi, and Mo Shan-chi had already arrived, and Cheng Jun-lin and Liu Yung-fu were due any day. When the enemy units were complete, they would come to more than twenty thousand men. At this news Commander Cheng realized that his troops could not cope with the enemy, and did not dare to attack. The following dawn he led his troops in the direction of Yunghu [Wingwu]. This day there were several small engagements along the line of march. At night they reached Yunghu and camped. This was the fifth day after the engagement at Shawan.

At the outset Commander Cheng had ordered all his troops to observe all army regulations carefully. Consequently the villagers along the line of march welcomed our forces with food and water, and stood by the roadside to greet them. The noise of firecrackers followed the noise of guns. There were many who gave money and donated beef and mutton. Old villagers said with admiration, "Revolutionary armies of the past were never this well-behaved. This is truly a righteous army." Our numbers swelled by several thousand.

On the morning of the sixth day our army marched out of Yunghu, proceeded for a few hours and then suddenly saw a large enemy force. This force was made up of units that had reformed after retreating from Tanshui and other units that had been sent from Huichou. They numbered about five or six thousand, and our numbers were about the same. Only about one thousand of our men had guns, but their spirits were extremely high and they were truly anxious to destroy the enemy completely. Those who had guns vied with each other to be first, and charged the enemy fiercely. After the battle had raged for several hours the enemy suffered a great defeat and their men fled in all directions; some toward Huichou, some toward Tanshui, and others toward Paimanghua [Pakmongfa]. The enemy commander Liu Wan was severely wounded. Our men pursued the enemy in all four directions. We took five or six hundred guns, tens of thousands of rounds of ammunition, and more than thirty horses. We also took several hundred enemy prisoners; they all cut their queues and joined us as labor troops.

That night our units were reformed and marched toward Paimanghua. They arrived at dawn and found no enemy. The townspeople welcomed the troops with rejoicing and an additional five or six thousand comrades joined us. Now we were more than ten thousand in all. Our men stayed there all day to collect supplies and to make preparations for the march to Amoy. This was the seventh day. The next morning the army began its advance in the direction of Amoy at dawn. No enemy troops were encountered along the way. Now the numbers were very large. The men had no training in marching, and consequently progress was very slow. Villages and houses along the line of march were very few and small, and there were not enough to provide assistance. Every night the men had no place to stay. So it went until the tenth day. That night they reached Pengkang and for the first time they were able to sleep in houses again. They found no enemy soldiers there. At dawn on the eleventh day they saw the enemy along the river. Our troops used the town of Pengkang as their stronghold, and fought several engagements. The enemy troops involved now numbered more than seven thousand; none of them would surrender. Our troops were forced to defend their stronghold, and they fought all through the night. It was the same on the twelfth day; the other side would not give up. At night our side sent out a small detachment to attack the enemy camp, and the fighting went on until dawn. The enemy force finally retreated a little. All of our troops then left their stronghold and attacked the enemy. A fierce fight raged for several hours, and then the enemy troops fled. After the sun set our forces reformed and again entered Pengkang, collected their supplies, and prepared for departure. However, this day's fighting had depleted our supplies of ammunition. And since we still had a long way to march, we were unable to pursue the enemy. The shortage of ammunition was a source of real concern for the high command. The only hope was to make rapid progress toward Amoy and receive supplies there. But that too was a vain hope. How serious Nakamura's crime had been!

On the fourteenth day the army marched again, and spent the night at Santoshu. On the fifteenth comrades came from a number of villages, and very many joined the army. Its total size was now about twenty thousand men. That day parties were sent out to seek supplies. But from Santoshu to Meilin there were not any large villages within a distance of four or five days' travel, and the commanders were concerned about lack of supplies. On the sixteenth the force set out from Santoshu and reached Paisha at night.

On the seventeenth day, as the force was about to set out, there was a man who had come from Hong Kong by way of Haiphong. He had an order from Sun: "The situation has changed suddenly and it is unlikely that there will be any outside help. Consequently, even if you reach Amoy I probably won't be able to do anything for you. I hope the Commander-in-Chief will decide what to do with respect to military affairs." In other words, he hadn't been able to send the ammunition because of Nakamura. Sun hadn't been able to reach the interior because of the situation in Taiwan. This news caused an immediate drop of morale throughout the army. The commanders gathered to discuss it. They all said, "Since we cannot get supplies at Amoy anymore we should retreat along the shore, cross the bay, get back to our mountain base at Sanchout'ien, and try to find some way to order ammunition from Hong Kong. After that we can turn to the northwest and join our comrades at Hsinan and Boca Tigris; then we should take Canton and set up a government." At this point the local people who had joined us scattered and returned to their homes, and only the thousand or so men who had Western rifles stayed with the force. They divided into two groups, one by land and one by water, and headed for Tap'eng Bay. At that time the Sanchout'ien mountain base had still not fallen into the hands of the enemy. However, the naval commander, Ho Chang-ch'ing, had just taken Hengkang by leading some troops from Shench'ou. This gave some comrades the idea of taking Hengkang with the idea of capturing the commander. But our army had no equipment, it was running out of food, and it did not have access to ammunition. In the end they had to give up the idea and disband. Alas! Who was responsible for this failure?

Throughout this whole affair only four of our men were killed. They can truly be called martyrs of the revolutionary army. But what I shall truly never forget are the deaths of Shih Chien-yu, Yang Fei-hung, and our Japanese comrade Yamada Yoshimasa. Shortly after I had been injured by Uchida and while I was still convalescing at Tomeka's house, Sun came to visit me to show me a letter. It turned out to be news of the death of Shih Chien-ju. It said that he had been captured by government soldiers in the city of Canton, who immediately beheaded him and displayed his head. Alas, that it should have come to this! A lad of eighteen, he had a beautiful, jewel-like countenance; he was as soft and gentle as a dove, and he was the first to participate in our secret plans for a Huichou revolutionary army. He worked his way into the city of Canton by himself to set fires, and on another occasion he threw a bomb into a high mandarin's residence, killing twenty people and striking fear into the hearts of the officials. By doing this he diverted attention from the Huichou revolutionary army, but he was discovered, arrested, and sentenced to be beheaded.

Prior to this, when we had been expelled from Hong Kong and were about to sail for Japan again, many Chinese and Japanese comrades had come to the pier to see us off. Shih came too. When we parted Kiyofuji gave him a Japanese sword. He accepted it joyfully, and was about to leave with it, but the police surveillance was very strict. After some worry, he finally thrust one end up his sleeve and covered the rest with a Western umbrella he was carrying; the sight of him standing there, looking back and laughing while he waved goodbye with his free arm, is still with me. And now he is dead.

Some months after the Huichou matter was over the commander of the defeated forces, Cheng Shih-liang, came to Japan. He had changed from Ch'ing to Western dress, cut his queue, got a haircut, and looked like a different person. I was moved beyond measure. He brought a sad report: "When the revolutionary army neared Huichou the Japanese comrade Yamada came to join and help us, but he disappeared during the retreat of our troops to Sanchout'ien. We are very worried about him." Two years passed after that, and there was not an inkling of what had happened to him. We were really concerned about him. He had traveled in China for many years, and knew it very well. He was modest, gentle, quiet; his purpose was high and his dedication great. When he heard about the Huichou affair he went there alone from Shanghai to join the movement. From that one can see how committed he was. What heaven is he in now? I hope he is well.

A few months later there was another tragic report. "Our revolutionary commander Yang Fei-hung was killed in his Hong Kong house by an assassin." More detailed reports followed. The government had put a price of forty thousand *taels* on his head and searched for him everywhere, and some base outlaw had responded to this. The Hong Kong government had gone to great efforts to arrest the assassin, whereupon the Governor General of Kwangtung and Kwangsi, who had instigated the murder, afraid that the details would be discovered, had himself ordered the murderer apprehended and executed. Is Yang's spirit consoled in his grave? If all China does not return to the virtue of the sacred emperors, how can our comrades sleep in peace? When will that day come? Whenever will it come?

As I look back, half of my life has been a dream, and a failed dream at that. And the most painful parts of that have been the Philippine and Huichou incidents. Each of them failed in the manner that I have described. When I look back at this, I am so furious with Nakamura that I could eat his meat and drink his blood. And not only I! It must be no less true of all our comrades who shared the same ideals to say nothing of Sun himself. However, when I think carefully, I conclude that this all sprang from my own lack of foresight and lack of virtue, and I cannot put the entire blame on Nakamura alone. Indeed, the fault is more mine than his. It is easier to find fault with somebody else than with yourself. Ah, how I wish I could withdraw from the world.

It would be good to retire from this secular world. But what would happen to my children? They have no place to live, nothing to eat, nothing to wear, and their fate lies with my wife's family. What hurt this has brought my wife! I cannot abandon them and go to enjoy a hermit's life alone. In the past I have followed my path through the kindnesses of many people. Up until today I have been responsible for the ruin or near ruin of two or three households: Specifically, the teahouse Matsuei; the Taiyōkan inn; the Hong Kong [brothel?] Shichiban; and more recently Tomeka. All these have suffered because of me. However much I might wish to withdraw from this world, I cannot at the same time withdraw from these people, who have been so good to me.

Indeed, Tomeka is now nearly bankrupt. She has often taken her finest and most treasured clothes to the pawnshop. Because of this violent disputes have broken out between her and her mother on a number of occasions. "At your age! You're foolish enough to let yourself be cheated by a man as if you were a young prostitute!" her mother keeps scolding her. And the daughter answers her mother, "You don't deserve a daughter's respect! Who asked me to become a geisha? Why didn't you leave me as I was?" I have considered leaving that house any number of times, but I have hesitated. I love the girl deeply, and yet I am also bound by claims of loyalty. Meanwhile Tomeka's household is poorer and poorer, her clothes are at the pawnshop, and she is unable to work at her arts with the samisen and play games with stupid guests. So I am more and more torn between duty and love.

When I first moved into Tomeka's house and became a parasite, I had the expectation of going to the continent again soon to involve myself in stirring up troubles there. But circumstances have not allowed this, and while I was idling the time flew. Even then I retained the hope of working out some secret plan with ______ and ______ but those plans too came to nothing. My fate has now run its course. Yet it cannot be exhausted forever. How was I to change it? I went first of all to Tomeka to tell her of my new dream.

[28]

I SING OF FALLEN FLOWERS

THERE IS NOTHING MORE PAINFUL FOR A PERSON than his inability to live up to others' expectations of him. It is like a *sumō* champion who disappoints his supporters. When he first enters the ring and postures in all directions, the shouts and claps of his supporters are like thunder and hail. What are his thoughts at that time? Of course his only concern is the satisfaction of his supporters, and he does not think about his own fate. I had always clung to my great purpose and high hope. Tomeka, naturally, did not understand what I had in my mind. Nevertheless there is no doubt that she played the role of the wrestler's fan on my behalf. That is, the reasons she bore with me in expectation and affection through four years of hardship and agony are explained partly by love and partly by anticipation. Indeed, I was exactly like a *sumō* wrestler she patronized. But for her I was more just than a favorite wrestler. Nevertheless my determination worked out in ways she had not expected and it produced only disappointment for her. That is, I left the world of respectable society and determined to devote myself to the world of the lowly. I explained this to Tomeka. She was thunderstruck and naturally showed her disappointment. She consoled me in her tears. "I know this is a time of suffering for you," she said, "but accept reality as it is; stay with us while you wait for things to change." When she saw that my mind was made up, she said, "You must have some deeper purpose in this; I don't understand your reasons, but I accept them. But please keep this from my mother until you are ready to put your plan into action." Alas that even Tomeka, who had insisted that her mother "wait and see what he's going to do" now had to keep her mouth shut and bow her head before her mother! And not only in front of her mother. She was ridiculed by any number of her friends and customers, she became the butt of gossip among her relatives. Alas, whose fault was that?

On March 23, 1903, I went to the storytellers' theater, the Happōtei, in Shiba, Atago Shitamachi, to see Tochūken Kumoemon. He was currently the outstanding *naniwabushi* chanter, the lead man of the Aishinsha. When I went to the Happōtei it happened that Tochūken was not there because he had gone to Yokohama. I gave my card to one of his disciples and that night I went a second time and asked for a meeting. He admitted me to the backstage room, and I bowed and asked permission to become his student. He laughed and did not answer; he didn't seem to believe that my request was serious. It was natural that he did not take me seriously. I had never met him before, I had no connection with him, and I had come without even bringing an introduction. I was sorry about my rashness. Accidentally, I saw a copy of the *Niroku shinpō* where we were sitting. I picked it up and showed him a chapter of this book, and said, "In this I have written the story of my life, and I recollect with regret that half my life now is gone. The meaning of this is that I want to retire from the world and enter the world of *naniwabushi* chanting. I hope that you will understand the meaning of this and grant my request." He seemed a little more understanding, and looked at me and said, "Granted." Then he asked me where I lived. I wrote it out for him. He said, "Tomorrow I have business near your home. I will stop in on my way by to have a talk." Then food and sake were served, and we drank several small bottles. I left, having arranged the second meeting.

The next day Kumoemon came together with his wife. We talked in my four-and-one-half-mat room upstairs. I waited on him as if he were my teacher. At first he cocked his head, but afterwards he struck his knee and said, "This is no pretense." His wife nodded and laughed. She said, "At first I thought this was a joke, but now that I see this scene I have no more doubt." My teacher Kumoemon continued to speak: "Actually the reason we came was to examine the situation and determine your sincerity." Then Tomeka served sake and food. I rinsed a sake cup and offered it to my teacher, saying, "We should pledge our master-disciple relationship." He said, "No, let's make it an elder brother-younger brother relationship. You can learn this art from me, and I can learn wisdom from you." My master's mind seemed at ease for the first time, and I could begin to put my hope into action. So we drank several small bottles of sake together and parted after we were pleasantly drunk.

Tomeka's mother and her younger brother, however, now realized for the first time that I had made a basic shift. I could hear their voices, and I could hear the sounds of complaint. Tomeka came upstairs and implored me through her tears: "I beg of you to give this up and change your mind." I stood my ground stubbornly.

The next day (and after) Tomeka's mother began bustling around. Tomeka, however, was quiet and sorrowful. She would sigh and say, "Must I go back to doing such disagreeable work?" I had to bear this reproach for some ten days. Once again I was bound by ties of duty and affection.

On April 3 I finally moved out of Tomeka's house into my teacher's house. I now became one of Tochūken's students and Tomeka went back to being a geisha. It is considered smart to say, "Love doesn't last. Only sex lasts." There is some truth in it. Nevertheless the loyalty and affection I have for Tomeka continue to live in my heart; both are unlimited.

Ah, worldly affairs and human affairs seem a dream once one has gained enlightenment. But they are also a dream without enlightenment. When we pursue a dream in a world of dreams, we enter yet another dream.

So let me sing of fallen flowers.
Let me act out a play of fallen flowers.
Let me gather the flowers of Musashino.
How can they console me?
Ah, how can they console me?

APPENDIX: FOUR PREFACES TO ORIGINAL EDITION

[I. Author's Preface]

I am fond of music by nature. I enjoy all forms, east and west, and all modes. That includes *Gidayū,*[1] of course; also *Hōkai bushi,*[2] *Ahodarakyō*[3] and *Shinnai.*[4] Of the many forms of singing there is not one that does not raise my spirits, regardless of whether they are considered vulgar or not. Unfortunately I do not sing very well myself.

I remember a line from *naniwa-bushi*[5] I knew as a child:

> Call on your patron, "Help! Help!"
> He's so chivalrous he helps everybody.
> People praise him, women worship him—
> Our famous Chōbei of Edo!

That's all. But when I'm depressed these lines make me feel better. During the ten or more years that I have known the hardships of life while involving myself in world affairs, my abilities in *naniwa-bushi* improved somewhat. When my spirit was restless I would drink sake, sing that snatch of ballad, and find myself able to relax.

A few years ago I returned from south China and visited Tōyama Mitsuru. He treated me to food and drink, and as I became exhilarated by sake I sang for joy. Tōyama laughed and said, "If you had become a *naniwa-bushi* chanter you'd be the world's best by now." Later, after I had come back from Hong Kong with K'ang Yu-wei, I went to Tōyama's house with the Chinese revolutionary

[1] A style of chanting, accompanied by samisen music, developed for the puppet theater in Tokugawa times.

[2] Ballad chant drawing its themes from popular Chinese drama that was popular in mid-Meiji years.

[3] Satirical chanting modeled on Buddhist mendicants that was popular in Tokugawa-Meiji years.

[4] A form of minstrel music associated particularly with the pleasure quarters, and considered rather coarse.

[5] A musical product of the Meiji period with declarative rhetoric, derived from chanted sermons and addresses of earlier periods.

Ch'en Shao-pai. Tōyama handed me a lute, and Ch'en composed this poem:

> The woman of Hsünyang, now a melancholy vagrant,
> Bids farewell with the strum of her p'i-p'a,
> As when the minstrel from Wu came to beg for food
> at the gate,
> Adding the sound of his flute.[6]
> The ruddy faces of heroes have aged and beauty has
> faded,
> They rest in autumn grasses cherishing their memories.
> Take my lute, let it be your companion on the road,
> Plucking its strings will always overcome your
> melancholy.

Was his poem an omen? Did he know I would become a ballad chanter later?

Some people say a man's determination should be fixed on a long-range goal; others say that unless you realize your limitations you will meet frustration throughout your whole life. The first position makes for boldness, and the other for timidity. The one risks total failure, and the second runs the danger of wasting one's life. I have erred on the side of the former.

I have always thought that no one could foresee the limits of human possibility; if a man decided to be content with something trivial, it would mean wasting his natural talents. I aspired to great deeds that would help the masses.

There are also people who say, "Ideals are all very well, but it is impossible to realize them." To this I say, "Ideals are to be carried out. If they cannot be carried out they remain dreams." I believed in righteousness for all mankind, and therefore I hated the present state of affairs in which the strong devour the weak. I believed that all the

[6] Ch'en's allusions are to Po Chü-i's (772-846) "Lute Song" describing a celebrated courtesan from the capital whose lute he heard in a provincial city where she had settled with a tea merchant, and to the Spring and Autumn period tale of the beggar minstrel Wu Yun.

world was one family, and therefore I deplored the present competition between nations. The things I hated had to be destroyed; if not, it would all be an empty dream. I thought it would take direct action to achieve these aims, and therefore I committed myself to world revolution.

From the outset I was a person who refused to recognize the limitations of human capability. I believed that true self-knowledge was required in human life—what the Buddhists call the achievement of Buddhahood through the appreciation of human nature, and what the Christians call the pursuit of self-perfection through the realization of the perfection of God. I believed that the only path to this was through study, and therefore I saw the importance of the diffusion of education and learning. Unfortunately, however, society is unequal; there are many poor and only a few are wealthy, and education requires time and money. If one were to set out to plan the diffusion of education it would be necessary to change the conditions of life of the poor, so that drew me back to the social revolution.

I was an advocate of freedom and rights for the individual, and consequently I did not like the doctrines about equality of property and I did not approve of socialism. But when it came to landholding, I felt that land was not something produced by man; it was rather the gift of heaven to all men, and therefore it should not be monopolized by a small number of people. It was my hope that the recovery of the rights to land could be arranged on the basis of this just principle, and that the hardships of the poor could then be changed. How was this to be carried out? It seemed to me that there was no way this could be done through debate, but that it would require direct action to get it done.

But alas, my ideals were far removed from the real world; they were separated from it by more than a thousand miles. Still I was not content to hold them as ideals alone; I was resolutely determined to see them realized. I thought there were times when things moved backward a hundred generations in a morning, and other times when they shot forward a hundred generations in an evening. I was convinced that it must sometimes be possible to propel them forward. This could be done only by the application of force, and the outcome would be decided by the degree to which such use of force was in harmony with heaven's purpose. If it proved impossible to succeed in this manner, furthermore, it would all end up as some kind of empty dream. Therefore I wanted to choose China as the place to apply that force. I thought of it as an enormous country with a large population; it was a place ready for revolution. I would either carry it out myself or help others who were of the same mind to carry it out; together we would establish a polity appropriate to my ideals and set it up as a model for order throughout the world, thereby carrying out my hopes.

Yet I was also conscious of the fact that there were racial differences and prejudices among peoples, and for that reason I decided that I would go into the Chinese interior to steep myself in the language and customs of that country and carry out my objectives as though I were a Chinese. But I wasn't able to carry this out in the way I had planned, and instead I drifted around vainly in tropical countries. Ultimately I was able to enter the country of my dreams through the kindness of Mr. Inukai. Now I was able to look for someone of the necessary stature, and finally I made the acquaintance of Mr. Sun Yat-sen. From then on I followed his heroic plans faithfully for many years. There followed our Philippine involvement, imprisonment in Singapore, my expulsion from the Straits Settlements and then from Hong Kong, the revolution at Huichou, the case of Nakamura Haizan, and the conflict with my comrades; all my projects failed. And so in the end I became a disciple of Tōchūken in the art of *naniwa-bushi*, and all my ideals have ended as empty dreams. Alas, did Tōyama's words and Ch'en's poem constitute omens of what lay ahead for me? Did they or didn't they? Whatever the case, I shall not regret that it all ended this way.

When I committed myself to the *naniwa-bushi* group I did not have the courage to tell my old friends what I was going to do. I was ashamed that I could not repay the obligations I had incurred and that my life had come to this. On one occasion I happened to go to the house of Ichiki on personal business; Kōmuchi was there too, and we sat drinking for a while. When the talk came to focus and Kōmuchi found out about my decision, he raised his voice and threw his sake cup down, and said, "What a coward you are! I'm not going to drink with the likes of you; I'd rather pour it on the floor." I was flushed with sake myself, forgot my manners, and shouted, "I don't need a self-serving politician's sake!" We argued violently all night. The next morning a disciple of his came to see me and told me that Kōmuchi had come home and gone to bed crying "If there was only some way I could help him! Bring him here! Bring him here!" When I heard this I was so overcome with emotion that I cried too; I really couldn't help feeling guilty. A few days later I got a letter from Mr. Inukai. It read, "The other day Ichiki came and told me that you've joined some sort of *naniwa-bushi* troupe. I can't believe this is true. Rumors are often wrong, and I certainly hope this one is." The letter went on, "The other day Mr. Miyoshi of Chikuzen came to visit me. He told me that he had become a merchant. He's no longer a wild-haired activist, and that's something we can be glad about. Are you really going to be the only one to drop out to chant *naniwa-bushi*? I can't understand how you came to that." I couldn't reply. And then a few days later Kojima Kazuo came. He said, "Mr. Inukai and his wife sent me to tell you to stop this. You probably won't want to, but I think you ought to reconsider. Why don't you dress normally again, and come and really drink with us again?" I didn't respond, and Kojima left in tears. Truly, I couldn't help feeling guilty.

A day after I had moved in with Tōchūken I went to Tōyama's house with my teacher and told Tōyama the truth. Tōyama smiled and said to me, "It doesn't make any difference, but a lot of people are going to talk. It's all right with me if they talk you into giving it up, and it's all right with me if you refuse; either way it's all right. I'll provide the calligraphy for the posters for your first performance." Truly, I couldn't help feeling guilty.

So many of my old friends, and even many people I didn't know at all, spoke to me, or wrote to me, to sympathize with me and encourage me. This moved me deeply. Still, my decision to join a *naniwa-bushi* group did not represent as big a decision as many of my friends thought it did. I just decided to take it up because I like it. That's why I felt ashamed, even toward the people who expressed sympathy with my decision. Ah, can it be that in these thirty-three years I have more or less learned what my limitations are?

When I decided to become an entertainer I had no money and I could not afford anything. Therefore I wrote a letter to a chivalrous woman named Miura in Kumamoto and appealed to her generosity. She sent me the sum I asked for, and she also wrote, "You don't seem old enough to retire from the world to me. How did you come to a decision like this? I hope you will change your mind. Please let me hear from you. I enclose enough to cover things like rickshaw fare and the like." I swallowed my tears while using what she sent, and was able to begin my new life against her kind advice. I want to express my gratitude to her here.

Alas, human life is primarily a stage dream. This thirty-three years' dream is only the first part of it. I now become a foolish fellow who prattles about his dream in public. I have no right to complain if the wise ridicule me.

August, 1902 — TŌTEN MIYAZAKI TORAZŌ

[II. Sun Yat-sen Preface]

It is said that during the Sui there was a knight errant of Tunghai who was known as Ch'iu Jan. He had traveled all over China and visited all the great heroes; in Lingshih he met Li Ching, and in Taiyuan he met Li Shih-min. Together they discussed all the important matters of the realm. Since he recognized unusual ability in Li Shih-min, Ch'iu Jan advised Li Ching to help Li Shih-min accomplish his great achievement. Afterwards Li Shih-min rose in revolt to put an end to the confusion of the Sui and founded the house of T'ang, becoming known as T'ai Tsung. It is said that in the fulfillment of these intentions the help of his chivalrous friend was of great importance.[1]

Miyazaki Torazō is such a knight errant of the present day. His knowledge is extensive, his ideals are out of the ordinary. He is one who hastens to help another's need; he is a man of benevolence and righteousness. He laments the oppression of the yellow race, and he grieves because of China's increasing weakness. He has repeatedly visited the Chinese mainland to visit our valorous comrades, and it has been his heartfelt desire to bring about with us the great achievement of our age—the revival of Asia. When he heard that I was planning to build a new China by setting up a republican government he hastened to join me. We planned together in closest harmony and he energetically urged us on. In comparison with Ch'iu Jan, he has done even more.

Unfortunately I do not have the character of T'ai Tsung and I lack the masterly strategy of Li Ching. It is a grievous imposition on his kindness that the activities up to this point have brought no results.

[1] Sun's reference is to a T'ang dynasty novel, *Ch'iu Jan k'e-ch'uan*, by Chang Shuo (667-730).

When he finished his recent travels, he returned to his country and set down his experiences for the consideration of those who will feel concern for the rise or decline of Asia and the existence of the yellow race in the future. I approved of his plan, and in view of his unparalleled efforts I add this preface to show my respect for him.

August, 1902 SUN YAT-SEN (China)

[III. Kiyofuji Kōshichirō Introduction]*

My friend Tōten
    is a man of chivalry and high purpose,
    rich in plans, unusual in speech.
His purpose has been to liberate the masses;
    he has had a grand design of awakening
    first Asia, and then the world.
His intensity can move mountains,
    his argument has the force of a rushing wave.
Alas, the time of opportunity has not yet arrived for him;
    he has lost ten years in struggle,
    half his life has fallen like a flower in evening of the day.
He is a lonely man,
    left looking at his wine-stained gown after guests have left.
As he thinks back over failures of thirty-three years,
    all in vain, only sincerity remains to him.
He has written this tale of his former dreams
    sitting reflecting in the light of his lamp at midnight.
Yet he has not retreated to a mountain
    or withdrawn from the world.
Instead he put aside shame and smiled
    and became a disciple of Kumoemon.
Kumoemon is extraordinarily gifted in *naniwa-bushi*
    and well known among the people.

Nature endowed Tōten with a splendid voice.
    He can be expected to develop this high art,
    use it to reveal the thoughts he has in his heart,
    and give utterance to basic human nature in his performance.
He can be at ease in all places,
    not deterred by pride or concerned with reputation.
Will he not see all human life a tumultuous dream,
    that neither wealth nor fame matter?

* Written in Chinese.

A great hermit sage can live in a city,
and a lesser sage can live in a country village;
among humans there can be sages who are not sages,
who accomodate the noble and ignoble,
and swallow all the world.
Ah! Everything is transient, so let us first
bring on the sake barrel;
this night we purify our spirits with drink,
as we raise our cups the spring warmth will return.
Flowers drop and rain drops fall
In everything we see, late spring makes the hour sad.

Some days after Tōten joined Tōchūken
I had the chance to call on him.
He welcomed me.
Through four afternoon hours
We raised our cups and talked about the past
But not at all of present things.
Our emotions were boundless,
I composed this poem.

Now, hearing that his book, *Sanjū-sannen no yume*, is to be published, I offer my poem as preface.

1902. Don'u KIYOFUJI KŌSHICHIRŌ

[IV. Takeda Hanshi Preface]*

The Thirty-Three Years' Dream

Tōten originally came from a leading family
    and practiced martial arts and reading books.
Thirty-three years have passed
    and we anticipate as many more.
Nine times nine make the number eighty-one,
    but three times three do not make ten.
Sincerity produces restlessness and discontent,
    and discontented often choose the life of chivalry.
The showy play at mating dance,
    and many abandon themselves to sex.
Some acclaim such men as heroes,
    but they are only ordinary men.
The dreams of arrogant kings and princes
    when they awake, can make quiet sages envy.
A knight of purity and nobility
    comes once in five hundred years.
A dream? Ah, 'tis but a dream.
    Then shall we seek the dream behind the dream?
A voice along a jeweled road,
    A dream that wakes us from the dream.

At Tōchūken's studio,
pleasantly intoxicated,
taking turns making Chinese couplets about Tōten's title, *Thirty-three Years' Dream*, in response to his *naniwa-bushi*.

Summer, 1902 MUKAYUGOSEI (Takeda Hanshi)

* Written in Chinese.

[Index of Names]

Library of Congress Cataloging in Publication Data

Miyazaki, Tōten, 1870-1922.
My thirty-three years' dream.

(Princeton library of Asian translations)
Translation of: Sanjūsannen no yume. 1967.
Includes index.
1. Miyazaki, Tōten, 1870-1922. 2. Revolutionists—China—Biography. 3. Revolutionists—Japan—Biography. 4. Sun, Yat-sen, 1866-1925. 5. Japanese—China. 6. China—History—19th century. I. Title. II. Series.
DS884.M5A313 951'.03'0924 [B] 81-47925
ISBN 0-691-05348-0 AACR2